THE HISTORY OF FREEMASONRY

ITS LEGENDS AND TRADITIONS

ITS CHRONOLOGICAL HISTORY

BY ALBERT GALLATIN MACKEY, M.D., 33°

VOLUME FOUR

PART 2. - HISTORY OF FREEMASONRY

CHAPTER XXIX

ORGANIZATION OF THE GRAND LODGE OF ENGLAND

WE have now reached the most interesting portion of the history of Freemasonry. We are getting away from the regions of legend and tradition, and are passing into the realm of authentic records. And though at this early period there is a sparseness of these records, and sometimes a doubtfulness about their meaning, which will occasionally compel us to build our hypothesis on the foundation of plausible conjecture and reasoning, still, to whatever conclusions we may come, they will, of course, be more satisfactory to the mind than if they were wrought out of mere mythical and traditionary narratives.

It has already been shown that the Guild or Fraternity of Freemasons from the earliest period of its history had admitted into its connection persons of rank and influence who were not workmen of the Craft.

In this usage it followed the example of the Roman Colleges of Artificers, whose patrons were selected to secure to the corporations a protection often needed, from the oppressive interference of the government.

Thus, when after the decadence of the Roman Empire, architecture, which had fallen into decline, began to revive, the Masons were employed in the construction of religious edifices, the dignitaries of the Church naturally became closely connected with the workmen, while many of the monks were operative masons. Bishops and abbots superintended the buildings, and were thus closely connected with the Guild.

This usage was continued even after the Freemasons had withdrawn from all ecclesiastical dependence, and up to the 18th century non-operatives were admitted into full membership of the Fraternity, under the appellation of Gentlemen or Theoretic Masons, or as Honorary Members. The title of Speculative Freemasons was a word of later coinage, though it is met with, apparently with the same meaning, in one of the oldest Records, the Cooke MS. But this is a solitary instance, and the word never came into general use until some time after the organization of the Grand Lodge in 1717.

It is here used for the sake of convenience, in reference to the early period, but without any intention to intimate that it was then familiar to the Craft. The fact existed, however, though the special word was apparently wanting.

The natural result of this commingling of Operative and Speculative Masons in the same Fraternity, was to beget a spirit of rivalry between the two classes. This eventually culminated in the dissolution of the Guild of Operative Freemasons as distinguished from the Rough Masons or Rough Layers, and the establishment on its ruin of the Society of Speculative Freemasons, which at London, in the year 1717, assumed the title of "The Grand Lodge of Free and Accepted Masons."

We are without any authentic narrative of the rise and progress of the contentions between the rival classes in England, because in that country the records of the Operative Lodges before the close of the 17th century have been lost. But the sister kingdom of Scotland has been more fortunate. There the minutes of the Lodges of Edinburgh and Kilwinning exhibit abundant evidence of the struggle for pre-eminence which terminated in the year 1736 in the establishment of the speculative "Grand Lodge of Scotland."

As the subject-matter to be treated in this chapter is the history of the establishment at London, in the year 1717, of the Grand Lodge of England, it will be proper as a preliminary step that some notice should be taken of the condition of Freemasonry during the first decade of the 18th century in the south of England.

The lodges then existing in the kingdom consisted, it is supposed, both of Operative and non-Operative members. We have positive evidence of this in some instances, and especially as respects the lodges in London.

Preston gives the following account of the condition of the institution in the beginning of the 18th century:

"During the Reign of Queen Anne, masonry made no considerable progress. Sir Christopher Wren's age and infirmities drawing off his attention from the duties of his office (that of Grand Master), the lodges decreased, and the annual festivals were entirely neglected. The old Lodge of St. Paul and a few others continued to meet regularly, but consisted of few members."[1]

Anderson, upon whose authority Preston had made this statement, says that "in the South the lodges were more and more disused, partly by the neglect of the Masters and Wardens and partly by not having a noble Grand Master at London, and the annual Assembly was not duly attended."[2]

As the statement so often made by Anderson and other writers of his school, that there was, anterior to the seventeenth year of the 18th century, an annual Assembly of the Craft in England over which a Grand Master presided, has been proved to be apocryphal, we must attribute the decline of Operative Freemasonry to other causes than those assigned by Dr. Anderson.

I have heretofore attempted to show that the decline in the spirit of Operative Freemasonry was to be attributed to the decadence of Gothic Architecture. By this the Freemasons were reduced to a lower level than they had ever before occupied, and were brought much nearer to the "Rough Masons" than was pleasing to their pride of "cunning." They thus lost the pre-eminence in the Craft which they had so long held on account of their acknowledged genius and the skill which in past times they had exhibited in the art of building.

But whatever may have been the cause, the fact is indisputable that at the beginning of the 18th century the Freemasons had lost much of their high standing as practical architects and had greatly diminished in numbers.

In the year 1716 there were but four lodges of Operative Masons in the city of London. The minutes of these lodges are not extant, and we have no authentic means of knowing what was their precise condition.

But we do know that among their members were many gentlemen of education who were not Operative Masons, but belonged to the class of Theoretic or Speculative Freemasons, which, as I have previously said, it had long been the custom of the Operative Freemasons to admit into their Fraternity.

Preston, in his Illustrations of Masonry, in a passage already cited, speaking of the decline of the lodges in the first decade of the 18th century, makes this statement:

---

[1] "Illustrations of Masonry," Jones's edit., 1821, p. 189. a
[2] "Constitutions," edit. 1738, p. 108.

"To increase their numbers, a proposition was made, and afterwards agreed to, that the privileges of Masonry should no longer be restricted to Operative Masons, but extend to men of various professions, provided they were regularly approved and initiated into the Order."

For this statement he gives no authority. Anderson, who was contemporary with the period of time when this regulation is said to have been adopted, makes no allusion to it, and Preston himself says on a preceding page that "at a general assembly and feast of the Masons in 1697 many noble and eminent brethren were present, and among the rest, Charles, Duke of Richmond and Lennox, who was at that time Master of the lodge at Chichester."[3]

The statement appears, therefore, to be apochryphal. Such a proposition would certainly have been wholly superfluous, as there is abundant evidence that in England in the 17th century "men of various professions" had been "regularly approved and initiated into the Order."

Elias Ashmole, the Antiquary, states in his Diary that he and Colonel Mainwaring were initiated in a lodge at Warrington in 1646, and he records the admission of several other non-Operatives in 1682 at a lodge held in London.

Dr. Plott, in his Natural History of Staffiordshire, printed in 1686, states that "persons of the most eminent quality did not disdain to be of the Fellowship."

In the first and second decades of the 18th century Operative Freemasonry appears, judging from extant records, to have been in the following condition:

In the northern counties there were several lodges of Operative Freemasons, which had a permanent character, having rules for their government, and holding meetings at which new members were admitted.

Thus Preston speaks of a lodge which was at Chichester in 1697, of which the Duke of Richmond and Lennox was Master; there was a lodge at Alnwick in Northumberland, whose records from 1701 are extant;[4] and there was at least one lodge, if not more, in the city of York whose preserved minutes begin on March 19, 1712.[5] We have every

---

[3] "Illustrations of Masonry," p. 189, Jones's edit.
[4] Bro. Hughan has published excerpts from the minutes. See Mackey's "National Freemason," vol iii., p. 233.
[5] See Hughan's History of Freemasonry in York, in his " Masonic Sketches and Reprints," p. 55. See also an article by him in the Voice of Masonry, vol. xiii., p. 571.

reason to suppose that similar lodges were to be found in other parts of the kingdom, though the minutes of their transactions have unfortunately been lost.

In London there were four operative lodges. These were the lodges which in 1717 united in the formation of the Speculative Grand Lodge of England, an act that has improperly been called the "Revival."

All the lodges mentioned consisted of two classes of members, namely, those who were Operative Freemasons and who worked in the mystery of the Craft, and those who were non-Operative, or, as they were sometimes called, Gentlemen Freemasons.

The ceremony of admission or initiation was at this time of a very simple and unpretentious character. There was but one form common to the three ranks of Apprentices, Fellows, and Masters, and the division into degrees, as that word is now understood, was utterly unknown.[6]

From the close of the 17th century the Operative lodges were gradually losing their prestige. They were no longer, as Lord Lindsay has denominated their predecessors of the Middle Ages, "parliaments of genius;" their architectural skill had decayed; their geometrical secrets were lost; and the distinction which had once been so proudly maintained between the Freemasons and the "rough layers" was being rapidly obliterated.

Meantime the men of science and culture who had been admitted into their ranks, thought that they saw in the principle of brotherhood which was still preserved, and in the symbolic teachings which were not yet altogether lost, a foundation for another association, in which the fraternal spirit should remain as the bond of union, and the doctrines of symbolism, hitherto practically applied to the art of architecture, should be in future directed to the illustration of the science of morality.

Long afterward the successors of these founders of Speculative Freemasonry defined it to be "a system of morality, veiled in allegory and illustrated by symbols."

Feeling that there was no congenial companionship between themselves and the uncultured men who composed the Operative element of the Association, the gentlemen of education and refinement who constituted the Theoretic element or the Honorary membership of

---

[6] This subject will be fully discussed in a future chapter on the history of the origin of the three Craft degrees, and the statement here made will be satisfactorily substantiated.

the four lodges then existing in the city of London, resolved to change the character of these lodges, and to withdraw them entirely from any connection with Operative or Practical Masonry.

It was in this way that Speculative Freemasonry found its origin in the desire of a few speculative thinkers who desired, for the gratification of their own taste, to transmute what in the language of the times would have been called a club of workmen into a club of moralists.

The events connected with this transmutation are fully recorded by Dr. Anderson, in the second edition of the Constitutions, and as this is really the official account of the transaction, it is better to give it in the very language of that account, than to offer any version of it.

The history of the formation of the Grand Lodge of Free and Accepted Masons of England, is given in the following words by Dr. Anderson, who is said to have been one of the actors in the event:

"King George I. entered London most magnificently on 20 Sept., 1714, and after the rebellion was over, A.D. 1716, the few lodges at London, finding themselves neglected by Sir Christopher Wren, thought fit to cement under a Grand Master as the centre of union and harmony, viz., the lodges that met.

"1, At the 'Goose and Gridiron Ale-house' in St. Paul's Churchyard.

"2. At the 'Crown Ale-house' in Parker's Lane near Drury Lane.

"3. At the ' Apple Tree Tavern ' in Charles Street, Covent Garden.

"4. At the 'Rummer and Grapes Tavern' in Channel Row, Westminster.

"They and some old brothers met at the said Apple Tree, and having put into the chair the oldest Master Mason (now the Master of a Lodge) they constituted themselves a Grand Lodge, pro tempore, in Due Form, and forthwith revived the Quarterly Communication of the Officers of Lodges (called the Grand Lodge) resolved to hold the Annual Feast and then to choose a Grand Master from among themselves, till they should have the honor of a noble brother at their head.

"Accordingly on St. John Baptist's day, in the 3d year of King George I., A.D. 1717, the Assembly and Feast of the Free and Accepted Masons was held at the foresaid ' Goose and Gridiron Ale-house.'

"Before dinner, the oldest Master Mason (now the Master of a Lodge) in the Chair, proposed a list of proper candidates, and the brethren by a majority of hands elected

"Mr. Anthony Sayer, Gentleman, Grand Master of Masons,

Capt. Joseph Elliott Mr. Jacob Lamball, Carpenter Grand Wardens, who being forthwith invested with the badges of office and power by the said oldest Master, and installed, was duly congratulated by the Assembly who paid him the homage.

"Sayer, Grand Master, commanded the Masters and Wardens of Lodges to meet the Grand Officers every quarter in communication at the place appointed in his summons sent by the Tyler."[7]

Such is the account of the transmutation of the four Operative to four Speculative lodges, given by Dr. Anderson, who is believed, with George Payne, Esq., and Dr. Desaguliers, to have been principally instrumental in effecting the transmutation.

Meager as are the details of so important an event which Anderson, as a contemporary actor, might easily have made more copious, they suggest several important points for our consideration.

We see that the change to be effected by the establishment of the Speculative Grand Lodge was not too hastily accomplished.

The first meeting in which it was resolved to organize a Grand Lodge took place some months before the actual organization occurred.

Anderson says that the four lodges met in 1716 and "revived the Quarterly Communication of the officers of lodges."

Preston says that they met in February, 1717, and that at this meeting "it was resolved to revive the Quarterly Communications of the Fraternity."

This is a more accurate statement than that of Anderson. The meeting in February, 1717, was merely preliminary. A resolution was adopted, or perhaps more correctly speaking, an agreement was entered into, to organize a Grand Lodge. But this agreement was not carried into execution until four months afterward. There could have been no Grand Lodge without a Grand Master, and the Grand Master was not elected until the 24th of June following. The apparent disagreement of the dates assigned to the preparatory meeting, Anderson saying it was in 1716, and Preston that it was in February, 1717, is easily reconciled.

Anderson in his narrative used the Old Style, in which the year began on March 25th, consequently February would fall in 1716. Preston used the New Style, which begins the year on January 1st, and thereby February fell in 1717. The actual period of time referred to by both authors is really the same.

In an anonymous work[8] published in 1764 it is said that six lodges were engaged in the organization of the Grand Lodge, but as the two additional lodges are not identified, it is better to reject the statement as untruthful, and to abide by the authority of Anderson,

---

[7] "Constitutions," 1738 edition. pp. 109, 110.
[8] "The Complete Freemason, or Multa Paucis, for Lovers of Secrets."

who, as Bro. Hughan says, "clearly wrote at a time when many personally knew as to the facts narrated and whose Book of Constitutions was really the official statement issued by the Grand Lodge."

The fact that four lodges were engaged in the act of transmuting Operative into Speculative Freemasonry by organizing a Grand Lodge, while admitted as an historical fact by Lawrence Dermott, is used by him as an objection to the legality of the organization.

"To form," he says, "what Masons mean by a Grand Lodge, there must have been the Masters and Wardens of five regular lodges that is to say, five Masters and ten Wardens, making the numbs of installed officers fifteen."[9]

But although Dermott very confidently asserts that this "is well known to every man conversant with the ancient laws, usages, customs, and ceremonies of Master Masons,"[10] there can be no doubt that this point of law so dogmatically proclaimed was the pure invention of Dermott's brain, and is entitled to no weight whatever.

As the Grand Lodge which was established in 1717 was the first one ever known, it was impossible that there could be any "ancient laws" to regulate its organization.

It is noteworthy that each of these premier lodges met at a tavern or ale-house. During the last century Freemasons' lodges in England almost universally had their lodge-rooms in the upper part of taverns. The custom was also adopted in this country, and all the early lodges in America were held in the upper rooms of buildings occupied as taverns.

The custom of meeting in taverns was one that was not confined to the Masonic Brotherhood. The early part of the 18th century was, in London, as we have already seen, the era of clubs. These societies, established some for literary, some for social, and some for political purposes, always held their meetings in taverns. " Will's Coffee House " is made memorable in the numbers of the Spectator as the rendezvous of the wits of that day.

It will also be noticed that these four lodges were without names, such as are now borne by lodges, but that they were designated by the signs of the taverns in which they held their meetings. Half a century elapsed before the lodges in England began to assume distinctive names. The first lodge to do so was Friendship Lodge No. 3, which is so styled in Cole's List of Lodges for 1767.

---

[9] "Ahiman Rezon " p. 13.
[10] Ibid., p. 14

No difficulty or confusion, however, arose from this custom of designating lodges by the signs of the taverns in which they held their meetings, for it seldom happened that more than one lodge ever met at any tavern. "The practice," says Gould, "of any one tavern being common as a place of meeting, to two or more lodges, seems to have been almost unknown in the last century."[11]

Two of the four taverns in which these four original lodges were held, and two of the lodges themselves, namely, the "Apple Tree," where the design of separating the Speculative from the Operative element was inaugurated, and the "Goose and Gridiron," where that design was consummated by the organization of the new Grand Lodge, particularly claim our attention.

But it will be more convenient while engaged on this subject to trace the fate and fortune of the whole four.

In this investigation I have been greatly aided by the laborious and accurate treatise of Bro. Robert Freke Gould, of London, on the Four Old Lodges. After his exhaustive analysis there is but little chance of unearthing any new discoveries, though I have been able to add from other sources a few interesting facts.

The lodge first named on Anderson's list met at the "Goose and Gridiron Ale-house," and it was there that, on the 24th of June, 1717, the Grand Lodge of England was established. Elmes says that "Sir Christopher Wren was Master of St. Paul's Lodge, which during the building of the Cathedral of St. Paul's, met at the 'Goose and Gridiron' in St. Paul's Churchyard, and is now the Lodge of Antiquity, acting by immemorial prescription; and he regularly presided at its meetings for upward of eighteen years."[12]

Dr. Oliver says that Dr. Desaguliers, who may be properly reputed as the principal founder of modern Speculative Freemasonry, was initiated into the ceremonies of the Operative system, such as they were, in the lodge that met at the "Goose and Gridiron," and the date assigned for his admission is the year 1712.

Larwood and Hotten in their History of Sign Boards, copying from a paper of the Tatler, say that the Tavern was originally a Music house, with the sign of the "Mitre." When it ceased to be a Music house the succeeding landlord chose for his sign a goose stroking the bars of a gridiron with his foot in ridicule of the "Swan and Harp," which was a common sign for the early music houses.[13] I doubt the truth of this

---

[11] "The Four Old Lodges," by Robert Freke Gould, p. 13.
[12] Elmes's "Sir Christopher Wren and his Times," quoted in the Keystone
[13] "History of Sign Boards," p. 445.

origin, and think it more likely that the "Swan and Harp" degenerated into the "Goose and Gridiron" by the same process of blundenng, so common in the history of signs which corrupted "God encompasseth us" into the "Goat and Compasses" or the "Belle Sauvage" into the "Bell and Savage."

In the list of lodges for 1725 to 1730 contained in the Minute Book of the Grand Lodge of England, Lodge No. 1 is still recorded as holding its meetings at the "Goose and Gridiron," whence, however, it not very long after removed, for in the next list, from 1730 to 1732, it is recorded as being held at the "King's Arms," in St. Paul's Churchyard.

The "King's Arms" continued to be its place of meeting (except a short time in 1735, when it met at the "Paul's Head," Ludgate Street) until 1768, when it removed to the "Mitre." Eight years before, it assumed the name of the "West India and American Lodge." In 1770 it became the "Lodge of Antiquity." Of this lodge the distinguished Masonic writer, William Preston, was a member. In 1779 it temporarily seceded from the Grand Lodge, and formed a schismatic Grand Lodge. The history of this schism will be the subject of a future chapter.

At the union of the two Grand Lodges of "Moderns" and "Ancients," it lost its number "One" in drawing lots and became number's Two," which number it still retains, though it is always recognized as the "premier lodge of England," and therefore of the world.

The "Goose and Gridiron Tavern" continued to be the place of meeting of the Grand Lodge until 1721, when in consequence of the need of more room from the increase of lodges the annual feast was held at Stationers' Hall.[14] The Grand Lodge never returned to the "Goose and Gridiron." It afterward held its quarterly communications at various taverns, and the annual assembly and feast always at some one of the Halls of the different Livery Companies of London. This migratory system prevailed until the Freemasons were able to erect a Hall of their own.

The second lodge which engaged in 1717 in the organization of the Grand Lodge, met at the "Crown Ale-house" in Parker's Lanes near Drury Lane. According to Bro. Gould, it removed about 1723 to the "Queen's Head," Turnstile, Holborn; to the "Green Lettuce," Brownlow Street, in 1725;[15] thence to the "Rose and Rummer" in 1728, and to the "Rose and Buffer" in 1729. In 1730 it met at the "Bull and Gate," Holborn, and appearing for the last time in the list for 1736, was struck off the roll in 1740.

---

[14] Anderson's "Constitutions," 2d edit., p. 112.
[15] Gould's "Four Old Lodges," p. 6.

But it had ceased to exist before that year, for Anderson, in the list published by him in 1738, says: "The Crown in Parker's Lane, the other of the four old Lodges, is now extinct."[16]

The third lodge engaged in the Grand Lodge organization was that which met at the "Apple Tree Tavern " in 1717. It was there that in February of that year the Freemasons who were preparing to sever the connection between the Operative and Theoretic Masons, took the preliminary steps toward effecting that design. From the "Apple Tree" it removed about 1723 to the Queen's Head," Knave's Acre; thence in 1740 to the George and Dragon," Portland Street, Oxford Market; thence in 1744 to the "Swan" in the same region. In the lists from 1768 to 1793 it is described as the Lodge of Fortitude. After various other migrations, it amalgamated, in 1818, with the Old Cumberland Lodge, and is now the Fortitude and Old Cumberland Lodge No. 12 on the roll of the United Grand Lodge of England. [17]

Of this third or "Apple Tree" Lodge, Anthony Sayer, the first Grand Master of England, was a member, and most probably was in 1717 or had been previously the Master. In 1723 he is recorded as the Senior Warden of the Lodge, which is certainly an evidence of his Masonic zeal.

The last of the four old Lodges which constituted the Grand Lodge met in 1717 at the "Rummer and Grapes Tavern," Westminster. It moved thence to the "Horn Tavern," Westminster, in 1723. It seemed to be blessed with a spirit of permanency which did not appertain to the three other lodges, for it remained at the "Horn" for forty-three years, not migrating until 1767, when it went to the "Fleece," Tothill Street, Westminster. The year after it assumed the name of the Old Horn Lodge. In 1774 it united with and adopted the name of the Somerset House Lodge, and met at first at the "Adelphi" and afterward until 1815 at "Freemasons' Tavern." In 1828 it absorbed the Royal Inverness Lodge, and is now registered on the roll of the United Grand Lodge of England as the Royal Somerset House and Inverness Lodge No. 4.[18]

George Payne, who was twice Grand Master, in 1718 and in 1720, had been Master of the original Rummer and Grapes Lodge. He must have been so before his first election as Grand Master in 1718, and he is recorded in the first edition of Anderson as having been its Master again in 1723. At one time the lodge received an important benefit from

---

[16] Anderson's " Constitutions," 2d edit., p. 185.
[17] Gould, "Four Old Lodges,"p.7.
[18] Ibid

this circumstance, as is shown by the following record taken by Entick from the Minutes of the Grand Lodge.

In 1747 the lodge, whose number had been changed to No. 2, was erased from the Books of Lodges for not obeying an order of the Quarterly Communication. But in 1753, the members having petitioned the Grand Lodge for restoration, Entick says in his edition of the Constitutions that "after a long debate, it was ordered that in respect to Brother Payne, late Grand Master, the Lodge No. 2 lately held at the 'Horn' in Palace Yard, Westminster, should be restored and have its former rank and place in the list of lodges."

Payne, who was a scholar, had done much for the advancement of Speculative Freemasonry, and the Grand Lodge by this act paid a fitting homage to his character and showed itself not unmindful of his services to the Fraternity.

Such are the facts, well authenticated by unquestioned historical authorities, which are connected with the establishment of the first Grand Lodge of Speculative Freemasons, not only in England, but in the world. Seeing that nothing analogous has been anywhere found in the records of Masonry, irrespective of its unauthenticated legends and traditions, it is proper, before proceeding to inquire into the condition of the Grand Lodge immediately subsequent to its organization at the "Goose and Gridiron Tavern," that the much discussed question, whether this organization was the invention of an entirely new system or only the revival of an old, and for a short time discontinued, one should be fairly considered.

To this important subject our attention will be directed in the following chapter.

CHAPTER XXX

WAS THE ORGANIZATION OF THE GRAND LODGE IN 1717 A REVIVAL?

It has been the practice of at Masonic writers from the earliest period of its literature to a very recent day, to designate the transaction which resulted in the organization of the Grand Lodge of England in the year 1717 as the "Revival of Freemasonry."

Anderson, writing in 1723, in the first edition of the Constitutions, says that "the freeborn British nation had revived the drooping Lodges of London," and in the year 1738, in the second edition of the same work, he asserts that the old Brothers who met at the "Apple Tree Tavern" "forthwith revived the Quarterly Communication of the Officers of Lodges, called the Grand Lodge."

This statement has been repeated by Preston, Calcott, Oliver, and all the older Masonic authors who have written upon the subject, until it has become an almost universal belief among the larger portion of the Fraternity that from some unknown or indefinite era until the second decade of the 18th century the Grand Lodge had been in a state of profound slumber, and that the Quarterly Communications, once so common, had long been discontinued, through the inertness and indifference of the Craft, while the lodges were drooping like sickly plants.

But in the year 1717, owing to the successful efforts of a few learned scholars, such as Desaguliers, Anderson, and Payne, the Grand Lodge had been awakened from its sleep of years, the Quarterly Communications had been renewed as of old, and the lodges had sprung into fresh and vigorous existence. Such was for a long time and indeed still is, to a diminished extent, the orthodox Masonic creed respecting the Revival of Freemasonry in the 18th century.

But this creed, popular as it is, has within a few years past been ruthlessly attacked by some of our more advanced thinkers, who are skeptical where to doubt is wise, and who are not prepared to accept legends as facts, nor to confound trading with history.

And now it is argued that before the year 1717 there never was a Grand Lodge in England, and, of course, there could have been no Quarterly Communications. Therefore, as there had not been a previous life, there could have been no revival, but that the Grand Lodge established in June, 1717, was a new invention, and the introduction of a system or plan of Freemasonry never before heard of or seen.

Which of these two hypotheses is the correct one, or whether there is not a mezzo termine - a middle point or just mean between the two - are questions well worthy of examination.

Let us first inquire what was the character of the four Lodges, and indeed of all the lodges in England which were in existence at the time of the so- called "Revival," or had existed at any previous time. What was the authority under which they acted, what was their character, and how was this character affected by the establishment of a new Grand Lodge?

As to the authority under which the four old lodges, as well as all others that existed in England, acted, it must be admitted that they derived that authority from no power outside of themselves "The authority," says Bro. Hughan, "by which they worked prior to the advent of the Grand Lodge was their own. We know of no other prior to that period for England."[19]

Preston admits that previous to the year 1717 "a sufficient number of Masons met together within a certain district, with the consent of the sheriff or chief magistrate of the place, were empowered to make Masons and practice the rites of Masonry without Warrant of Constitution.'[20]

Bro. Hughan substantially repeats this statement in the following language:

"A body of Masons in any district or town appear usually to have congregated and formed lodges, and they had the 'Ancient Charges' or Rolls to guide them as to the rules and regulations for Masons generally. There were no Grand Masters or Grand Lodges before 1716-

---

[19] See Voice of Masonry, vol. xiii., p. 571.
[20] Preston's "Illustrations," p. 191, note.

17, and so there were no authorities excepting such as the annual assemblies and the 'Old Charges' furnished in England."

He admits that "there were laws for the government of the lodges apparently, though unwritten, which were duly observed by the brotherhood."

This view is confirmed, impliedly, at least, by all the Old Constitutions in manuscript, from the most ancient to the most recent. In none of these (and the last of them has a date which is only three years prior to the so- called " Revival") do we find any reference whatever to a Grand Lodge or to a Grand Master. But they repeatedly speak of lodges in which Masons were to be " accepted," and the counsels of which were to be kept secret by the Fellows.

The only allusion made to the manner of organizing a lodge is contained in the Harleian MS., which prescribes that it must consist of not less than five Freemasons, one of whom must be a master or warden of the limit or division wherein the lodge is held.

From this regulation we are authorized, I think, to conclude, that in 1670, which is the date of the Harleian MS., nothing more was necessary in forming a lodge in which "to make Masons or practice the rites of Masonry," as Preston gives the phrase, than that a requisite number should be present, with a Master or Warden working in that locality.

Now the Master, as the word is here used, meant a Freemason of the highest rank, who was engaged in building with workmen under him, and a Warden was one who having passed out of his apprenticeship, had become a Fellow and was invested with an authority over the other Fellows, inferior only to that of the Master. The word and the office are recognized in the early English Charters as pertaining to the ancient guilds. Thus the Charters granted in 1354 by Edward III. gave the London Companies the privilege to elect annually for their government "a certain number of Wardens." In 1377 an oath was prescribed called the "Oath of the Wardens of the Crafts," which contained these words: "Ye shall swere that ye shall wele and treuly oversee the Craft of ____ whereof ye be chosen Wardeyns for the year." In the reign of Elizabeth the presiding officer began to be called the Master, and in the reign of James I., between 1603 and 1625, the guilds were generally governed by a Master and Wardens. The government of lodges by a Master and Wardens must have been introduced into the guilds of Masons in the 17th century, and this is rendered probable by the fact that in the Harleian MS. just quoted, and whose coniectural date is 1670, it is provided "that for the future the sayd Society,

Company and Fraternity of Free Masons shall be regulated and governed by One Master & Assembly & Wardens as the said Company shall think to choose, at every yearely General Assembly."

A similar officer in the Sullen or Lodges of the old German Freemasons was called the Parlirer.

We arrive, then, at the conclusion that in the 17th century, while there were permanent lodges in various places which were presided over by a Master and Wardens, any five Freemasons might open a temporary or "occasional" lodge for the admission of members of the Craft, provided one of these five was either the Master or a Warden of a permanent lodge in the neighborhood.

I know of no other way of reasonably interpreting the 26th article contained in the Harleian Constitutions.

But nowhere, in any of the Old Constitutions, before or after the Harleian, even as late as 1714, which is the date of the Papworth MS., do we find the slightest allusion to any exterior authority which was required to constitute either permanent or temporary lodges.

The statement of Preston is thus fully sustained by the concurrent testimony of the old manuscripts. Therefore, when Anderson in his first edition gives the form of constituting a new lodge and says that it is "according to the ancient usages of Masonry,"[21] he indulges in a rhetorical flourish that has no foundation in truth. There is no evidence of the slightest historical value that any such usage existed before the second decade of the 18th century.

But immediately after what is called the Revival the system of forming lodges which had been practiced was entirely changed. Preston says that among a variety of regulations which were proposed and agreed to at the meeting in 1717, was the following:

"That the privilege of assembling as Masons, which had been hitherto unlimited, should be vested in certain lodges or assemblies of Masons convened in certain places; and that every lodge to be hereafter convened, except the four old lodges at this time existing, should be legally authorized to act by a warrant from the Grand Master for the time being granted to certain individuals by petition, with the consent and approbation of the Grand Lodge in communication; and that without such warrant no lodge should be hereafter deemed regular or constitutional."[22]

We have this regulation on the evidence of Preston alone, for according to the unfortunate usage of our early Masonic writers, he cites

---

[21] Anderson's "Constitutions," 1st edition, p. 71.
[22] Preston, "Illustrations," p. 191.

no authority. It is not mentioned by Anderson, and the preserved minutes of the Grand Lodge of England extend no farther than the 25th of November, 1723.

Still, as Preston gives it within quotation marks, and as it bears internal evidence in its phraseology of having been a formal regulation adopted at or very near the period to which Preston assigns it, we may accept it as authentic and suppose that he had access to sources of information no longer extant. As the Grand Lodge was organized in 1717 in the rooms of the lodge of which Preston afterward became a member, it is very possible that that lodge may have had in its possession the full records of that meeting, which were in existence when Preston wrote, but have since been lost.[23]

At all events the "General Regulations," compiled by Grand Master Payne in 1720, and approved the next year by the Grand Lodge, contain a similar provision in the following words:

"If any set or number of Masons shall take upon themselves to form a lodge without the Grand Master's warrant, the regular lodges are not to countenance them, nor own them as fair Brethren and duly formed, nor approve of their acts and deeds; but must treat them as rebels, until they humble themselves, as the Grand Master shall, in his prudence, direct; and until he approve of them by his warrant."[24]

If we compare the usage by which lodges were brought into existence under the wholly Operative rules, and that adopted by the Speculative Freemasons after the organization of the Grand Lodge in 1717, we will very clearly see that there was here no revival of an old system which had fallen into decay and disuse, but the invention of one that was entirely new and never before heard of.

The next point to be examined in discussing the question whether or not the transactions of 1717 constituted a Revival will be the character of the lodges before and after those transactions as compared with each other.

During the 17th century, to go no farther back, and up to the second decade of the 18th, all the lodges of Freemasons in England were Operative lodges, that is to say, the larger portion of their members were

---

[23] Findel ("History," p. 140), says the regulation was adopted at a later period, in 1723 This he had no right to do. Preston is our only authority for the regulation, and his statement must be taken without qualification or wholly rejected. Findel was probably led into his error by seeing the General Regulation above quoted, which was very similar This was published in 1723, but it had been adopted by the Grand Lodge in 1721.

[24] "General Regulations," art. viii. Anderson, 1st edition, p. 60.

working Masons, engaged in building according to certain principles of architecture with which they alone were acquainted.

They had admitted among their members persons of rank or learning who were not Operative Masons or builders by profession, but all their laws and regulations were applicable to a society of mechanics or workingmen.

There are no minutes in England, as there are in Scotland, of lodges prior to the beginning of the 18th century. They have all been lost, and the only one remaining is that of the Alnwick Lodge, the records of which begin in the year 1701.

But the "Old Charges" contained in the manuscript Constitutions which extend from 1390 to 1714, of which more than twenty have been preserved, supply us (especially the later ones of the 17th century) with the regulations by which the Craft was governed during the ante-revival period.

It is unnecessary to quote in extenso any one of these Old Constitutions. It is sufficient to say that they bear the strongest internal evidence that they were compiled for the use of purely Operative Masons.

They were wholly inapplicable to any merely moral or speculative association. Excepting those clauses which directed how the craftsmen were to conduct themselves both in the lodge and out of it, so that the reputation of the Brotherhood should not be injured, they were mainly engaged in prescribing how the Masons should labor in their art of building, so that the employer might be "truly served." The same regulations would be just as applicable, mutatis mutandis, to a Guild of Carpenters, of Smiths, or any other mechanical trade, as to one of Masons.

But while these lodges were wholly Operative in their character and design, there is abundant evidence, as I have heretofore shown, that they admitted into their companionship persons who were not Masons by profession. The article in the Harleian Constitutions, to which reference has just been made, while stating that a lodge called to make a Mason must consist of five Free Masons, adds that one of them at least shall be "of the trade of Free Masonry." The other four, of course, might be non- operatives, that is to say, persons of rank, wealth, or learning who were sometimes called Theoretic and sometimes Gentlemen Masons.

But in the laws enacted for the government of the Craft, no exceptional provision was made in them, by which any difference was created in the privileges of the two classes.

The admission of these Theoretic Masons into the Fraternity did not, therefore, in the slightest degree affect the Operative character of the Craft, except in so far as that the friendly collision with men of education must have given to the less educated members a portion of refinement that could not fail to elevate them above the other Craft Guilds.

Yet so intimate was the connection between these Operative Freemasons and their successors, the Speculatives, that the code of laws prepared in 1721 by Anderson at the direction of the Grand Lodge, and published in 1723, under the title of The Charges of a Free-Mason, for the use of the Lodges in London, was a transcript with no important variations from these Old Constitutions, or as Anderson calls them, the "Old Gothic Constitutions."

As these "Charges" have now been accepted by the modern Fraternity of English-speaking Freemasons as the basis of what are called the Landmarks of the Order, to make them of any use it has been found absolutely necessary to give them a symbolic or figurative sense.

Thus, "to work," which in the Operative Constitution signifies "to build," is interpreted in the Speculative system as meaning "to confer degrees;" the clause which prescribes that "all the tools used in working shall be approved by the Grand Lodge" is interpreted as denoting that the ritual, ceremonies, and by-laws of every lodge must be subjected to the supervision of the Grand Lodge. Thus every regulation which clearly referred to a fraternity of builders has, in the course of the modifications which were necessary to render it applicable to a moral association, been made to adopt a figurative sense.

Yet the significant fact that while in the government of Speculative Freemasonry the spirit and meaning of these "Old Charges" have been entirely altered, the words have been carefully retained is an important and irrefutable proof that the Speculative system is the direct successor of the Operative.

So when the Theoretic or Gentleman Masons had, in the close of the 17th and the beginning of the 18th century, acquired such a preponderance in numbers and in influence in the London lodges that they were able so to affect the character of those lodges as to divert them from the practice of an Operative art to the pursuit of a Speculative science, such change could not be called a Revival, if we respected the meaning of that word. Nothing of the kind had been known before; and when the members of the lodges ceased to pay any attention to the craft or mystery of practical stonemasonry, and resolved to treat it thenceforth in a purely symbolic sense, this act could be deemed nothing else but a new departure in the career of Freemasonry.

The ship was still there, but the object of the voyage had been changed.

Again: we find a third change in the character of the Masonic society when we compare the general government of the Craft as it appears before and after the year 1717.

This change is particularly striking in respect to the way in which the Craft were ruled in their Operative days, compared with the system which was adopted by the Speculative Freemasons.

It has already been said that prior to the year 1717, there never were Grand Masters or a Grand Lodge except such as were mythically constructed by the romantic genius of Dr. Anderson.

The only historical records that we have of the condition of Freemasonry in England and of the usages of the Craft during the three centuries which preceded the 18th, are to be found in the old manuscript Constitutions.

A thoroughly careful examination of these documents will show that neither in the Legend of the Craft, which constitutes the introductory portion of each Constitution, nor in the "Charges" which follow, is there the slightest allusion, either in direct language or by implication, to the office of Grand Master or to the body now called a Grand Lodge.

But it can not be denied that there was an annual convocation of the Craft, which was called sometimes the "Congregations" sometimes the "Assembly," and sometimes the "General Assembly." We must accept this as an historical fact, or we must repudiate all the manuscript Constitutions from the 14th to the 18th century. In all of them there is an unmistakable allusion to this annual convocation of the Craft, and regulations are made concerning attendance on it.

Thus the Halliwell MS. says that "every Master who is a Mason must be present at the general congregation if he is duly informed where the assembly is to be holden; and to that assembly he must go unless he have a reasonable excuse."

The precise words of this most ancient of all the Old Masonic Constitutions, dating, as it does, not later than toward the close of the 14th century, are as follows:

That every mayster, that ys a mason, Must ben at the generate congregracyon, So that he hyt reasonably y-tolde Where that the semble' schal be holde; And to that semble' he must nede gon, But he have a resonabul skwsacyon.

The Cooke MS., which is about a century later, has a similar provision. This manuscript is important, inasmuch as it describes the character of the Assembly and defines the purposes for which it was to be convoked.

It states that the Assembly, or, as it is there called, the Congregation, shall assemble once a year, or at least once in three years, for the examination of Master Masons, to see that they possessed sufficient skill and knowledge in their art.

An important admission in this manuscript is that the regulation for the government of this Assembly "is written and taught in our book of charges."

All the subsequent Constitutions make a similar statement in words that do not substantially vary.

The Harleian MS., whose date is about the last quarter of the 17th century, says that Euclid gave the admonition that the Masons were to assemble once a year to take counsel how the Craft could best work so as to serve their Lord and Master for his profit and their credit, and to correct such as had offended. And in another MS., much earlier than the Harleian, it is said that the Freemasons should attend the Assembly, and if any had trespassed against the Craft, he should there abide the award of the Masters and Fellows.

This Assembly met that statutes or regulations might be enacted for the government of the Craft, and that controversies between the craftsmen might be determined.

It was both a legislative and a judicial body, and in these respects resembled the Grand Lodge of the present day, but in no other way was there any similitude between the two.

Now, leaving out of the question the legendary parts which ascribe the origin of this annual assembly to Euclid or Athelstan or Prince Edwin, which, of course, are of no historical authority, it is impossible to believe that all these Constitutions should speak of the existence of such an Assembly at the time of writing, and lay down a regulation in the most positive terms, that every Mason should attend it, if the whole were a mere figment of the imagination.

We can account for the mythical character of a legend, but we cannot for the mythical character of a law which has been enacted at a specified time for the government of an association, which law continues to be repeated in all the copies of the statutes written or published for more than three centuries continuously.

In the establishment of a Grand Lodge with quarterly meetings and an annual one in which a Grand Master and other Grand Officers were elected for the following year, we find no analogy to anything that had existed previous to the year 1717. We cannot, therefore, in these points call the organization which took place in. that year a "Revival." It was, rather, a radical change in the construction of the system.

Another change, and a very important one, too, which occurred a short time after the establishment of the Grand Lodge of England in 1717, was that which had reference to the ritual or forms of initiation. During the purely Operative period of Freemasonry it is now well known that there was but one esoteric system of admission to the brotherhood of the Craft. This we also know was common to the three classes of Masters, Fellows, and Apprentices. There was, in fact, if we may use the technical language of modern Freemasonry, but one degree practiced by the Operative Craft.

When the Theoretic members of the London lodges dissociated from the Operatives in the year 1717 and formed the Speculative system, they, of course, at first accepted the old method of admission. But in the course of two or three vears they adopted another system and fabricated what are now called the three degrees of ancient Craft Masonry, each one of which was exclusively appropriated as a form of initiation to one of the three classes and to that one only. What had formerly been a division of the Fraternity into three classes or ranks became now a division into three degrees.[25]

This was a most important change, and as nothing of the kind was known to the Craft in the years prior to the establishment of the Grand Lodge, it certainly can not be considered a correct use of the word to call an entire change of a system and the adoption of a new one a revival of the old.

Bro. W.P. Buchan, in numerous articles published in the London Freemason, about 1870, attacked what has been called the Revival theory with much vigor but with exaggerated views. He contends that "our system of degrees, words, grips, signs, etc., was not in existence until about A.D. 1717, and he attributes the present system to the inventive genius of Anderson and Desaguliers. Hence he contends that modern Freemasonry was simply a reconstruction of an ancient society, viz., of some old Pagan philosophy. This he more fully explains in these words:

"Before the 18th century we had a renaissance of Pagan architecture; then to follow suit in the 18th century we had a renaissance

---

[25] it is not necessary to enter at this time into an examination and defense of this hypothesis, as the history of the fabrication of the three degrees will be made the subject of a future chapter.

in a new dress of Pagan mysticism; but for neither are we indebted to the Operative Masons, although the Operative Masons were made use of in both cases."[26]

There is in this statement a mixture of truth and error. It is undoubtedly true that the three degrees into which the system is now divided were unknown to the Freemasons of the 17th century, and that they were an invention of those scholars who organized the Grand Lodge of Speculative Freemasonry, mainly of Dr. Desaguliers, assisted perhaps by Anderson and Payne. But there were signs of recognition, methods of government, legends, and some form, though a simple one of initiation, which were in existence prior to the 18th century, which formed the kernel of the more elaborate system of the modern Freemasons.

Bro. Hughan calls attention to the fact, if there were need of proofs, in addition to what has been found in the authentic accounts of the mediaeval Freemasons, that in the Tatler, published in 1709, is a passage in which the writer, speaking of a class of men called the "Pretty Fellows," says that "they have their signs and tokens like the Freemasons."[27]

In fact, Bro. Buchan admits that the "elements or ground work" of the system existed before the year 1717.

This is in fact the only hypothesis that can be successfully maintained on the subject.

The Grand Lodge of Speculative Freemasons, which was organized at the "Goose and Gridiron Tavern" in London in the year 1717, was a new system, founded on the older one which had existed in England years before, and which had been derived from the Operative Freemasons of the Middle Ages.

It was not, as Hyneman[28] has called it, a Revolution, for that would indicate a violent disruption, and a sudden and entire change of principles.

It was not a Revival, as most of the earlier writers have entitled it, for we should thus infer that the new system was only a renewal without change of the old one.

But it was a gradual transition from an old into a new system - of Operative into Speculative Freemasonry - in which Transition the

---

[26] London Freemason, September 29, 1871.
[27] Voice of Masonry, April, 1873.
[28] In a work abounding in errors, entitled "Ancient York and London Grand Lodges," by Lem Hyneman, Philadelphia, 1872. Its fallacies as a contribution to Masonic history have been shown by the incisive but courteous criticism of Bro. Hughan.

later system has been built upon the earlier, and the practical art of building has been spiritualized into a theoretic science of morality, illustrated by a symbolism drawn principally from architecture.

We thus recognize the regular descent of the modern Speculative Freemasons from their older Operative predecessors, and we answer the question which forms the heading of the present chapter.

But it has been said that in one sense at least we may with propriety apply the word "Revival" to the transactions of the early part of the 18th century. Operative Freemasonry, and what very little of the Speculative element that had been engrafted on it, had, we are told, begun to decline in England in the latter part of the 17th century.

If we may rely on the authority of Preston, the fraternity at the time of the revolution in 1688 was so much reduced in the south of England, that no more than seven regular lodges met in London and its suburbs, of which two only were worthy of notice.[29] Anderson mentions seven by their locality, and says that there were "some more that assembled statedly."[30]

These were, of course, all purely Operative lodges. Thus one of them, Anderson tells us, was called upon to give architectural counsel as to the best design of rebuilding St. Thomas's Hospital,[31] a clear evidence that its members were practical builders.

But this decline in the number of the lodges may possibly be attributed to local and temporary causes. It was certainly not accompanied, as might have been expected, with a corresponding decline in the popularity of the institution, for if we may believe the same authority, " at a general assembly and feast of the Masons in 1697, many noble and eminent brethren were present."[32]

But admitting that there was a decline, it was simply a decline of the Operative lodges. And the act of 1717 was not to revive them, but eventually to extinguish them and to establish Speculative lodges in their place; nor was it to revive Operative Freemasonry, but to establish for it another and an entirely different institution.

We arrive, therefore, again at the legitimate conclusion that the establishment of the Grand Lodge of England in June, 1717, was not a revival of the old system of Freemasonry, which soon after became extinct, but its change into a new system.

---

[29] Preston, "Illustrations.
[30] Anderson, "Constitutions," 2d edition, p. 107.
[31] Ibid., p. 106.
[32] Preston, " Illustrations," p. 189.

What remained of the Operative Freemasons who did go into the new association were merged in the Masons' Company, or acted henceforward as individual craftsmen unconnected with a guild.

CHAPTER XXXI

THE EARLY YEARS OF SPECULATIVE FREEMASONRY IN ENGLAND

In the feast of St. John the Baptist, the 24th of June, in the year 1717, the principal members of the four old Operative Lodges in London, who had previously met in February and agreed to constitute a Grand Lodge of Free and Accepted Masons, assembled at the "Goose and Gridiron Tavern" in St. Paul's Churchyard with some other old Masons, and there and then organized the new Grand Lodge.

This was accomplished by electing a Grand Master and two Grand Wardens, after which the Brethren proceeded to partake of a dinner, a custom which has ever since been continued under the name of the Grand Feast.

As the written minutes in the record book of the Grand Lodge do not begin before November, 1723, we are indebted for all that we know of the transactions on that eventful day to the meager account contained in the 2d edition of Dr. Anderson's Constitutions, with a few additional details which are given by Preston in his Illustrations.

Preston cites no authority for the facts which he has stated. But as the meeting of the Grand Lodge was held in the room of the lodge which afterward became the Lodge of Antiquity, and of which Preston was a prominent member, it is not improbable that some draft of those early proceedings may have been contained in the archives of that lodge, which have been since lost. To these Preston would naturally, from his connection with the lodge, have had access. If such were the case, it is very certain that he must have made use of them in compiling his history.

I am disposed, therefore, from these circumstances, together with the consideration of the character of Preston, to accept his statements as authentic, though they are unsupported by any contemporary authority now extant.[33]

The first indication of a change, though not purposely intended, by which the Operative system was to become eventually a Speculative one, is seen in the election as presiding officers of three persons who were not Operative Masons.

Mr. Anthony Sayer, the first Grand Master, is described by Anderson in his record of the election by the legal title of "Gentleman," a title which, by the laws of honor, was bestowed upon one who can live without manual labor and can support himself without interfering in any mechanical employment. Such a person, say the heralds, "is called Mr., and may write himself Gentleman."[34]

"Anthony Sayer, Gentleman," as he is described in the record, was undoubtedly a mere Theoretic member of the Masonic association and not an Operative Mason.

Of the two Grand Wardens who were elected at the same time, one was Captain Joseph Elliot. Of his social position we have no further knowledge that what is conveyed by the title prefixed to his name, which would indicate that he was of the military profession, probably a retired or half-pay officer of the army.

The other Grand Warden was Mr. Jacob Lamball, who is designated as being a Carpenter.

Thus we see that the first three officers of the Grand Lodge were not Operative members of the Craft of Masonry.

The choice, however, of a Carpenter, a profession closely connected with that of the Masons, affords proof that it was not intended to confine the future Speculative society altogether to persons who were not mechanics.

At the succeeding election in 1718 George Payne, Esq., was elected Grand Master. He was an Antiquary and scholar of considerable ability, and was well calculated to represent the Speculative character of the new association.

---

[33] Preston is, however, sometimes careless, a charge to which all the early Masonic writers are amenable. Thus, he says that Sayer appointed his Wardens. But these officers were, like the Grand Master, elected until 1721, when, for the first time, they were appointed by the Grand Master.

[34] "Laws of Honor," p. 286.

The Wardens were Mr. John Cordwell and Mr. Thomas Morrice. The former is described as a Carpenter and the latter as a Stonecutter.

While the choice of these officers was an evident concession to the old Operative element, the election of Payne was a step forward in the progressive movement which a few years afterward led to the total emancipation of Speculative Freemasonry from all connection with practical building. Northouck attests that "to the active zeal of Grand Master Payne the Society are under a lasting obligation for introducing brethren of noble rank into the fraternity."[35]

From the very beginning the Grand Lodge had confined its selection of Grand Masters to persons of good social position, of learning, or of rank, though for a few years it occasionally conferred the Grand Wardenship on Operative Masons or on craftsmen of other trades.

In the year 1719 Dr. John Theophilus Desaguliers was elected Grand Master, and Anthony Sayer and Thomas Morrice Grand Wardens. Desaguliers was a natural philosopher of much reputation and a Fellow of the Royal Society. Sayer had been the first Grand Master, and Morrice, who was a stonecutter or Operative Mason, had been a Warden the previous year.

In 1720 Payne was again elected Grand Master, and Thomas Hobby and Richard Ware were chosen as Grand Wardens. Hobby, like his predecessor, Morrice, was an Operative Mason or stonecutter, and Ware was a mathematician.

In 1721 the Duke of Montagu was elected Grand Master. He was the first nobleman who had served in that capacity, and from that day to the present the throne of the Grand Lodge of England, as it is technically styled, has without a single exception been occupied by persons of royal or noble rank.

In this year the office of Deputy Grand Master was created, and the power of choosing him as well as the Grand Wardens was taken from the Grand Lodge and invested in the Grand Master, a law which still continues in force.

Accordingly, the Duke of Montagu appointed John Beal, a physician, his Deputy, and Josiah Villeneau, who was an upholsterer, and again Thomas Morrice, his Wardens.

The Duke of Wharton, who was Grand Master in 1722, appointed Dr. Desaguliers his Deputy, and Joshua Timson and James

---

[35] Northouck's " Constitutions anno 1784," p. 207. Entick ("Constitutions," 1756, p. 190) had made a similar remark.

Anderson his Wardens. Timson was a blacksmith and Anderson a clergyman, well-known afterward as the Compiler of the first and second editions of the Book of Constitutions.

In 1723 the Earl of Dalkeith was Grand Master, Desaguliers again Deputy, and Francis Sorrel, Esq., and John Senex, a bookseller, Wardens.

From 1717 to 1722 the claims of the Operative Masons to hold a share of the offices had, as Gould[36] remarks, been fairly recognized. The appointment of Stonecutters, Carpenters, and other mechanics as Grand Wardens had been a concession by the Speculative members to the old Operative element.

But in 1723 the struggle between the two, which is noticed in the records of the society only by its results, terminated in the complete victory of the former, who from that time restricted the offices to persons of rank, of influence, or of learning. From the year 1723 no Operative Mason or workman of any trade was ever appointed as a Warden. In the language of Gould, "they could justly complain of their total supercession in the offices of the society.

This silent progress of events shows very clearly how the Freemasons who founded the Speculative Grand Lodge in 1717 on the principles and practices of Operative Freemasonry as they prevailed in the four Lodges of London, gradually worked themselves out of all connection with their Operative brethren and eventually made Freemasonry what it now is, a purely Speculative, philosophical, and moral institution.

Upon the coalition of the four Lodges into one supervising body, the next step in the progress to pure Speculative Freemasonry was to prevent the formation of other lodges which might be independent of the supervision of the Grand Lodge, and thus present an obstacle to the completion of the reformation.

This could only be accomplished by a voluntary relinquishment, on the part of the four Lodges, of their independency and an abandonment of their privileges.

The conference at the "Apple Tree Tavern" in February, 1717, and that at the "Goose and Gridiron" in June of the same year, were what, at the present day, would be called mass-meetings of the Craft. They resembled in that respect the General Assembly spoken of in the old manuscript Constitutions, and every Freemason was required to

---

[36] "Four Old Lodges," p. 33.

attend if it were held within a reasonable distance,[37] and if he had no satisfactory excuse for his absence.

Attendance at these conferences which resulted in the establishment of the Grand Lodge was open, not only to all the members of the four Lodges, but to other Masons who were not, to use a modern phrase, affiliated with any one of them.

"The Lodges," that is, the members of them, says Anderson, "with some old Brothers." Preston calls them more distinctively some other old Brethren." Both of these phrases, of course, indicate that these "old Brethren" were not among the members of the four Lodges, but were Freemasons who had either, on account of their age, retired from active participation in the labors of the Craft, or who had been members of other lodges which were then extinct.

At the preliminary meeting in February, they voted, says Preston, "the oldest Master Mason then present into the Chair." Anderson, writing in 1738, adds "now the Master of a Lodge," by which I suppose he meant that the oldest Master Mason who presided in 1717 became in 1738 the Master of a Lodge. I know of no other way of interpreting the significance of the particle "now." They then "constituted themselves a Grand Lodge pro tempore in due form."

This "due form," I think, could have amounted to no more than a formal declaration of the intention to establish a Grand Lodge, which intention was carried out in the following June by the election of a Grand Master and Wardens.

The Freemasons of America are familiar with the methods pursued in the organization of a Grand Lodge in a territory where none had previously existed. Here a certain number of lodges, not less than three, assemble through their three principal officers and constitute a Convention, which proceeds to the election of a Grand Master and other officers, directs the lodges to surrender the Warrants under which they had been working to the Grand Lodges from which they had originally received them, and then issues new ones. The new Grand Lodge thus becomes " an accomplished fact."

But this was not the method adopted in the establishment of the Grand Lodge of England in the year 1717. Instead of the representation of the four Lodges being restricted to the Masters and Wardens of each, all the members, down to the youngest Entered Apprentice, together with Masons who were not affiliated with any lodge, met together.

---

[37] In most of the Constitutions that distance is defined to be not more than fifty miles.

The chair, according to Preston, in the preliminary meeting in February had been taken by the oldest Master Mason present. At this meeting the oldest Master Mason, who at the same time was Master of one of the four Lodges, presided. Then the Grand Lodge was duly organized by the election of its first three officers.

But now it became necessary to secure the sovereignty of the new Grand Lodge as the future supervising body of the Craft, and to prevent any additional lodges being established without its authority, so that the system might be perfected in the future according to the method which was originally designed by its founders.

Almost the first regulation which was adopted at the meeting in June, 1717, was to effect this object.

Hitherto, as we have already seen, the Operative Freemasons possessed a privilege derived from the Old Constitutions of the Guild (and which is formally enunciated in the Harleian MS.) of assembling in lodges for the purpose of "making Masons" under very simple provisions. There was no necessity for a Warrant or permission from a superior Masonic body to make such an assembly legal.

But now it was resolved that this privilege should be abolished. No number of Masons were hereafter to assemble as a lodge without the consent of the Grand Lodge, expressed by the granting of a Warrant of Constitution or Charter authorizing them to constitute or form themselves into a lodge. Without such Warrant, says Preston, no lodge should hereafter be deemed regular or constitutional.

From this regulation, however, the four Lodges which had cooperated in the formation of the Grand Lodge were excepted. They, so long as they existed, were to be the only lodges working without a Warrant and deriving their authority to do so from "immemorial usage."

The effect of this regulation was to throw an insurmountable obstacle in the way of any new lodge being formed which was not Speculative in its character and in perfect accord with the new system, from whose founders or their successors it was to derive its existence.

Hence it was the most fatal blow that had as yet been struck against the continuance of the Guild of purely Operative Freemasonry. No purely Operative nor half Operative and half Speculative lodges, we may be sure, would thereafter be erected.

From this time all lodges were to consist of Speculative Freemasons only and were to form a part of the new non-Operative system, of which the first organized Grand Lodge was the head and exercised the sovereign power.

It is true that Preston tells us that long before this period a regulation had been adopted by which "the privileges of Masonry should no longer be restricted to Operative Masons," but allowed to men of various professions; and it is also well known that there hardly ever was a time in the history of Operative Freemasonry when Theoretic or non-Operative persons were not admitted into the guild.

But this was taking a step farther, and a very long step, too. Membership in the new society was no longer a privilege extended by courtesy to Theoretic Masons. It was to be a franchise of which they alone were to be possessors. Operative Masons, merely as such, were to be excluded. In other words, no Operative Mason was to be admitted into the Fraternity because he was an Operative. He was, on his admission, to lay aside his profession, and unite with the others in the furtherance of the purely speculative design of the Institution.

So it has continued to the present day, and so it must continue as long as the system of Speculative Freemasonry shall last. Operative Freemasonry, "wounded in the house of its friends," has never covered from the blow thus inflicted.

Operative Masonry, for building purposes, still lives and must always live to serve the needs of man.

But Operative Freemasonry, as a Guild, is irrecoverably dead.

It is impossible to say for how long a time the meetings of the Grand Lodge continued to be attended by all the members of the particular lodges, or, in other words, when these assemblies ceased, like those of the old Operative Freemasons, to be mass-meetings of the Craft.

But the rapidly growing popularity of the new Order must have rendered such meetings very inconvenient from the increase of members.

Anderson says that in 1718 Several old Brothers that had neglected the Craft visited the lodges; some noblemen were also made Brothers and more new lodges were constituted."[38]

Northouck, writing in reference to the same period, says that the Free and Accepted Masons "now began visibly to gather strength as a body,"[39] and we are told that at the annual feast in 1721 the number of lodges had so increased[40] that the General Assembly required more room, and therefore the Grand Lodge was on that occasion removed to

---

[38] Anderson, "Constitutions," 2d ed., p. 110.
[39] Northouck, "Constitutions," p. 207.
[40] There were at that time twenty lodges, and the number of Freemasons who attended the annual meetings and feast was one hundred and fifty.

Stationers' Hall, nor did it ever afterward return to its old quarters at the "Goose and Gridiron Tavern."

This unwieldiness of numbers would alone be sufficient to suggest the convenience of changing the constitution of the Grand Lodge from a mass-meeting of the Fraternity into a representative body.

This was effected by the passage of a regulation dispensing with the attendance of the whole of the Craft at the annual meeting, and authorizing each lodge to be represented by its Master and two Wardens.

We have no positive knowledge of the exact date when this regulation was adopted. It first appears in the "General Regulations" which were compiled by Grand Master Payne in 1720, and approved by the Grand Lodge in 1721. The twelfth of these Regulations is in these words:

"The Grand Lodge consists of, and is formed by, the Masters and Wardens of all the regular, particular lodges upon record, with the Grand Master at their head, and his Deputy on his left hand, and the Grand Wardens in their proper places."

Preston says that the Grand Lodge having resolved that the four old Lodges should retain every privilege which they had collectively enjoyed by virtue of their immemorial rights, the members considered their attendance on the future Communications of the Grand Lodge unnecessary. They "therefore, like the other lodges, trusted implicitly to their Master and Wardens, resting satisfied that no measure of importance would be adopted without their approbation."[41]

But he adds that the officers of the four old Lodges "soon began to discover" that the new lodges might in time outnumber the old ones and encroach upon their privileges. They therefore formed a code of laws, the last clause of which provided that the Grand Lodge in making any new regulations should be bound by a careful observation of the old landmarks.

It is unfortunate that in treating this early period of Masonic history Preston should be so careless and confused in his chronology as to compel us to depend very much upon inference in settling the sequence of events.

It may, however, I think, be inferred from the remarks of Preston, and from what little we can collect from Anderson's brief notices, that the Grand Lodge continued to be a mass-meeting, attended by all the Craft, until the annual feast on the 24th of June, 1721. At that communication Anderson records that the Grand Lodge was composed

---

[41] "Illustrations," p. 193

of "Grand Master with his Wardens, the former Grand officers, and the Master and Wardens of the twelve lodges."[42] In all subsequent records he mentions the number of lodges which were represented by their officers, though the Grand Feast still continued to be attended by as many Masons as desired to partake of the dinner and, I suppose, were willing to pay their scot.[43]

It was, therefore, I think, not till 1721 that the Grand Lodge assumed that form which made it a representative body, consisting of the Masters and Wardens of the particular lodges, together with the officers of the Grand Lodge.

That form has ever since been retained in the organization of every Grand Lodge that has directly or indirectly emanated from the original body.

This was another significant token of the total disseverance that was steadily taking place between the Operative and the Speculative systems.

Hitherto we have been occupied with the consideration of the transactions recorded as having taken place at the annual meetings. We are now to inquire when these meetings began to be supplemented by Quarterly Communications.

Here an historical question presents itself, which, so far as I am aware, has not been distinctly met and treated by any of our Masonic scholars. They all seem to have taken it for granted on the naked authority of Anderson and Preston, that the Quarterly Communications were coeval with the organization of the Grand Lodge in the year 1717

Is this an historical fact? I confess that on this subject a shadow of doubt has been cast that obscures my clearness of vision.

Anderson says, and Preston repeats the statement, that at the preliminary meeting in February, 1717, at the "Apple Tree Tavern," it was resolved if to revive the Quarterly Communications."

But these two authorities (and they are the only ones that we have on the subject) differ in some of the details. And these differences are important enough to throw a doubt on the truth of the statement.

Anderson says in one place that in February, 1717, they "forthwith revived the Quarterly Communications of the officers of lodges called the Grand Lodge."[44]

---

[42] "Constitutions," 2d edition, p. 112.

[43] The only qualification for attendance on the feast was that the guests must be Masons: therefore waiting brethren were appointed to attend the tables, "for that no strangers must be there." - "Constitutions," 2d ed., p. 112.

[44] Anderson, " Constitutions," 2d edition, p. 109

Afterward he says that at the meeting in June, 1717, Grand Master Sayer "commanded the Masters and Wardens of lodges to meet the Grand officers every quarter in communication, at the place he should appoint in his summons sent by the Tyler."[45]

Preston says that in February "it was resolved to revive the Quarterly Communications of the Fraternity."[46] Immediately after he adds that in June the Grand Master "commanded the Brethren of the four Lodges to meet him and his Wardens quarterly in communication."[47]

Thus, according to Preston, the Quarterly Communications were to apply to the whole body of the Fraternity; but Anderson restricted them to the Masters and Wardens of the lodges.

The two statements are irreconcilable. A mass-meeting of the whole Fraternity and a consultation of the Masters and Wardens of the lodges are very different things.

But both are in error in saying that the Quarterly Communications "were revived," for there is no notice of or allusion to Quarterly Communications in any of the old records which speak only of an annual General Assembly of the Craft, and sometimes perhaps occasional assemblies for special purposes.

There can be no doubt that such was the usage among the English mediaeval guilds, a usage which must have been applicable to the Freemasons as well as to other Crafts. "The distinction," says J. Toulmin Smith, "between the gatherings (congregations) and general meetings (assemblies) is seen at a glance in most of the ordinances. The guild brethren were bound to gather together, at unfixed times, for special purposes; but besides these gatherings upon special summons, general meetings of the guilds were held on fixed days in every year for the election of officers, holding their feasts, etc."[48]

I do not see any analogy in these gatherings of local guilds to the Quarterly Communications of the Grand Lodge spoken of by Anderson. The analogy is rather to the monthly meetings of the particular lodges as contrasted with the annual meeting of the Grand Lodge.

But if, as Anderson and Preston say, the Quarterly Communications were "forthwith revived" in 1717, it is singular that there is no record of any one having been held until December, 1720.

---

[45] Ibid., p. 110.
[46] Preston, " Illustrations," p. 191.
[47] Ibid.
[48] "English Guilds," p. 128, note.

After that date we find the Quarterly Communications regularly recorded by Anderson as taking place at the times appointed in the Regulations which were compiled in 1720 by Grand Master Payne, namely, "about Michaelmas, Christmas, and Lady Day," that is, in September, December, and March.

The word "about" in the 12th Regulation permitted some latitude as to the precise day of meeting.

Accordingly, we find that Quarterly Communications were held in 1721 in March, September, and December; in 1722, in March, but the others appeared to have been neglected, perhaps in consequence of irregularities attendant on the illegal election of the Duke of Wharton; in 1723 there were Quarterly Communications in April and November, and the December meeting was postponed to the following January; in 1724 they occurred in February and November; in 1725 in May, November, and December, and so on, but with greater regularity, in all the subsequent proceedings of the Grand Lodge as recorded in the Book of Constitutions by Anderson, son, and by his successors Entick and Northouck in the subsequent editions.

Looking at the silence or the records in respect to Quarterly Communications from 1717 to 1720; then to the regular appearance of such records after that year, and seeing that in the latter year the provision for them was first inserted in the General Regulations compiled at that time by Grand Master Payne, I trust that I shall not be deemed too skeptical or too hypercritical, if I confess my doubt of the accuracy of Anderson, who has, whether wilfully or carelessly, I will not say, attributed the establishment of these Quarterly Communications to Grand Master Sayer, when the honor, if there be any, properly belongs to Grand Master Payne.

The next subject that will attract our attention in this sketch of the early history of the Grand Lodge, is the method in which the laws which regulated the original Operative system were gradually modified and at length completely changed so as to be appropriate to the peculiar needs of a wholly Speculative Society.

When the four old Lodges united, in the year 1717, in organizing a Grand Lodge, it is very evident that the only laws which governed them must have been the "Charges" contained in the manuscript Constitutions or such private regulations adopted by the lodges, as were conformable to them.

There was no other Masonic jurisprudence known to the Operative Freemasons of England, at the beginning of the 18th century, than that which was embodied in these old Constitutions. These were familiar to the Operative Freemasons of that day, as they had been for centuries before to their predecessors.

Though never printed, copies of them in manuscript were common and were easily accessible. They were often copied, one from another - just as often, probably, as the wants of a new lodge might require.

Beginning at the end of the 14th century, which is the date of the poetical Constitutions, which were first published by Mr. Halliwell, copies continued to be made until the year 1714, which is the date of the last one now extant, executed before the organization of the Grand Lodge.[49][50]

Now in all these written Constitutions, extending through a period of more than three centuries, there is a very wonderful con-formity of character.

The poetic form which exists in the Halliwell MS. was apparently never imitated, and all the subsequent manuscript Constitutions now extant are in prose. But as Bro. Woodford has justly observed, they all "seem in fact to be clearly derived from the Masonic Poem, though naturally altered in their prose form, and expanded and modified through transmission and oral tradition, as well as by the lapse of time and the change of circumstances."

While these old constitutions contained, with hardly any appreciable variation, the Legend of the Craft, which was conscientiously believed by the old Operative Free Masons as containing the true history of the rise and progress of the brotherhood, they embodied also that code of laws by which the fraternity was governed during the whole period of its existence.

Though these Constitutions commenced, so far as we have any knowledge of them from personal inspection, at the close of the 14th century, we are not to admit that there were no earlier copies. Indeed, I have formerly shown that the Halliwell Poem, whose conjectural date is 1390, is evidently a compilation from two other poems of an earlier date.

The Freemasons who were contemporary with the organization of the Grand Lodge held those old manuscript Constitutions, as their predecessors had done before them, in the greatest reverence. The fact that the laws which they prescribed, like those of the Medes and Persians, had invested them with the luster of antiquity, and as they had

---

[49] I take no notice here of the Krause MS., which pretends to contain the Constitutions enacted by Prince Edwin, in 926, because I have not the least doubt that it is a forgery of comparatively recent times.
[50] Preface to Hughan's "Old Charges of British Freemasons," p. 13.

always remained written, and had never been printed, the Craft looked upon them as their peculiar property and gave to them much of an esoteric character.

This false estimate of the true nature of these documents led to an inexcusable and irreparable destruction of many of them.

Grand Master Payne had in 1718 desired the brethren to bring to the Grand Lodge "any old writings and records concerning Masons and Masonry in order to show the usages of ancient times."[51] These, it was suspected, were to be used in the preparation and publication of a contemplated Book of Masonic Constitutions, and the Masons became alarmed at the threatened publicity of what they had always deemed to be secret.

Accordingly, in 1720, "at some private lodges," says Anderson, "several valuable manuscripts (for they had nothing yet in print) concerning their lodges, Regulations, Charges, Secrets, and Usages (particularly one writ by Mr. Nicholas Stone, the Warden of Inigo Jones) were too hastily burnt by some scrupulous brothers, that those papers might not fall into strange hands."[52]

Northouck, commenting on this instance of vandalism, which he strangely styles an act of felo de se, says that it surely "could not proceed from zeal according to knowledge."

Of course, it was zeal without knowledge that led to this destruction, the effects of which are felt at this day by every scholar who attempts to write an authentic history of Freemasonry.

The object of Grand Master Payne in attempting to make a collection of these old writings was undoubtedly to enable him to frame a code of laws which should be founded on what Anderson calls the Gothic Constitutions. Several copies of these Constitutions were produced in the year 1718 and collated.

The result of this collation was the production which under the title of "The Charges of a Free-Mason" was appended to the first edition of the Book of Constitutions.

This is the first code of laws enacted by the Speculative Grand Lodge of England, and thus becomes important as an historical document.

As to the date and the authorship we have no other guide than that of inference.

---

[51] Anderson, "Constitutions," 2d edition, p. 110.
[52] Anderson, "Constitutions," 2d edition, p. 111.

There can, however, be little hesitation in ascribing the authorship to Payne and the time of the compilation to the period of his first Grand Mastership, which extended from June, 1718, to June, 1719.

In the title to these "Charges" it is said that they have been "extracted from the ancient records of lodges beyond sea and of those in England, Scotland, and Ireland, for the use of the lodges in London."

Now this admirably coincides with the passage in Anderson in which it is said that at the request of Grand Master Payne, in the year 1718, "several old copies of the Gothic Constitutions were produced and collated."

In fact, we thus identify the collation of the Gothic Constitutions in 1718 with the "Charges of a Free-Mason," published in the first edition of the Book of Constitutions.

Nor do I feel any hesitation in ascribing this collation of the old Constitutions and the compilation, out of it, of the "Charges" to Payne, whose genius lay in that way and who again exercised it, two years afterward, in the compilation of the "General Regulations," which took the place of the "Charges" as the law of the Speculative Grand Lodge.

The valuable services of George Payne in the incipient era of Speculative Freemasonry have not received from our historians the appreciation which is their just due. His reputation has been overshadowed by that of Desaguliers. Both labored much and successfully for the infant institution. But we should never forget that the work of Payne in the formation of its jurisprudence was as important as was that of Desaguliers in the fabrication of its ritual.[53]

But to resume the history of the progress of Masonic law.

The adoption in 1718 of the "Charges of a Free-Mason," with the direction that they shall be read as the existing law of the fraternity" at the making of new brethren," [54]is a very significant proof of what has before been suggested that at the time of the so-called "Revival" there was no positive intention to wholly dissever the Speculative from the Operative system.

---

[53] Dr. Oliver very inaccurately says in his "Revelations of a Square" that "at the annual assembly on St. John's day, 1721, Desaguliers produced thirty-eight regulations," but distinctly states that these regulations were "compiled first by Mr. George Payne, anno 1720, when he was Grand Master, and approved by the Grand Lodge on St. John Baptist's day, anno 1721." The venerable doctor had here forgotten the Ciceronian axiom - suum cuique tribuere.

[54] See the title of the "Charges" in the first edition of the "Book of Constitutions," p. 49.

These "Charges" are, as they must necessarily have been, originating as they did in the Old Constitutions, a code of regulations adapted only to a fraternity of Operative Freemasons and wholly inapplicable to a society of Speculatives, such as the institution afterward became.

Thus Masters were not to receive Apprentices unless they had sufficient employment for them; the Master was to oversee the lord's or employer's work, and was to be chosen from the most expert of the Fellow-Crafts; the Master was to undertake the lord's work for reasonable pay; no one was to receive more wages than he deserved; the Master and the Masons were to receive their wages meekly; were to honestly finish their work and not to put them to task which had been accustomed to journey; nor was one Mason to supplant another in his work.

The Operative feature is very plain in these regulations. They are, it is true, supplemented by other regulations as to conduct in the lodge, in the presence of strangers, and at home; and these are as applicable to a Speculative as they are to an Operative Mason.

But the whole spirit, and, for the most part, the very language of these "Charges," is found in the Old Constitutions of the Operative Masons.

They have, however, been always accepted as the foundation of the law of Speculative Masonry, though originally adopted at a time when the society had not yet completely thrown over its Operative character.

But to apply them to an exposition of the laws of Speculative Freemasonry, and to make them applicant to the government of the Order in its purely Speculative condition, modern Masonic jurists have found it necessary to give to the language of the "Charges" a figurative or symbolic signification, a process that I suspect was not contemplated by Payne or his contemporaries.

Thus, to work, is now interpreted as meaning to practice the ritual. The lodge is at work when it is conferring a degree. To receive wages is to be advanced from a lowes to a higher degree. To supplant another in his work, is for one lodge to interfere with the candidates of another.

In this way statutes intended originally for the government of a body of workmen have by judicial ingenuity been rendered applicable to a society of moralists.

The adoption of these "Charges" was a concession to the Operative element of the new society. The Grand Lodge of 1717 was the successor or the outcome of an old and different association. It brought into its organization the relics of that oid association, nor was it prepared in its inchoate condition to cast aside all the usages and habits of that ancient body.

Hence the first laws enacted by the Speculative Grand Lodge were borrowed from and founded on the manuscript Constitutions of the Operative Freemasons.

But the inapplicability of such a system of government to the new organization was very soon discovered.

Two years afterward Payne, untiring in his efforts to perfect the institution, which had honored him twice with its highest office, compiled a new code which was perfectly applicable to a Speculative society.

This new code, under the title of the "General Regulations," was compiled by Payne in 1720, and having been approved by the Grand Lodge in 1721, was inserted in the first edition of the Book of Constitutions, published in 1723.

Anderson says that he "has compared them with and reduced them to the ancient records and immemorial usages of the Fraternity, and digested them into this new method with several proper explications for the use of the lodges in and about London and Westminster.[55]

There certainly is some evidence of the handiwork of Anderson in some interpolations which must have been of a later date than that of the original compilation.[56] But as a body of law, it must be considered as the work of Payne.

This code has ever since remained as the groundwork or basis of the system of Masonic jurisprudence. Very few modifications have ever been made in its principles. Additional laws have been since enacted, not only by the mother Grand Lodge, but by those which have emanated from it, but the spirit of the original code has always been respected and preserved. In fact, it has been regarded almost in the light of a set of landmarks, whose sanctity could not legally be violated.

George Payne, the second and fourth Grand Master of the Grand Lodge of England, is therefore justly entitled to the distinguished reputation of being the lawgiver of modern Freemasonry.

If we compare the Charges adopted in 1718 with the Regulations approved in 1721, we will be struck with the great change

---

[55] Title prefixed to the General Regulations, in 1st edition of "Book of Constitutions," p. 58.
[56] This subject will be more fully discussed, and some of these interpolations will be pointed out, when we come, in a future chapter, to the consideration of the fabrication of the degrees.

that must have taken place in the constitution and character of a society that thus necessitated so important a modification in its principles of government.

The "Charges" were, as has already been shown, applicable to an association in which the Operative element preponderated. The Regulations are appropriate to one wholly Speculative in its design, and from which the Operative element has been thoroughly eliminated.

The adoption of the Regulations in 1721 was therefore an irrefutable proof that at that period the Grand Lodge and the lodges under its jurisdiction had entirely severed all connection with Operative Freemasonry.

We may, indeed, make this the epoch to which we are to assign the real birth of pure Speculative Freemasonry in England.

There were, however, many lodges outside of the London limit which still preserved the Operative character, and many years elapsed before the Speculative system was universally disseminated throughout the kingdom.

The minutes of a few of them have been preserved or recovered after having been lost, and they exhibit for the most part, as late as the middle of the 18th century, the characteristics which distinguished all English Masonic lodges before the establishment of the Grand Lodge. Their membership consisted of an admixture of Operative and Theoretic Masons. But the business of the lodge was directed to the necessities and inclinations of the former class.

A common feature in these minutes is the record of the indentures of Apprentices for seven years, to Master Masons who were members of the lodge.

Speculative Freemasonry, which took rapid growth in London after its severance from the Operative lodges, made slower progress in the provinces.

Of the rapidity of growth in the city and its suburbs we have every satisfactory evidence in the increase of lodges as shown in the official lists which were printed at occasional periods.

Thus, in 1717, as we have seen, there were but four Lodges engaged in the organization of the Grand Lodge.

These were the only Lodges then in London. At least no evidence has ever been produced that there were any others. These were all original Operative lodges.

Anderson says that "more new lodges were constituted" in 1719.

If he had been accurate in the use of his language, the qualifying adverb "more" would indicate that "new lodges" had also been constituted the year before.

In June, 1721, twelve lodges were represented in the Grand Lodge by their Masters and Wardens, showing, if there were no absentees, that eight new lodges had been added to the Fraternity since 1717.

In September of the same year Anderson records the presence of the representatives of sixteen lodges. Either four new lodges had been added to the list between June and September, or what is more likely, some were absent in the meeting of the former month.

In March, 1722, the officers of twenty-four lodges are recorded as being present, and in April, 1723, the number had increased to thirty.

But the number of lodges stated by Anderson to have been represented at the Communications of the Grand Lodge does not appear to furnish any absolute criterion of the number of lodges in existence. Thus, while the records show that in April, 1723, thirty lodges were represented in the Grand Lodge, the names of the Masters and Wardens of only twenty lodges are signed to the approbation of the Book of Constitutions, which is appended to the first edition of that work published in the same year.

Bro. Gould calls this "the first List of Lodges ever printed,"[57] but I deem it unworthy of that title, if by a "List of Lodges" is meant a roll of all those actually in existence at the time. Now, if this were a correct list of the lodges which were on the roll of the Grand Lodge at the time, what has become of the ten necessary to make up the number of thirty which are reported to have been represented in April, 1723, besides some others which we may suppose to have been absent?

Anderson did not think it worth while to explain the incongruity, but from 1723 onward we have no further difficulty in tracing the numerical progress of the lodges and incidentally the increase in the number of members of the Fraternity.

Engraved lists of lodges began in 1723 to be published by authority of the Grand Lodge, and to the correctness of these we may safely trust, as showing the general progress of the Institution.

The first of these lists is "printed for and sold by Eman Bowen, Engraver, in Aldersgate St." It purports to be a list of lodges in 1723, and the number of them amounts to fifty-one. In 1725 Pine, who was in some way connected, it is supposed, with Bowen, issued a list for 1725,

---

[57] The "Four Old Lodges," p. 2.

which contains, not the names, for the lodges at that time had no names, but the taverns or places of meeting of sixtyfour lodges, fifty-six of which were in London or its vicinity.

On November 27, 1723, the Grand Lodge commenced in its minute-book an official list of the lodges, which seems, says Bro. Gould, "to have been continued until 1729." The lodges are entered, says the same authority, in ledger form, two lodges to a page, and beneath them appear the names of members.

This list contains seventy-seven lodges. Supposing, as Gould does, that the list extended to 1729, it shows an increase in twelve years of seventy- three lodges, without counting the lodges which had become extinct or been merged into other lodges.

In the next official list contained in the minute-book of the Grand Lodge, and which extends to 1732, the number of lodges enumerated is one hundred and two, or an increase in fifteen years of ninety-eight lodges, again leaving out the extinct ones.

These examples are sufficient to show the steady and rapid growth of the society during the period of its infancy.

There is, however, another historical point which demands consideration. At what time did the formal constitution of lodges begin ?

It is at this day a settled law and practice, that before a lodge of Masons can take its position as one of the constituent members of a Grand Lodge, a certain form or ceremony must be undergone by which it acquires all its legal rights. This form or ceremony is called its Constitution, and the authority for this must emanate from the Grand Lodge, either directly, as in America, or indirectly, through the Grand Master, as in England, and is called the Warrant or Constitution.

The Constitutions of the Grand Lodge of England, which are in force at the present day, say: " In order to avoid irregularities, every new lodge should be solemnly constituted by the Grand Master with his Deputy and Wardens."[58]

This regulation has been in force at least since January, 1723, the very words of the clause above quoted having been taken from the form of constitution practiced by the Duke of Wharton, who was Grand Master in that year, and which form is appended to the first edition of the Book of Constitutions.

Anderson says that in 1719 "more new lodges were constituted;"[59] and Preston states that at the meeting of the Grand Lodge in 1717 a regulation was agreed to that "every lodge, except the four old Lodges at

---

[58] "Constitutions of the Ancient Fraternity of Free and Accepted Masons," p.124.
[59] Anderson, "Constitutions." 2d edition, p. 110.

this time existing, should be legally authorized to act by a warrant from the Grand Master for the time being, granted to certain individuals by petition, with the consent and approbation of the Grand Lodge in communication; and that without such warrant no lodge should be hereafter deemed regular or constitutional."[60]

Now I think that on the establishment of the new Grand Lodge, when the only lodge then existing in London had united in the enterprise of modifying their old and decaying system, and of renovating and strengthening it by a closer union, it may be fairly conceded that the members must, at a very early period, have come to the agreement that no new members should be admitted into the society unless consent had been previously obtained for their admission. This would naturally be the course pursued by any association for the purpose of self-preservation from the annoyance of uncongenial companions.

If any number of craftsmen availing themselves of the privilege of assembling as Masons in a lodge, which privilege had hitherto been unlimited and, as Preston says, was inherent in them as individuals, and which was guaranteed to them by the old Operative Constitutions, there is, I think, no doubt that such a lodge would not have been admitted into the new Fraternity in consequence of this spontaneous and automatic formation.

The new society would not recognize it as a part of its organization, at least until it had made an application and been accepted as a co-partner in the concern.

The primitive lodges which are said by Anderson to have been "constituted" between the years 1717 and 1723 may or may not have originated in this way. There is no record one way or the other.

But it is, I think, very certain that the present method of constituting lodges was not adopted until a regulation to that effect was enacted in 1721. This regulation is found among those which were compiled by Payne in 1720, and approved the following year by the Grand Lodge.

It is a part of the eighth regulation, and it prescribes that "if any Set or Number of Masons shall take upon themselves to form a lodge without the Grand Master's warrant, the regular lodges are not to countenance them nor own them as fair brethren and duly formed" until the Grand Master "approve of them by his warrant, which must be specified to the other lodges, as the custom is when a new lodge is to be registered in the list of lodges."

---

[60] "Illustrations," p. 192

This regulation was followed in 1723 by a form or "manner of constituting new lodges," which was practiced by the Duke of Wharton when Grand Master, and which was probably composed for him by Dr. Desaguliers, who was his Deputy.

It would seem, then, that new lodges were not constituted by warrant until the year 1721, the date of the Regulation, nor constituted in form until 1723, during the administration of the Duke of Wharton. Prior to that time, if we may infer from the phraseology of the Regulation, lodges when accepted as regular were said to be "formed," and were registered in the "List of Lodges."[61]

This presumption derives plausibility from the authentic records of the period.

In the earlier "Lists of Lodges" authoritatively issued, there is no mention of the date of Constitution of the lodges. In all the later lists the date of Constitution is given. In none of them, however, is there a record of any lodge having been constituted prior to the year 1721. Thus, in Pine's list for 1740, engraved by order of the Grand Officers, and which contains the names and numbers of one hundred and eighty-one lodges, four are recorded as having been constituted in 1721, five in 1722, and fourteen in 1723. No lodge is recorded there as having been constituted between the years 1717 and 1721.

It is, then, very clear that the system of constituting lodges was not adopted until the latter year; that it was another result of the legal labors of Payne in legislating for the new society, and another and an important step in the disseverance of Speculative from Operative Freemasonry.

We next approach the important and highly interesting subject of the early ritual of the new institution. But this will demand for its thorough consideration and full discussion the employment of a distinct chapter.

---

[61] In an article published in Mackey's National Freemason in 1873 (vol. ii., p. 288), Bro. Hughan has said "that it is a fact that no constituted lodge dates at an earlier period than the Revival of Masonry, 1717." I suspect my learned brother wrote these lines currente calamo, and without his usual caution. It will be seen from the text that there is no record of any constituted lodge dating prior to 1721.

CHAPTER XXXII

THE EARLY RITUAL OF SPECULATIVE FREEMASONRY

THE ritual is an important part of the organization of Speculative Freemasonry. It is not a mere garment intended to cover the institution and conceal its body from unlawful inspection. It is the body itself and the very life of the institution. Eliminate from Freemasonry all vestiges of a ritual and you make it a mere lifeless mass. Its characteristic as a benevolent or as a social association might continue, but all its pretensions as a speculative system of science and philosophy would be lost.

As a definition of this important and indispensable element in the Masonic system, it may be said that the ritual is properly the prescribed method of administering the forms of initiation into the society, comprising not only the ceremonies but also the explanatory lectures, the catechismal tests, and the methods of recognition.

Every secret society, that is to say, every society exclusive in its character, confining itself to a particular class of persons, and isolating itself by its occult organization from other associations and from mankind in general, must necessarily have some formal mode of admission, some meaning in that form which would need explanation, and some method by which its members could maintain their exclusiveness.

Every secret society must, then, from the necessity of its organization, be provided with some sort of a ritual, whether it be simple or complex.

The Operative Freemasonry of the Middle Ages is acknowledged to have been a secret and exclusive society or guild of architects and builders, who concealed the secret processes of their art from all who were not workers with them.

As a secret association, the old Operative Freemasons must have possessed a ritual. And we have, to support this hypothesis, not only logical inference but unquestionable historical evidence.

German archaeologists have given us the examination or catechism which formed a part of the ritual of the German Steinmetzen or Stonecutters.

The Sloane MS. No. 3329 contains the catechism used by the Operative Freemasons of England in the 17th century. A copy of this manuscript has already been given in a preceding parts of the present work, and it is therefore unnecessary to reproduce it here.

As the Sloane MS. has been assigned to a period between 1640 and 1700, we may safely conclude that it contains the ritual then in use among the English Operative Freemasons. At a later period it may have suffered considerable changes, but we infer that the ritual exposed in that manuscript was the foundation of the one which was in use by the Operative lodges which united in the formation of the Grand Lodge in the year 1717.

If the new society did not hesitate to adopt, at first, the old laws of the Operative institution, it is not at all probable that it would have rejected the ritual then in use and frame a new one. Until the Grand Lodge was securely seated in power, and the Operative element entirely eliminated, it would have been easier to use the old Operative ritual. In time, as the Operative laws were replaced by others more fitting to the character of the new Order, so the simple, Operative ritual must have given way to the more ornate one adapted to the designs of Speculative Freemasonry.

But during the earlier years of the Grand Lodge, this old Operative ritual continued to be used by the lodges under its jurisdiction.

The precise ritual used at that time is perhaps irretrievably lost, so that we have no direct, authentic account of the forms of initiation, yet by a careful collation of the historical material now in possession of the Fraternity, we may unravel the web, to all appearance hopelessly entangled, and arrive at something like historic truth.

It was not until 1721 that by the approval of the "Charges" which had been compiled the year before by Grand Master Payne, the Grand Lodge took the first bold and decisive step toward the[62] total

---

[62] See Part II., chap. xii., p. 626.

abolishment of the Operative element, and the building upon its ruins a purely Speculative institution.

The ritual used by the four old Lodges must have been very simple. It probably consisted of little more than a brief and unimpressive ceremony of admission, the communication of certain words and signs, and instruction in a catechism derived from that which is contained in the Sloane MS. But I do not doubt that this catechism, brief as it is, was greatly modified and abridged by the lapse of time, the defects of memory, and the impossibility of transmitting oral teachings for any considerable length of time.

It is probable that Dr. Desaguliers, the great ritualist of the day, may have begun to compose the new ritual about the same time that Payne, the great lawmaker of the day, began to compile his new laws.

What this ritual was we can only judge by inference, by comparison, and by careful analysis, just as Champollion deciphered the Egyptian hieroglyphics by a collation of the three inscriptions of the Rosetta Stone.

For this purpose we have a very competent supply of documents which we may employ in a similar comparison and analysis of the primitive ritual of the Speculative Freemasons.

Thus we have had the book called The Grand Mystery, which was published just a year after the appearance of the first edition of Anderson's Book of Constitutions.

Dr. Oliver, it is true, calls this production a "catchpenny."[63] It would be great folly to assert that it did not contain some shadowing forth of what was the ritual at the time of its publication. When, a few years afterward, Samuel Prichard published his book entitled Masonry Dissected, which is evidently based on The Grand Mystery, and in fact an enlargement of it, showing the improvements and developments which had taken place in the ritual, Dr. Anderson replied to it in the pamphlet entitled A Defense of Masonry.

---

[63] "Revelations of a Square," chap. ii., note 6. But in a posthumous work entitled "The Discrepancies of Freemasonry," published by Hogg & Co. in 1874 (page 79), he treats it with more respect, and says that it was the examination or lecture used by the Craft in the 17th century, the original of which, in the handwriting of Elias Ashmole, was given to Anderson when he made his collections for the history contained in the "Book of Constitutions." All this is very possibly correct, but as Oliver must have derived his information from some traditional source in his own possession solely, and as he has cited no authentic authority, we can hardly make use of it as an historical fact.

In this work it will be remarked that Anderson does not directly deny the accuracy of Prichard's formulas, but only attempts to prove, which he does very successfully, that the ceremonies as they are described by Prichard were neither "absurd nor pernicious."

The truth is that Anderson's Defense is a very learned and interesting interpretation of the symbols and ceremonies which were described by Prichard, and might have been written, just in the same way, if Anderson had selected the ritual as it was then framed on which to found his commentaries.

Krause accepted both of these works, as he gave them a place in his great work on The Three Oddest Documents of the Masonic Brotherhood.

For myself, I am disposed to take these and similar productions with some grains of allowance, yet not altogether rejecting them as utterly worthless. From such works we may obtain many valuable suggestions, when they are properly and judiciously analyzed.

Krause thinks that The Grand Mystery was the production of one of the old Masons, who was an Operative builder and a man not without some learning.

This is probably a correct supposition. At all events, I am willing to take the work as a correct exposition, substantially, of the condition of the ritual at the time when it was published, which was seven years after what was called the "Revival" in London.

It will give us a very correct idea of the earliest ritual accepted by the Speculative Masons from their Operative brethren, and used until the genius of Desaguliers had invented something more worthy of the Speculative science.

Adopting it then as the very nearest approximation to the primitive ritual of the Speculative Freemasons, it will not be an unacceptable gift, nor useless in prosecuting the discussion of the subject to which this chapter is devoted.

It has not often been reprinted, and the original edition of 1724 is very scarce. I shall make use of the almost fac-simile imitation of that edition printed in 1867 by the Masonic Archaeological Society of Cincinnati, and under the supervision of Brother Enoch T. Carson, from whose valuable library the original exemplar was obtained.

The title of the pamphlet is as follows:

"The Grand Mystery of Free-Masons Discover'd. Wherein are the several Questions, put to them at their Meetings and Intstallations: As also the Oath, Health, Signs and Points to know each other by. As they were found in the Custody of a Free-Mason who Dyed suddenly.

And now Publish'd for the Information of the Publick. London :- Printed for T. Payne near Stationer's-Hall 1724 (Price Six Pence) "

THE CATECHISM.[64]

1. Q. Peace be here. A. I hope there is.
2. Q. What a-clock is it? A. It is going to Six or going to Twelve.[65]
3. Q. Are you very busy?[66]
A. No.
4. Q. Will you give or take? A. Both; or which you please.
5. Q. How go Squares?[67] A. Straight.
6. Q. Are you Rich or Poor? A. Neither.
7. Q. Change rrle that. [68]A. I will.
8. Q. In the name of, &c., [69]are you a Mason?
9. Q. What is a Mason? A. A Man begot of a Man, born of a woman, Brother to a king.

---

[64] The object of this reprint being only to give the reader some idea of what was the earliest form of the ritual that we possess, the Preface, the Free-Mason's Oath, A FreeMason's Health and the signs to know a Free Mason have been omitted as being unnecessary to that end. The questions have been numbered here only for facility of reference in future remarks.

[65] This may be supposed to refer to the hours of labor of Operative Masons who commenced work at six in the morning and went to their noon-meal at twelve. This is the first indication that this was a catechism originally used by Operative Free Masons.

[66] Otherwise, "Have you any work? " Krause suggests that it was the question addressed to a traveling Fellow who came to the lodge. "Every Mason," say the Old Constitutions," shall receive or cherish strange Fellows when they come over the Country and sett them on work." - Landsdowne MS.

[67] Halliwell, in his Dictionary, cites "How gang squares?" as meaning "How do you do?" He also says that "How go the squares?" means, how goes on the game, as chess or draughts, the board being full of squares. Krause adopts this latter interpretation of the phrase, but I prefer the former.

[68] Here it is probable that the grip was given and interchanged. The mutilation of this catechism which Krause suspects is here, I think, evident. The answer " I will " and the expression "In the name of, &c.," are connected with the interchange of the grip. The answer to the question "Are you a Mason?" is omitted, and then the catechism goes on with the question "What is a Mason?"

[69] The omission here can not be supplied. It was a part of the formula of giving the grip. Krause suggests that the words thus omitted by the editor of the catechism might be "In the name of the Pretender" or probably "In the name of the King and the Holy Roman Catholic Church." But the former explanation would give the catechism too modern an origin and the latter would carry it too far back. However, that would suit the hypothesis of Dr. Krause. I reject both, but can not supply a substitute unless it were " In the name of God and the Holy Saint John."

10. Q. What is a Fellow? A. A Companion of a Prince.
11. Q. How shall I know that you are a Free-Mason ? A. By Signs, Tokens, and Points of my Entry.
12. Q. Which is the Point of your Entry ? A. I hear[70] and conceal, under the penalty of having my Throat cut, or my Tongue pulled out of my Head.
13. Q. Where was you made a Free-Mason ? A. In a just and perfect Lodge.
14 Q. How many make a Lodge ? A. God and the Square with five or seven right and perfect Masons, on the highest Mountains, or the lowest Valleys in the world.[71]
15. Q. Why do Odds make a Lodge ? A. Because all Odds are Men's Advantage.[72]
16. Q. What Lodge are you of ? A. The Lodge of St. John.[73]
17. Q. How does it stand ? A. Perfect East and West, as all Temples do.
18. Q. Where is the Mason's Point ?[74] A. At the East-Window, waiting at the Rising of the Sun, to set his men at work.
9. Q. Where is the Warden's Point ?
A. At the West-Window, waiting at the Setting of the Sun to dismiss the Entered Apprentices.
20. Q. Who rules and governs the Lodge, and is Master of it ? A. Irah, Iachin or the Right Pillar.[75]

---

[70] The Sloane MS., in which the same answer occurs, says, "I heal and conceal," to heal being old English for to hide. It is very clear that the word hear is a typographical error.

[71] Krause thinks that in this answer an old and a new ritual are mixed. God and the Square he assigns to the former, the numbers five and seven to the latter. But the Harleian MS. requires five to make a legal lodge.

[72] We must not suppose that this was derived from the Kabbalists. The doctrine that God delights in odd numbers, "numero Deus impare gaudet" (Virgil, Ed. viii.), is as old as the oldest of the ancient mythologies. It is the foundation of all the numerical symbolism of Speculative Freemasonry. We here see that it was observed in the oldest ritual.

[73] This hieroglyphic appears to have been the early sign for a lodge, as the oblong square is at the present day.

[74] I find this question thus printed in all the copies to which I have had access. But I have not the slightest doubt that there has been a typographical error, which has been faithfully copied. I should read it "Where is the Master's point?" The next question confirms my conviction. The Master sets the Craft to work, the Warden dismisses them. This has been followed by the modern rituals.

[75] Various have been the conjectures as to the meaning of the word Irah. Schneider, looking to the theory that modern Freemasonry was instituted to

21. Q. How is it govern'd?
A. Of Square and Rule.
22. Q. Have you the Key of the Lodge ? A. Yes, I have.
23. Q. What is its virtue ? A. To open and shut, and shut and open.
24. Q. Where do you keep it ? A. In an Ivory Box, between my Tongue and my Teeth, or within my Heart, where all my Secrets are kept.
25. Q. Have you the Chain to the Key ? A. Yes, I have.
26. Q. How long is it ? A. As long as from my Tongue to my Heart.[76]
27. Q. How many precious Jewels ? A. Three; a square Asher, a Diamond, and a Square.
28. Q. How many Lights ? A. Three; a Right East, South and West.[77]
29. Q. What do they represent ? A. The Three Persons: Father, Son, and Holy Ghost.[78]
30. Q. How many Pillars? A. Two; Iachin and Boaz.
31. Q. What do they represent ? A. A Strength and Stability of the Church in all Ages.[79]
32. Q. How many Angles in St. John's Lodge ? A. Four bordering on Squares.
33. Q. How is the Meridian found out ? A. When the Sun leaves the South and breaks in at the West-End of the Lodge.

---

secure the restoration of the House of Stuart, supposes the letters of the word to be the initials of the Latin sentence "Iacobus Redibit Ad Hereditatem" - James shall return to his inheritance. Krause thinks it the anagram of Hiram, and he rejects another supposition that it is the Hebrew Irah, reverence or holy fear, i.e., the fear of God. It may mean Hiram, but there is no need of an anagram. The wonted corruption of proper names in the old Masonic manuscripts makes Irah a sufficiently near approximation to Hiram, who is called in the Old Constitutions, Aynon, Aman, Amon, Anon, or Ajuon. The German Steinmetzen called Tubal Cain Walcan.

[76] Speaking of tests like this, Dr. Oliver very wisely says: "These questions may be considered trivial.

[77] The Bauhutten or Operative lodges of the Germans probably had, says Krause, only three windows corresponding to the cardinal points, and the three principal officers of the lodge had their seats near them so as to obtain the best light for their labors.

[78] This is ample proof that the earliest Freemasonry of the new Grand Lodge was distinctly Christian. The change of character did not occur until the adoption of the "Old Charges" as printed in Anderson's first edition. But more of this in the text.

[79] There is an allusion to strength in the German Steinmetzen's catechism: "What is the Strength of our Craft?" Strength continued to be symbolized as a Masonic attribute in all subsequent rituals and so continues to the present day.

34. Q. In what part of the Temple was the Lodge kept? A. In Solomon's Porch,[80] at the West-End of the Temple, where the two Pillars were set up.
35. Q. How many Steps belong to a right Mason? A. Three.
36. Q. Give me the Solution. A. I will . . . The Right Worshipful, Worshipful Master and Worshipful Fellows of the Right Worshipful Lodge from whence I came, greet you well.
That Great God to us greeting, be at this our meeting profoundest mysteries of the Craft. . . . A single Masonic question, how puerile soever it may appear, is frequently in the hands of an expert Master of the Art, the depository of most important secrets." On "The Masonic Tests of the Eighteenth Century " in his "Golden Remains," vol. iv.,pp. 14, 15. and with the Right Worshipful Lodge from whence you came, and you are. [81]
37. Q. Give me the Jerusalem Word.[82] A. Giblin.
38. Q. Give me the Universal Word. A. Boaz.
39. Q. Right Brother of ours, your Name? A. N. orM. Welcome Brother M. or N. to our Society.
40. Q. How many particular Points pertain to a Free-Mason? A. Three; Fraternity, Fidelity, and Tacity.
41. Q. What do they represent? A. Brotherly Love, Relief and Truth among all Right Masons; for all Masons were ordain'd at the Building of the Tower of Babel and at the Temple of Jerusalem.[83]
42. Q. How-many proper Points? A. Five: Foot to Foot, Knee to Knee, Hand to Hand, Heart to Heart, and Ear to Ear. [84]

---

[80] An allusion to the Temple of Solomon is common in all the old Constitutions. But no hypothesis can be deduced from this of the Solomonic origin of Freemasonry. The subject is too important to be discussed in a note.

[81] It is most probable that this answer was given on the three steps which were made while the words were being said.

[82] The "Jerusalem Word" was probably the word traditionally confined to the Craft while they were working at the Temple, and the "Universal Word" was that used by them when they dispersed and traveled into foreign countries. The old "Legend of the Craft" has a tradition to that effect which was finally developed into the Temple Allegory of the modern rituals.

[83] Of this answer Krause gives the following interpretation - "Perhaps the Tower of Babel signifies the revolution under and after Cromwell, and the Temple of Jerusalem the restoration of the Stuart family in London" -which may be taken for what it is worth and no more, especially as the stories of the Tower and the Temple formed prominent points in the Craft legend which was formulated some two centuries at least before the time of Cromwell or of the restored Stuarts.

43. Q. Whence is an Arch derived ? A. From Architecture.[85]
44. Q. How many Orders in Architecture ? A. Five: The Tuscan, Doric, Ionic, Corinthian, and Composite.
45. Q. What do they answer ? A. They answer to the Base, Perpendicular, Diameter, Circumference, and Square.
46. Q. What is the right Word, or right Point of a Mason ? A. Adieu.

End of the Catechism.

Such is this important document, but of whose real value different opinions have been expressed. Oliver, as we have seen, calls it a "catchpenny." This epithet would, however, refer to the motives of the printer who gave the public the work at sixpence a copy and not to the original writer against whom no such charge, nor no such mercenary views should be imputed. The Rev. Mr. Sidebotham, who reprinted it in the Freemasons' Monthly Magazine, for August, 1855, from a copy found among the collection of Masonic curiosities deposited in the Bodleian Library, calls it "only one of the many absurd attempts of ignorant pretenders;" but his attempts to prove absurdities are themselves absurd.

The learned Mossdorf who, in 1808, found a copy of the second editions in the Royal Library at Leipsic, which Dr. Krause reprinted in his Three Oldest Documents of the Masonic Fraternity, designates it as a delicately framed but very bitter satire against the old lodges in London, which had just established the Grand Lodge. But a perusal of the document will disclose nothing of a satirical character in the document itself, and only a single paragraph of the preface in which

---

[84] At first glance this answer would seem to be adverse to the theory that the Third was not known in the year 1717, unless it were to be supposed that the passage was an interpolation made subsequent to the year 1720.
But the fact is that, as Krause remarks these expressions were not originally a symbol of the Master's degree (Meisterzeichen), but simply a symbol of Fellowship, where heart and heart and hand and hand showed the loving-kindness of each brother. Afterward, under the title of "The Five Points of Fellowship," it was appropriated to the Third Degree and received the symbolic history which it still retains.
[85] Here, say Schneider and Krause, is a trace of Royal Arch Masonry. Not so. Architecture was the profession of the Operative Freemasons and became naturally a point in the examination of a craftsman. Such as this catechism evidently was.

the design of the institution is underrated, and the depreciation illustrated by a rather coarse attempt at a witticism.[86]

But the preface was the production of the editor or printer, and must not be confounded with the catechism, which is free from anything of the kind. The very title, which might be deemed ironical, was undoubtedly an assumed one given to the original document by the same editor or printer for the purpose of attracting purchasers.

Bro. Steinbrenner, of New York, who has written one of our most valuable and interesting histories of Freemasonry, [87]thus describes it, and has given it what I think must have been its original title.

"The oldest fragment of a ritual or Masonic lecture in the English Language [88] which we have met with is the 'Examination upon Entrance into a Lodge,' as used at the time of the Revival."

Dr. Krause is the first writer who seems to have estimated this old catechism at anything like its true value. He calls it a remarkable document, and says that after a careful examination he has come to the conclusion that it was written by one of the old Operative Masons, who was not without some scholarship, but who esteemed Masonry as an art peculiarly appropriate to builders only, and into which a few non-Masons were sometimes admitted on account of their scientific attainments.

He thinks that this catechism presents the traces of a high antiquity, and so far as its essential constituent parts are concerned, it might have derived its origin from the oldest York ritual, probably as early as the 12th or 13th century.

I am not inclined to accept all of the Krausean theory on the subject of the origin or of the antiquity of this document. It is not necessary for the purpose of employing it in the investigation of the primitive ritual adopted by the Speculative Freemasons when they organized their Grand Lodge, to trace its existence beyond the first decade of the 18th century, though it might be reasonably extended much farther back.

---

[86] It was the 2d edition, 1725, with which Mossdorf was acquainted, and to this were annexed "Two Letters to a Friend," which are not contained in the 1st edition. These gave him the opinion of the satirical character of the work.
[87] "The Origin and Early History of Masonry," by G. W. Steinbrenner, Past Master. New York, 1864.
[88] When Steinbrenner wrote the above the Sloane MS. No. 3339 had not been discovered. And yet it is doubtful whether it and the original manuscript of "The Grand Mystery" are not contemporaneous.

The statement in the preface or introduction, that the original manuscript was printed, and had "been found in the custody of a Freemason who died suddenly," may be accepted as a truth. There is nothing improbable about it, and there is no reason to doubt the fact.

Connecting this with the date of the publication, which was just seven years after the establishment of the Grand Lodge, and only four years after what is supposed to be the date of the fabrication of the three degrees; and comparing it with the Sloane MS. 3329, where we shall find many instances of parallel or analogous passages; and seeing that the Sloane MS. was undeniably an Operative ritual, since its acknowledged date is somewhere between the middle and the close of the 17th century; considering all these points, I think that we may safely conclude that the original manuscript of the printed document called The Grand Mystery was the "Examination upon Entrance into a Lodge" of Operative Freemasons.

The following inferences may then be deduced in respect to the character of this document with the utmost plausibility:

1. That it was a part, and the most essential part, of the ritual used by the Operative Freemasons about the close of the 17th and the beginning of the 18th century, and if anything was wanting toward a complete ritual it was supplemented by the Sloane MS. No. 3329

2. That it was the ritual familiar to the four Lodges which in 1717 united in the establishment of the Speculative Grand lodge of England.

3. That on the establishment of that Grand Lodge it was accepted as the ritual of the Speculative Freemasons and so used by them until they perfected the transition from wholly Operative to wholly Speculative Freemasonry by the fabrication of degrees and the development of a more philosophical ritual, composed, as it has always been conjectured, by Desaguliers and Anderson, but principally always by the former.

Having premised these views, we may now proceed to investigate, with some prospect of a satisfactory result, the character and condition of Speculative Freemasonry so far as respects a ritual during the earliest years of the Grand Lodge.

In the first place, it may be remarked that internal evidence goes to prove that this catechism is appropriate solely for Operative Freemasons. It was undoubtedly constructed at a time when Speculative Freemasonry, in the modern sense, was not in existence, and when the lodges which were to use it were composed of Operatives the Theoretic members not being at all taken into consideration.

This is very clearly shown by various passages in the catechism. Thus, Question 2 alludes to the hours of labor; Question 3 is an inquiry whether the brother who is being examined is in want of work, because the old Operative Constitutions directed the Craft "to receive or cherish strange Fellows when they came over the country and set them to work." Hence, in view of this hospitable duty, the visitor is asked if he is busy, that is to say, if he has work to occupy and support him.

Questions 18 and 19 make reference to the time and duty of setting the men to work, and of dismissing them from labor.

Questions 14 and 21 refer to the square and rule as implements of Operative Masonry employed in the lodge. Question 27 speaks of the ashlar, and 43 and 44 of the orders of architecture. All of these are subjects appropriate and familiar to Operative Masons, and indicate the character of the catechism.

The next point that calls for attention is that in this Operative ritual there is not the slightest reference to degrees. They are not mentioned nor alluded to as if any such system existed. The examination is that of a Freemason, but there is no indication whatever to show that he was a Master, Fellow, or an Apprentice. He could not probably have been the last, because, as a general rule, Apprentices were not allowed to travel.

The German Steigmetzen, however, sometimes made an exception to this regulation, and the Master who had no work for his Apprentice would furnish him with a mark and send him forth in search of employment.

If a similar custom prevailed among the English Freemasons, of which there is no proof for or against, the wandering Apprentice woulds on visiting a strange lodge, doubtless make use of this catechism. There is nothing in its text to prevent him from doing so, for, as has already been said, there is no mention in it of degrees.

There does not seem to be any doubt in the minds of the most distinguished Masonic scholars, with perhaps a very few exceptions, that in the Operative ritual there were no degrees, the words Apprentice, Fellow, and Master referring only to gradations of rank. It is also believed that the ceremonies of admission were exceedingly simple, and that all these ranks were permitted to be present at a reception.

According to this catechism a lodge consisted of five or seven Masons, but it does not say that they must be all Master Masons.

The Sloane M S. says that there should be in a lodge two Apprentices, two Fellow-Crafts, and two Master Masons.

The Statutes of the Scottish Masons explicitly require the presence of two Apprentices at the reception of a Master.

The Old Constitutions, while they have charges specially for Masters and Fellows, between whom they make no distinction, have other "charges in general" which, of course, must include Apprentices, and in these they are commanded to keep secret "the consells of the lodge," from which it is to be inferred that Apprentices formed a constituent part of that body.

It has been usual to say that from 1717 to 1725 there were only Apprentices' lodges. The phraseology is not correct. They were lodges of Freemasons, and they so continued until the fabrication of a system of degrees. After that period the lodges might properly be called Apprentice lodges, because the first degree only could be conferred by them, though Fellow-Craft and Master Masons were among their members, these having until 1725 been made in the Grand Lodge exclusively.

The fact that this ritual, purposely designed for Operative Freemasons only, and used in the Operative lodges of London at the beginning of the 18th century, was adopted in 1717 when the four Lodges united in the organization of a Grand Lodge, is, I think, a convincing proof that there was no expressed intention at that time to abandon the Operative character of the institution, and to assume for it a purely Speculative condition.

I use the word "expressed" advisedly, because I do not contend that there was no such covert intention floating in the minds of some of the most cultivated Theoretic Freemasons who united with their Operative brethren in the organization.

But these Theoretic brethren were men of sense. They fully appreciated the expediency of the motto, festina lente. They were, it is true, anxious to hasten on the formation of an intellectual society, based historically on an association of architects, but ethically on an exalted system of moral philosophy; they perfectly appreciated, however, the impolicy of suddenly and rudely disrupting the ties which connected them with the old Operative Freemasons. Hence, they fairly shared with these the offices of the Grand Lodge until 1723, after which, as has been shown, no Operative held a prominent position in that body. The first laws which they adopted, and which were announced in the "Charges of a Free Mason," compiled by Payne and Anderson about 1719, had all the features of an Operative Code, and the ritual of the Operative Freemasons embodied in the document satirically called The Grand Mystery was accepted and used by the members of the Speculative Grand

Lodge until the fabrication of degrees made it necessary to formulate another and more philosophical ritual.

But it is not necessary to conclude that when the system of degrees was composed, most probably in 1720 and 1721, principally by Dr. Desaguliers, the old Operative ritual was immediately cast aside. In all probability it continued to be used in the lodges, where the Fellow-Crafts and Masters' degrees were unknown, until 1725, the conferring of them having been confined to the Grand Lodge until that year. There were even Operative lodges in England long after that date, and the old ritual would continue with them a favorite. This will account for the publication in 1724, with so profitable a sale as to encourage the printing of a second edition with appendices in 1725.

But the newer ritual became common in 1730 or a little before, and the able defense of it by Anderson in the 1738 edition of the Book of Constitutions shows that the old had at length been displaced, though some of its tests remained for a long time in use among the Craft, and are continued, in a modified form, even to the present day.

The early Operative ritual, like the Operative laws and usages, has made an impression on the Speculative society which has never been and never will be obliterated while Freemasonry lasts.

The next feature in this Operative ritual which attracts our attention is its well-defined Christian character. This is shown in Question 29, where the three Lights of the Lodge are said to represent "The Three Persons, Father, Son, and Holy Ghost."

Originating as it did, and for a long time working under ecclesiastical control, being closely connected with the Church, and engaged exclusively in the construction of religious edifices, it must naturally have become sectarian.

In the earliest times, when the Roman Catholic religion was the prevailing faith of Christendom, Operative Freemasonry was not only Christian but Roman Catholic in its tendencies. Hence, the oldest of the manuscript Constitutions contains an invocation to the Virgin Mary and to the Saints. In Germany the patrons of the Freemasons were the Four Crowned Martyrs.

But when in England the Protestant religion displaced the Roman Catholic, then the Operative Freemasons, following the sectarian tendencies of their countrymen, abandoned the reference to the Virgin and to the Saints, whose worship had been repudiated by the reformed religion, and invoked only the three Persons of the Trinity. The Harleian MS. commences thus: "The Almighty Father of Heaven with the Wisdom of the Glorious Sonne, through the goodness of the

Holy Ghost, three persons in one Godhead, bee with our beginning & give us grace soe to governe our Lives that we may come to his blisse that never shall have end."

All the other manuscript Constitutions conform to this formula, and hence we find the same feature presented in this catechism, and that in the ritual used when the Grand Lodge was established the three Lights represented the three Persons of the Trinity.

Operative Freemasonry never was tolerant nor cosmopolitan. It was in the beginning ecclesiastical, always Christian, and always sectarian.

Of all the differences that define the line of demarcation between Operative and Speculative Freemasonry, this is the most prominent.

The Theoretic Freemasons, that is, those who were non-Masons, when they united with their Operative fellow-members in the organization of a Grand Lodge, did not reject this sectarian character any more than they did the ritual and the laws of the old association.

But the non-Masonic or non-Operative element of the new Society was composed of men of education and of liberal views. They were anxious that in their meetings a spirit of toleration should prevail and that no angry discussions should disturb the hours devoted to innocent recreation. Moreover, they knew that the attempt to revive the decaying popularity of Freemasonry and to extend its usefulness would not be successful unless the doors were thrown widely open to the admission of moral and intellectual men of all shades of political and religious thought. Hence, they strove to exclude discussions which should involve the bitterness of partisan politics or of sectarian religion.

Dr. Anderson describes the effect produced by this liberality of sentiment when he says, speaking of this early period of Masonic history: "Ingenious men of all faculties and stations, being convinced that the cement of the lodge was love and friendship, earnestly requested to be made Masons, affecting this amicable fraternity more than other societies then often disturbed by warm disputes."[89]

Thus it was that the first change affected in the character of the institution by which the ultimate separation of Speculative from Operative Freemasons was foreshadowed, was the modification of the sectarian feature which had always existed in the latter.

Therefore, in 1721, the Grand Lodge, "finding fault" with the "Old Gothic Constitutions" or the laws of the Operative Freemasons,

---

[89] "Book of Constitutions," 2d edition, p. 114

principally, as the result shows, on account of their sectarian character, instructed Dr. Anderson "to digest them in a new and better method."

This task was duly accomplished, and the "Charges of a Freemason," which were published in the first edition of the Book of Constitutions, announce for the first time that cosmopolitan feature in the religious sentiments of the Order which it has ever since retained.

"Though in ancient times," so runs the first of these " Charges," "Masons were charged in every country to be of the religion of that country or nation, whatever it was; yet it is now thought more expedient only to oblige them to that religion in which all men agree, leaving their particular opinions to themselves."

In consequence of this declaration of tolerance, the ritual which was framed after the old Operative one, exemplified in The Ground Mystery, ceased to derive any of its symbolism from purely Christian dogmas, though it can not be denied that Christian sentiments have naturally had an influence upon Speculative Freemasonry.

But the institution, in all the countries into which it has since extended, has always, with a very few anomalous exceptions, been true to the declaration made in 1721 by its founders, and has erected its altars, around which men of every faith, if they have only a trusting belief in God as the Grand Architect of the universe, may kneel and worship.

But before this sentiment of perfect toleration could be fully developed, it was necessary that the tenets, the usages, and the influence of the Operative element should be wholly eliminated from the new society. The progress toward this disruption of the two systems, the old and the new, would have to be slow and gradual.

Very justly has Bro. Gould remarked that "Speculative Masonry was, so to speak, only on its trial during the generation which succeeded the authors of the Revival. The institution of a society of Free and Accepted Masons on a cosmopolitan and unsectarian basis was one thing; its consolidation, however, opposed as its practical working showed it to be to the ancient customs and privileges of the Operatives, was another and a very different affair."[90]

Therefore, as a matter of sheer policy, and also because it is probable that no intention of effecting such a change had, in the beginning, entered into the minds of the future founders of Speculative Freemasonry, it was deemed necessary to continue the use of the simple ritual which had so long been familiar to the Operatives, and it was accordingly so continued to be used until, in a few years, the opportune

---

[90] "The Four Old Lodges," p. 33.

time had arrived for the fabrication of a more complex one, and one better adapted to the objects of a Speculative Society.

As it appears, then, to be clearly evident that the Operative ritual was practiced by the Grand Lodge from 1717 until 1721 or 1722, and for a much longer period by many of the lodges under its jurisdiction, it is proper that we should endeavor, so far as the materials in our possession will permit, to describe the character of that ritual.

Masonic scholars who have carefully investigated this subject do not now express any doubt that the rite practiced by the mediceval Freemasons of every country, and which, under some modifications, was used by the Operative Freemasons when the Grand Lodge of England was established, was a very simple one, consisting of but one degree.

In fact, as the word degree literally denotes a step in progression, and would import the possible existence of a higher step to which it is related, it would seem to be more proper to say that the Operative rite was without degrees, and consisted of a form of admission with accompanying esoteric instructions, all of which were of the simplest nature.

Master, Fellow, and Apprentice were terms intended to designate the different ranks of the Craftsmen, which ranks were wholly unconnected with any gradations of ritualistic knowledge.

Masters were those who superintended the labors of the Craft, or were, perhaps, in many instances the employers of the workmen engaged on an edifice. Paley suggests that they were probably architects, and he says that they must have been trained in one and the same school, just as our clergy are trained in the universities, and were either sent about to different stations or were attached to some church or cathedral, or took up their permanent residence in certain localities.[91]

This description is very suitable to the most flourishing period of Gothic architecture, when such Craftsmen as William of Sens or Erwin of Steinbach were the Masters who directed the construction of those noble works of architecture which were to win the admiration of succeeding ages.

But in the 17th and the beginning of the 18th century, when there was a decadence in the old science of Gothic architecture, every Fellow who was appointed by an employer or selected by his brethren to govern a lodge and to direct the works of the Craftsmen, became by that appointment or selection a Master Mason.

---

[91] "Manual of Gothic Architecture," p. 209.

We know that this usage was for some time observed by the Speculative Freemasons, for in the form of constituting a new lodge as prescribed in 1723 by the Duke of Wharton, who was then Grand Master, it is said that the Master who is to be installed, "being yet among the Fellow-Craft," must be taken from among them, and be inducted into office by the Grand Master; by which act he became a Master Mason, and not by the reception of a degree; and the investiture of certain additional secrets.[92]

The Fellows were workmen who had served an apprenticeship of several years, and had at length acquired a knowledge of the trade. They constituted the great body of the Craft, as is evident from the constant reference to them in the Old Constitutions.

The Apprentices, as the etymology of the word imports, were learners.

They were youths who were bound to serve their Masters for a term of five or seven years, on the condition that the Master shall instruct them in the trade, that at the expiration of their term of service they might be admitted into the rank or class of Fellows.

As there was but one ceremony of admission common to all classes of the Craft, it follows that there could be no secrets of a ritual character which belonged exclusively to either of the three classes, and that whatever was known to Masters and Fellows must also have been communicated to Apprentices; and this is very evident from the well-known fact that the presence of members of each class was necessary to the legal communications of a lodge.

The Mason Word is the only secret spoken of in the minutes of the Scotch lodges, but the German and English rituals show that there were other words and methods of recognition besides an examination which constituted the esoteric instructions of Operative Masonry.

The most important of these points is, however, the fact that at the time of the organization of the Grand Lodge in 1717, and for a brief period afterward, there was but one degree, as it is called, which was known to the Operatives, and that for a brief period of three or four years this simple system was accepted and practiced by the founders of Speculative Freemasonry.

But the discussion of this fact involves a thorough investigation, and can not be treated at the close of a chapter.

---

[92] See the form in the 1st edition of Anderson, p. 71.

The inquiry, so far as it has advanced, has, I think, satisfied us that the Operative ritual was that which was at first adopted by the founders of Speculative Freemasonry.

When, afterward, they discarded this ritual as too simple and as unsuitable to their designs, they were obliged, in the construction of their new system, to develop new degrees.

The task, therefore, to which our attention must now be directed, is first to demonstrate that the primitive ritual accepted in 1717 by the Speculatives consisted of but one degree, if for convenience I may be allowed to use a word not strictly and grammatically correct; and, secondly, to point out the mode in which and the period when a larger ritual, and a system of degrees, was invented.

And these must be the subjects of the two following chapters.

CHAPTER XXXIII

THE ONE DEGREE OF OPERATIVE FREEMASONS

In the articles of union agreed to in 1813 by the two Grand Lodges of England, the "Moderns" and the "Ancients" as they were called, it was declared that "pure Ancient Masonry consists of three degrees and no more." If by Ancient Masonry it was intended to designate the system then existing, and no other and earlier one - if the character of antiquity was to be circumscribed within the one hundred preceding years, or thereabouts - then the declaration might be accepted as an historical truth. But if it was designed to refer by these words to the whole period of time, within which included the era of Operative, and of combined Operative and Speculative Freemasonry, as well as that later one when pure Speculative Masonry alone prevailed, then the assertion must be considered as apocryphal and as having no foundation in authentic history.

If our judgment on this subject were to be formed merely on the complete silence of the Old Records, we should be forced to the conclusion that until the close of the second decade of the 18th century, or about the year 1720, when the Speculative element was slowly disintegrating itself from the Operative, there was only one degree known as the word is understood in the present day.

We have evidence that the Operative Freemasons of Scotland in the 15th century adopted, to some extent, the secret ceremonies observed by the medieval builders of the continent.[93] we may therefore

---

[93] See Lyon, "History of the Lodge of Edinburgh," p. 234. This is evident from, the charter granted to the Masons and Wrights of Edinburgh in 1475, copied by Lyon (p. 230) from the Burgh Records of Edinburgh, where reference is made for their government to the customs "in the towne of Bruges."

refer to the records of the Scotch lodges for a correct knowledge of what was the degree system practiced, not only in Scotiand but on the continent, at that period.

Now we have abundant evidence by deduction from the records of the old Scottish lodges that there was in the 15th, 16th, and 17th centuries only one degree known to the brotherhood.

There were, it is true, three classes or ranks of Masons, namely, Masters, men who made contracts and undertook the work of building for employers; Fellow-Crafts or Journeymen employed by these Masters; and Entered Apprentices, who were received that they might be taught the art of building. But this difference of rank involved no difference of esoteric instruction. There was but one ceremony and one set of secrets for all, and common to and known by everyone, from the youngest Apprentice to the oldest Master. This is plainly deducible from all the Old Records.

Thus, in the Schaw statutes, whose date is December 28, 1498, it is enacted as follows:

"Item that na maister or fellow of craft be ressavit nor admittit without the number of sex maisters and twa enterit prenteissis the wardene of that lodge being one of the said sex."

The same regulation, generally, in very nearly the same words, is to be found in subsequent records, constitutions, and minutes of the 16th and 17th centuries.

Now what deduction must be drawn from the oft-repeated language of this statute? Certainly only this, that if two Apprentices were required to be present at the reception of a Fellow-Craft or a Master, there could have been no secrets to be communicated to the candidates as Fellow-Crafts or Masters which were not als ready known to the Apprentices. In other words, that these three ranks were not separated and distinguished from each other by any ceremonies or instructions which would constitute degrees in the modern acceptation of the term. In fact, there could have been but one degree common to all.

Upon this subject Bro. Lyon says: "It is upon Schaw's regulation anent the reception of Fellows or Masters, that we found our opinion that in primitive times there were no secrets communicated by lodges to either Fellows of Craft or Masters that were not known to Apprentices, seeing that members of the latter grade were necessary to the legal constitution of communications for the admission of Masters or Fellows."[94]

---

[94] "History of the Lodge of Edinburgh," p. 23.

We are confirmed in this conclusion by what is said in the same Old Records of the "Mason Word."

The Mason Word and what was connected with it appeared to constitute

the only secret known to the Masons of the centuries preceding the 18th. It was, however, not simply a word, but had other mysteries connected with it, as is apparent from an expression in the minutes of the Lodge of

Dunblane, where it is said that two Apprentices of the Lodge of Kilwinning being examined on their application for affiliation, were found to have " a competent knowlsedge of the secrets of the Mason Word."[95]

These secrets consisted also probably of a sign and grip. Indeed, the records of Haughfort Lodge in 1707 state the fact that there was a grip, and it is known that as early as the 12th century the German Masons used all these modes of recognition.[96]

There was also a Legend or Allegory, nothing, however, like the modern legend of the Third degree, which connected the Craft traditionally with the Tower of Babel and the Temple of Solomon. This Legend was contained in what we now call the Legend of the Craft or the Legend of the Guild. This is contained, with only verbal variations, in all the old manuscript Constitutions. That this Legend was always deemed a part of the secrets of the brotherhood, is very evident from the destruction of many of those manuscripts by scrupulous Masons in 1720, from the fear, as Anderson expresses it, that they might fall into strange hands.

But whatever were the secrets connected with the "Mason Word," there is abundant evidence that they were communicated in full to the Apprentice on his initiation.

First, we have the evidence of the Schaw statutes that two Apprentices were required to be present at the reception of a Mason or a Fellow-Craft. Then the minutes of the Lodge of Edinburgh for 1601, 1606, and 1637, referred to by Bro. Lyon, [97]show that Apprentices were present during the making of Fellow-Crafts. Again, we find the following

---

[95] "History of the Lodge of Edinburgh," p. 417.

[96] The English Masons in the beginning of the 18th century, and I suppose before that penod, had two words, the "Jerusalem Word" and the "Universal Word." See the Examination in the last chapter. The German Masons also had two words, at least.

[97] "History of the Lodge of Edinburgh," p. 74.

conclusive testimony in the Laws and Statutes of the Lodge of Aberdeen, adopted December 27, 1760:

"Wee Master Masons and Entered Prentises, all of us under. seryvers, doe here protest and vowe as hitherto we ehave done at our entrie when we received the benefit of the Mason Word," &c.[98]

From all of which we are authorized to entertain the opinion, in the language of Bro. Lyon, who has thoroughly investigated the subject, so far at least as relates to Scotland, "that 'the Word' and other secrets peculiar to Masons were communicated to Apprentices on their admission to the lodge, and that the ceremony of passing was simply a testing of the candidate's fitness for employment as a journeyman."[99]

In the English lodges of the same period, that is, up to the beginning of the 18th century, we find no indications of the existence of more than one degree common to the whole Craft. The Apprentices, however, do not occupy in the old English Constitutions so conspicuous a place as they do in the Scotch. We can, for instance, find no regulation like that in the Schaw statutes which requires Apprentices to be present at the making of Fellow-Crafts.

But in the oldest of the English Constitutions which have been unearthed by the labors of Masonic archaeologists - namely, the one known as the Halliwell MS., the date of which is supposed to be not later than the middle of the 15th century - we find indications of the fact that the Apprentices were in possession of all the secret knowledge possessed by the Masters and Fellows, and that they were allowed to be present at meetings of the lodge. Thus, the thirteenth article of that early Constitution says: " - gef that the mayster a prentes have Enterlyche thenne that he hym teche, And meserable poyntes that he hym reche, That he the crafte abelyche may conne,

Whersever he go undur the sonne."[100]

That is, if a Master have an Apprentice, he shall give him thorough instruction, and place him in the possession of such points as will enable him to recognize the members of the Craft wheresoever he may go. He was to be invested with the modes of recognition common to all, whereby a mutual intercourse might be held. It was not that he was to know just enough to prove himself to be an Apprentice, but he was to have such knowledge as would enable him to recognize in a stranger a Fellow-Craft or a Master - in other words, he was to have all that they had, in the way of recognition.

---

[98] "History of the Lodge of Edinburgh," p. 423.
[99] Ibid., p. 233
[100] Halliwell MS., lines 240 - 244.

But a more important admission, namely, that the Apprentice was permitted to be present at the meetings of a lodge of Masters and Fellows, and to participate in, or at least be a witness of, their private transactions, is found in the third point of this same Constitution, which is in the following words:

"The thrydee poynt must be severele, With the prentes knowe hyt wele, Hys mayster cownsel he kepe and close, And hys fellowes by hys goode purpose; The prevystye of the chamber telle he no mon, Ny yn the logge whatsever they done; Whatsever thon heryst or eyste hem do Telle hyt no mon, wherseyer thou go; The cownsel of halle and yeke of boure, Kepe hyt lvel to gret honoure, Lest hyt wolde torne thyself to blame, And brynge the craft ynto gret schame." [101]

That is, the Apprentice was directed to keep the counsel of his Master and Fellows, and to tell to no one the secrets of tlle chamber nor what he should see or hear done in the lodge.[102]

He was to keep the counsel of "hall and bower," a medizeval phrase denoting all sorts of secrets, and all this he was to observe lest he should bring the Craft into shame.

Now I do not think we need anything more explicit to prove that Apprentices were admitted to share the secrets of the Fellows and be present at the meetings of the lodge, all of which is a conclusive evidence against the existence of separate degrees.

The same reference to Apprentices as being in possession of the secrets of the Craft, which they were not to communicate unlawfully, is found in subsequent Constitutions, as late as 1693. In the York Constitutions, first published by Bro. Hughan in his History of Freemasonry in York, under the title of "The Apprentice Charge," it is said that "he shall keepe councell in all things spoken in Lodg or Chamber by any Masons, Fellowes or Fremasons."

The Masonic student, while carefully perusing the Old Records of the English Masons and comparing them with those of the Scotch, will be struck with one important difference between them. In the Scotch Statutes, Constitutions, and Minutes, the Apprentices assume a prominent position, and are always spoken of as a component and necessary part of the brotherhood.

Thus, the Schaw statutes prescribe the fee for the admission of Fellow-Crafts, followed immediately by another prescribing the fee for

---

[101] Halliwell MS., lines 275-286.
[102] Similar to this is "The Apprentice Charge" contained in the Lodge of Hope MS., the date of which is 1680. It says that the Apprentice "shall keep counsell in all things spoken in lodge or chamber by fellowes or free masons."

the admission of Apprentices; twice in the minutes of the Lodge of Edinburgh (1706 and 1709) it is recorded that a notary who was appointed for the purpose of acting as "clerk to the brethren masons" was initiated as Jane entered Apprentice and Fellow-Craft,"[103] and lastly, Apprentices were required to be present at the admission of Fellow-Crafts and Masters.

I think, therefore, that the most eminent Masonic historians of the present day have been justified in the conclusion to which they have arrived after a careful examination of old documents, that until a short time after the organization of the Grand Lodge in the year 1717, there is no evidence of the existence of more than one degree; that all the secrets were communicated to the Apprentices, and that the ceremony of passing to a Fellow-Craft was simply a testing of the candidate's fitness for employment as a journeyman.[104]

Bro. Hughan says that "no record prior to the second decade of the last century ever mentions Masonic degrees, and all the MSS. preserved decidedly confirm us in the belief that in the mere Operative (although partly Speculative) career of Freemasonry the ceremony of reception was of a most unpretentious and simple character, mainly for the communication of certain lyrics and secrets, and for the conservation of ancient customs of the Craft."[105]

In another place the same distinguished writer says: "I have carefully perused all the known Masonic MSS. from the 14th century down to A.D 1717 (of which I have eitherseen the originals or have certified copies), and have not been able to find any reference to three degrees."[106]

Bro. Findel says: "Originally it seems there was but one degree of initiation in the year 1717; the degrees or grades of Apprentice, Fellow, and Master were introduced about the year 1720."[107]

Bro. Lyon, also, who has thoroughly investigated the customs of the early Scottish lodges, in referring to the Schaw statute, which required two Apprentices to be present at the admission of Fellows, says that in 1693 "the lodge recognized 'passing,' i.e., a promotion to the fellowship, simply as an 'honour and dignity.'" And he adds:

---

[103] Lyon, " History of the Lodge of Edinburgh," p. 43.
[104] Such is the opinion of Bro. Lyon. See "History of the Lodge of Edinburgh," p. 233,
[105] Voice of Masonry, vol. xii., June, 1874, p. 340.
[106] Cited by Lyon in "History of the Lodge of Edinburgh," p. 211.
[107] "History of Freemasonry," p. 150, Lyon's Translation.

"If the communication by Mason Lodges of secret words or signs constituted a degree - a term of modern application to the esoteric observances of the Masonic body - then there was under the purely Operative regime only one known to Scotch lodges, viz., that in which, under an oath, Apprentices obtained a knowledge of the Mason Word and all that was implied in the expression."[108]

Even Dr. Oliver, who, of all writers, is the least skeptical in respect to Masonic traditions, acknowledges that there is no evidence of the existence of degrees in Freemasonry anterior to the beginning of the 18th century.

The only living Masonic scholar of any eminence who, so far as I am aware, denies or doubts this fact is the Rev. Bro. W. A. Woodford, and he asserts his opinion rather negatively, as if he were unwilling to doubt, than positively as if he were ready to deny the fact, that the old Operative system consisted of but one degree.

As Bro. Woodford is one whose learning and experience entitle his opinion on any point of Masonic history to a deferential consideration, it will be proper to examine the weight of his arguments on this subject.

In the year 1874 Bro. Hughan proposed, in the London Freemason, to defend in future communications three historical statements against anyone who should oppugn them.

One of these statements was made in the following words:

"The references to Masonic degrees (as we understand the term now) never occur in the ancient minutes; no rituals of degrees prior to 1720 are in existence, and whatever esoteric customs may have been communicated to Craftsmen before the last century, they do not appear to have necessitated the temporary absence of either class of members from the Lodge."[109]

To this challenge Bro. Woodford responded in a subsequent number of the same paper.[110]

The gist of our learned Brother's argument in reply appears to be that though, as Vaughan asserts, there may be no ritual evidence of the existence of the three degrees before 1720, yet "such a proposition need not be understood as asserting that they did not exist, but only that, so far, we have no ritual evidence of their distinct existence as now."

As a logical conclusion, it appears to me that such a disposition of the question is wholly untenable. It was an excellent maxim of the

---

[108] Lyon, " History of the Lodge of Edinburgh," p. 23.
[109] London freemason, June 27, 1874.
[110] Ibid., July 27, 1874.

schools, which has been adopted in philosophy, in physical science, and in law, thats "of things which do not appear and of things which do not exist, the reasoning is the same."[111]

We can only arrive at a correct judgment when we are guided by evidence; without it no judgment can be reasonably formed.

Dr. Hedge, in his excellent manual of logic, says: "The proof that the Romans once possessed Great Britain is made up of a rariety of independent arguments: as immemorial tradition; the testimony of historians; the ruins of Roman buildings, camps, and walls; Roman coins, inscriptions, and the like. These are independent arguments; but they all conspire to establish the fact."[112]

Now, if we apply this method of reasoning to the question of the existence of Masonic degrees prior to the year 1720, we shall see clearly how completely the affirmative proposition is without support. We have no immemorial tradition, no historical testimony, no allusion in old documents, such as the manuscript Constitutions, the minutes of the Scottish or of the very few English lodges that are extant, nor in the English or German Freemasons, which tend to prove the existence of degrees in the old system of Operative Freemasonry. On the contrary, we have abundant evidence in these Constitutions and minutes that the secrets of the Craft were common to the three classes, and that Apprentices were required to he present at the admission of Masters.

The other argument of Bro. Woodford is, that, "notwithstanding the Scotch lodges had an open court for their members, that does not preclude the possibility of the existence of other secrets and separate degrees."

It is possible, but it does not thence follow that it is true. In this investigation we seek not possibilities but facts, and, as Bro. Woodford, usually so careful and so accurate in his historical and archaeological inquiries, has supplied no proof of the hypothesis which he has advanced, it must be accepted as a mere assumption, and may be fairly met with a contrary one.

But the remarks of Bro. Hughan himself, in reply to the argument of Bro. Woodford, are so conclusive and throw so much light upon this interesting subject that I can not refrain from enriching the pages of this work with the very words of this eminent authority in Masonic archaeology.[113]

---

[111] De non apparentibus et de non existentibus, eadem est ratio.
[112] "Elements of Logic," by Levi Hedge, LL.D., Boston, 1827, p. 74
[113] Contained in article in the London Masonic Magazine for August, 1874.

"Now what do the old lodge minutes say on this subject ? we have had authorized excerpts from these valuable books published (with few exceptions). The whole of the volumes have been most diligently and carefully searched, the result made known, and every Masonic student furnished with the testimony of these important witnesses, all of which, from the 16th century to the first half of the second decade of the 18th century, unite in proving that there is no register of any assembly of Masons working ceremonies or communicating 'secrets' from which any portion of the Fraternity was excluded or denied participation; neither can there be found a single reference in these lodge minutes to justify one in assuming 'three degrees' to be even known to the brethren prior to A.D. 1716-1717.[114] Of course, there can be no doubt as to what may be termed grades in Ancient Masonry, Apprentices had to serve their 'regular time' before being accounted Fellow-Crafts, and then subsequently the office or position of Master Mason was conferred upon a select few; but no word is ever said about 'degrees.' All the members were evidently eligible to attend at the introduction of Fellow-Crafts and Master Masons, as well as at the admission of Apprentices; and so far as the records throw light on the customs of our early brethren, the Apprentices were as welcome at the election and reception of Masters - as the latter were required to participate in the initiation of the former.

"We are quite willing to grant, for the sake of argument, that a word may have been whispered in the ear of the Master of the lodge (or of Master Masons) on their introduction or constitution in the lodge; but supposing that such were the case (and we think the position is at least probable), the 'three degrees' are as far from being proved as before, especially as we have never yet traced any intimation, ever so slight, of a special ceremony at the 'passing' of Fellow-Crafts, peculiar to that grade, and from which Apprentices were excluded.

"If we have overlooked such a minute, we shall be only too glad to acknowledge the fact; but at present we must reiterate our conviction, that whatever the ceremonies may have been at the introduction of Fellow- Crafts and Master Masons anterior to the last century, they were not such as to require the exclusion of Apprentices from the lodge meetings; and in the absence of any positive information on the subject, we are not justified in assuming the existence of 'three degrees of Masonry' at that period; or, in other words, we can only fairly advocate that two have existed of which we have evidence, and whatever else we

---

[114] The learned Brother makes here a rather too liberal admission. I have found no evidence of the existence of three degrees in the year 1717, and it will be hereafter seen that their fabrication is assigned to a later date.

may fancy was known, should only be advocated on the grounds of probability. If the proof of 'three degrees' before 1717 is to rest on the authority of the Sloane MS. 3329, we shall be glad to give our opinion on the subject.

"With all respect, then, for our worthy Brother, the Rev. A. F. A. Woodford, whose exertions and contributions to Masonic literature have been continuous and most valuable for many years, we feel bound to state we do not believe according to the evidences accumulated that the 'three degrees were distinct grades in the Operative Order; but that the term Apprentice, Fellow-Craft, and Master Mason simply denoted Masonic, relative, or official positions.'"

If, then, there was originally but one degree, the one into which Freemasons of every class or rank were initiated, according to a very simple form, upon their admission to the Craft, it follows that the degree Fellow-Craft and Master Mason must be of comparatively recent origin. This is legitimately a logical conclusion that can not, I believe, be avoided.

And if so, then the next question that we have to meet and discuss is as to the time and the circumstances of the fabrication of these degrees

CHAPTER XXXIV

INVENTION OF THE FELLOW-CRAFT'S DEGREE

IT having been satisfactorily shown, first, that during the existence of pure Operative Freemasonry there was but one degree, or ritual, of admission, or system of secret working in a lodge, which was accessible in common to all the members of the Craft, Apprentices as well as Fellows and Masters; secondly, that in the year 1717, when the Speculative element began to assume a hitherto unknown prominence, though it did not at once attempt to dissever the connection with the Operative, the Grand Lodge then formed, accepted, and practiced for some time this system of a single degree; and thirdly, that in the year 1723 we have the authentic documentary evidence of the "General Regulations " published in that year, that two degrees had been superimposed on this original one, and that at that time Speculative Freemasonry consisted of three degrees; it follows as a natural inference, that in the interval of six years, between 1717 and 1723, the two supplemental degrees must have been invented or fabricated.

It must be here remarked, parenthetically, that the word degree, in reference to the system practiced by the Operative Freemasons, is used only in a conventional sense, and for the sake of convenience. To say, as is sometimes carelessly said, that the Operative Freemasons possessed only the Apprentice's degree, is to speak incorrectly. The system practiced by the Operatives may be called a degree, if you choose, but it was not peculiar to Apprentices only, but belonged in common to all the ranks or classes of the Fraternity.

When the Speculative branch wholly separated from the Operative, and three divisions of the Order, then properly called degrees, were invented, this ritual of the latter became the basis of them all. Portions of it were greatly modified and much developed, and became what is now known as the First degree, though it continued for many years to receive increments by the invention of new symbols and new ceremonies, and by sometimes undergoing important changes. Other portions of it, but to a less extent, were incorporated into the two supplemental degrees, the Second and the Third.

Thus it was that by development of the old ritual, and by the invention of a new one, the ancient system, or, conventionally speaking, the original degree of the Operatives, became the Entered Apprentice's degree of the Speculatives, and two new degrees, one for the Fellow-Crafts and one for the Master Masons, were invented.

Then the important and most interesting question recurs, When and by whom were these two new degrees invented and introduced into the modern system of Speculative Freemasonry?

The answer to this question which, at this day, would probably be given by nearly all the Masonic scholars who have, without preconceived prejudices, devoted themselves to the investigation of the history of Freemasonry, as it is founded on and demonstrated by the evidence of authentic documents, combined with natural and logical inferences and not traditionary legends and naked assumptions, is that they were the invention of that recognized ritualist, Dr. John Theophilus Desaguliers, with the co-operation of Dr. James Anderson, and perhaps a few others, among whom it would not be fair to omit the name of George Payne. The time of this invention or fabrication would be placed after the formation of the Grand Lodge in 1717, and before the publication of the first edition of its Book of Constitutions in 1723.

To the time and manner of the fabrication of the Fellow-Craft's degree the writers who have adopted the theory here announced have not paid so much attention as they have to that of the Master Mason. Recognizing the fact that the two supplementary degrees were fabricated between the years 1717 and 1723, they have not sought to define the precise date, and seem to have been willing to believe them to have been of contemporaneous origin.

But after as careful an investigation as I was capable of making, I have been led to the conclusion that the fabrication of the degree of Fellow- Craft preceded that of Master Mason by three or four years, and that the system of Speculative Freemasonry had been augmented by the addition of a new degree to the original one in or about the year 1719.

There is documentary evidence of an authentic character which proves the existence of a "Fellow-Craft's part" in the year 1720, while it is not until the year 1723 that we find any record alluding to the fact that there was a " Master's part."

Hence, in a chronological point of view, it may be said that the single degree or ritual in which, and in the secrets of which, all classes of workmen, from the Apprentice to the Master, equally participated, constituted, under various modifications, a part of Operative Freemasonry from the earliest times. The possession of those secrets, simple as they were, distinguished the Freemasons from the Rough Layers in England, from the Cowans in Scotland, and from the Surer, or Wall Builders, in Germany.

This degree, in its English form, was the only one known or practiced in London in the year 1717, at the era which has incorrectly been called the "Revival." The degree of Fellow-Craft, in the modern signification of the word degree, was incorporated into the system, probably a very few years after the organization of the Grand Lodge, and was fully recognized as a degree in the year 1719, or perhaps early in 1720.

Finally, the Third or Master's degree was added, so as to make the full complement of degrees as they now exist, between the years 1720 and 1723 - certainly not before the former nor after the latter period.

Of this theory we have, I think, documentary evidence of so authentic a character, that we must be irresistibly led to the conclusion that the theory is correct.

Bro. Lyon, in his History of thve Lodge of Edinburgh, cites a record which has a distinct relevancy to the question of the time when the Second degree originated. It is contained in the minutes of the Lodge of Dunblane, under the date of December 27, 1720, which is about sixteen years prior to the establishment of the Grand Lodge of Scotland.

The minute records that a lawyer, and therefore a Theoretic Mason, who had formerly been entered, had, after a due examination, been " duely passed from the Squair to the Compass and from ane Entered Prentiss to a Fellow of Craft." In commenting on this minute, Bro. Lyon says:

"It would appear from this that what under the modern ritual of the Fraternity is a symbol peculiar to the Second Degree, was, under the system which obtained in Scotland prior to the introduction of the Third Degree, the distinctive emblem of the Entered Apprentice step - and what is now a leading symbol in the degree of Master Mason, was then indicative of the Fellow-Craft, or highest grade of Lodge membership."[115]

This authentic record surely corroborates the theory just advanced that the Fellow-Craft's degree was formulated in London after the year 1717 and before the close of the year 1720. Here, I think, we are warranted in pursuing the following method of deduction.

If the first notice of the degree of Fellow-Craft being conferred in Scotland, as a degree, occurs in the record of a lodge in the last days of the year 1720; and if, as we know from other sources, that Scotland derived the expanded system of degrees from the sister kingdom; then it is reasonable to suppose that the degree must have been given in Scotland at as early a period after its fabrication in England as was compatible with a due allowance of time for its transmission from the lodges of the latter kingdom to those of the former, and for the necessary preparation for its legal adoption.

The degree must, of course, have been practiced in London for some time before it would be transmitted to other places, and hence we may accept the hypothesis, as something more than a mere presumption, that the Second degree had been invented by Desaguliers and his collaborators on the ritual of the new Grand Lodge in the course of the year 1719, certainly not later than the beginning of the year 1720.

Between the 24th of June, 1717, when the Grand Lodge was established, and the end of the year 1718, the period of less than eighteen months which had elapsed was too brief to permit the overthrow of a long-existing system, endeared to the Craft by its comparative antiquity. Time and opportunity were required for the removal of opposition, the conciliation of prejudices, and the preparation of rituals, all of which would bring us to the year 1719 as the conjectural date of the fabrication of the Second degree.

It is highly probable that the degree was not thoroughly formulated and legally introduced into the ritual until after the 24th of June, 1719, when Desaguliers, who was then Grand Master, and the Proto-Grand Master, Sayer, who was then one of the Grand Wardens, had, from their official positions, sufficient influence to cause the acceptance of the new degree by the Grand Lodge.

We can gather very little, except inferentially, from the meager records of Anderson, and yet he shows us that there was certainly an

---

[115] No reference is here made to the subsequent disseverment of the Third degree which resulted in the composition of the Royal arch degree, as that subject will be here- after fully discussed.

impetus given to the Order in 1719, which might very well have been derived from the invention of a new and more attractive ritual.

Anderson says, referring to the year 1719, that "now several old brothers, that had neglected the Craft, visited the lodges; some noblemen were also made brothers, and more new lodges were constituted."

The record of the preceding year tells us that the Grand Master Payne had desired the brethren to bring to the Grand Lodge any old writings concerning Masonry "in order to shew the usages of ancient times." Northouck, a later but not a discreditable authority, expanding the language of his predecessor, says that "the wish expressed at the Grand Lodge for collecting old manuscripts, appears to have been preparatory to the compiling and publishing a body of Masonical Constitutions."

I can see in this act the suggestion of the idea then beginning to be entertained by the Speculative leaders of the new society to give it a more elevated character by the adoption of new laws and a new form of ceremonies. To guide them in this novel attempt, they desired to obtain all accessible information as to old usages.

And now, some of the older Operative Craftsmen, becoming alarmed at what they believed was an effort to make public the secrets which had been so scrupulously preserved from the eyes of the profane by their predecessors, and who were unwilling to aid in the contemplated attempt to change the old ritual, an attempt which had been successful in the fabrication of a Second degree, and the modification of the First, resolved to throw obstructions in the way of any further innovations.

This will account for the fact recorded by Anderson that, between June, 1719, and June, 1720,[116] several valuable manuscripts concerning the ancient " regulations, charges, secrets, and usages " were "burnt by some scrupulous brothers, that those papers might not fall into strange hands."

The records do not say so, in as many words, but we may safely infer from their tenor that the conflict had begun between the old Operative Freemasons who desired to see no change from the ancient ways, and the more liberal-minded Theoretic members, who were anxious to develop the system and to have a more intellectual ritual - a conflict which terminated in 1723 with the triumph of the Theoretics

---

[116] Dr. Anderson, in his chronological records, counts the years from the installation of one Grand Master in June to that of the next in June of the following year.

and the defeat of the Operatives, who retired from the field and left the institution of Speculative Freemasonry to assume the form which it has ever since retained, as "a science of morality veiled in allegory and illustrated by symbols," a definition which would be wholly inapplicable to the old Operative system.

In the minute of the Dunblane Lodge which has been cited through Bro. Lyon, it was said that the candidate in being advanced from an Entered Apprentice to a Fellow-Craft had "passed from the Square to the Compass."

It is curious and significant that this expression was adopted on the Continent at a very early period of the 18th century, when the hautes grades or high degrees began to be manufactured. With the inventors of these new degrees the Square was the symbol of Craft Masonry, while the Compass was the appropriate emblem of what they called their more elevated system of instruction. Hence, instead of the Square which is worn by the Master of an Ancient Craft Lodge, the Master of a Lodge of Perfection substitutes the Compasses as the appropriate badge of his office.

But in Ancient Craft Masonry, with whose history alone we are now dealing, the Compass is at this day a symbol peculiar to the Third degree, while it would seem from the above-cited minute that in the beginning of the 18th century it was appropriate to the Fellow-Crafts.

In commenting on this phrase in the record of the Lodge of Dunblane, Bro. Lyon makes the following remarks:

"To some it will appear to favor the theory which attributes the existence of the Third degree to a disjunction and a rearrangement of the parts of which the Second was originally composed."

I have no objection to accept this theory in part. I believe, and the hypothesis is a very tenable one, that when the Second degree was fabricated, the secrets, the ritual, and instructions which were formerly comprised in the single degree which was then given to the whole Craft, indiscriminately, to Apprentices, to Fellows, and to Masters alike, were divided between the two degrees which were then formulated, with certain new additions; and that subsequently, when the Third degree was invented, there was a further disintegration, and a portion of that which had constituted the "part of a Fellow-Craft " was, with many new points, transferred to that of the Master.

I have thus, by what I believe to be a tenable hypothesis, sought to fix the time of the first expansion of the old ritual of the Operatives, which was for a short time made use of, in all its simplicity, by the Speculative Grand Lodge.

The next step in this expansion was the fabrication of the Third or Master Mason's degree. To the time when this important event took place and to the circumstances attending it we are now to direct our attention. This shall therefore be the subject to be treated in the following chapter.

CHAPTER XXXV

NON-EXISTENCE OF A MASTER MASON'S DEGREE AMONG THE OPERATIVE FREEMASONS

The history of the origin of the Third or Master's degree - that is, so much of it as refers to the precise time of its invention - has, at this day, been involved in much doubt, and been the source of earnest controversy in consequence of the searching investigations of recent scholars, whose incisive criticism has shown many theories to be untenable which were once held to be plausible.

Until within a few years the opinion was universally entertained that the Third degree must have been in existence from the time of the invention of the Masonic system, and at whatever period that event was placed, the doctrine was held as indisputable that the First, the Second, and the Third degrees must have had a contemporaneous origin, no one preceding the other in point of time, but all springing at the same epoch into form and practice.

The theory that Freemasonry originated at the Temple of Solomon was for a very long time a universally accepted proposition, constituting, in fact, the orthodox creed of a Freemason, and conscientiously adopted, not merely by the common and unlearned masses of the Fraternity, but even by Masonic scholars of distinguished reputation.

Consequent upon this theory was another, that at the same time the Master's degree was invented and that the builders of the Temple were divided into the same three classes distinguished as degreed which constitute the present system of Freemasonry.

This theory was derived from the esoteric narrative contained in the modern ritual of the Third degree. If this narrative is accepted as an authentic history of events which actually occurred at that time, then there need be no more difficulty in tracing the invention of the Third degree to the time of King Solomon than there can be in placing the origin of Freemasonry at the same remote period.

But unfortunately for the repose of those who would be willing to solve a difficult problem by the Alexandrian method of cutting the Gordian knot, rather than by the slower process of analytical investigation, the theory of the Temple origin of the Master's degree has now been repudiated by nearly all Masonic scholars. A few may be accepted who, like Bro. Woodford, still express a doubtful recognition of the possibility that the legend may be true.[117]

Thus Bro. Woodford, referring to the Temple legend, says: "As there is no a priori reason why an old Masonic tradition should not be true in the main, we see no reason to reject the world-wide story of King Solomon's protection of a Masonic association. Indeed, modern discovery seems to strengthen the reality of our Masonic legends, and we should always, as it appears to us, distinguish between what is possible and probable and what is actually provable or proved by indubitable evidence." In reply to this it must be remembered that of all the arguments in favor of an event, the possibility of its occurrence is the weakest that can be adduced. In dialectics there is an almost illimitable gulf between possibility and actuality. A hundred things may be possible or even probable, and yet not one of them may be actual. With the highest respect for the scholarship of our reverend Brother, I am compelled to dissent from the views he has here expressed. Nor am I prepared to accept the statement that "modern discovery seems to strengthen the reality of our Masonic legends." A contrary opinion now generally prevails, though it must be admitted that the modern interpretations of these legends have given them a value, as the expression of symbolic ideas, which does not pertain to them when accepted, as they formerly were, as truthful narratives.

The Temple legend, however, must be retained as a part of the ritual as long as the present system of Speculative Freemasonry exists, and the legendary and allegorical narrative must be repeated by the Master of the lodge on the occasion of every initiation into the mysteries of the Third degree, because, though it is no longer to be accepted as an historical statement, yet the events which it records are still recognized as a myth containing within itself, and independent of all question of probability, a symbolical significance of the highest importance.

---

[117] Kenning's "Masonic Cyclopedia," art. Temple of Solomon, p. 612.

This mythical legend of the Temple, and of the Temple Builder, must ever remain an inseparable part of the Masonic ritual, and the narrative must be repeated on all appropriate occasions, because, without this legend, Speculative Masonry would lose its identity and would abandon the very object of its original institution. On this legend, whether true or false, whether a history or a myths is the most vital portion of the symbolism of Freemasonry founded.

In the interpretation of a legendary symbol or an allegory it is a matter of no consequence to the value of the interpretation whether the legend be true or false; the interpretation alone is of importance. We need not, for instance, inquire whether the story of Hiram Abif is a narrative which is true in all its parts, or merely a historical myth in which truth and fiction are variously blended, or, in fact, only the pious invention of some legendmaker, to whose fertile imagination it has been indebted for all its details.

It is sufficient when we are occupied in an investigation of subjects connected with the science of symbolism, that the symbol which the legend is intended to develop should be one that teaches some dogma whose truth we can not doubt. The symbologist looks to the truth or fitness of the symbol, not to that of the legend on which it is founded. Thus it is that we should study the different myths and traditions which are embodied in the ritual of Freemasonry.

But when we abandon the role of the symbologist or ritualist, and assume that of the historian - when, for the time, we no longer interest ourselves in the lessons of Masonic symbolism, but apply our attention to the origin and the progress of the institution, then it really becomes of importance that we should inquire whether the narrative of certain supposed events which have hitherto been accepted as truthful, are really historical or merely mythical or legendary.

And, therefore, when the question is asked in an historical sense, at what time the Third degree was invented, and in the expectation that the reply will be based on authentic historical authority, we at once repudiate the whole story of its existence at the Temple of Solomon as a mere myth, having, it is true, its value as a symbol but being entitled to no consideration whatever as an historical narrative.

It is, however, most unfortunate for the study of Masonic history that so many writers on this subject, forgetting that all history must have its basis in truth, have sought rather to charm their readers by romantic episodes than to instruct them by a sober detail of facts. One instance of this kind may be cited as an example from the visionary speculations of Ragon, a French writer of great learning, but of still greater imagination.

In his Orthvodoxie Mafonnifue he has attributed the invention of all the degrees to Elias Ashmole, near the end of the 17th century. He says that the degree of Master Mason was formulated soon after the year 1648, but that the decapitation of King Charles I., and the part taken by Ashmole in favor of the House of Stuart, led to great modifications in the ritual of the degree, and that the same epoch saw the birth of the degrees of Secret Master, Perfect Master, Elect, and Irish Master, of all of which Charles the First was the hero, under the name of Hiram.[118]

Assertions like this are hardly worth the paper and ink that would be consumed in refuting them. Unlike the so-called historical novel which has its basis in a distortion of history, they resemble rather the Arabian Tales or the Travels of Gulliver, which owe their existence solely to the imaginative genius of their authors.

Still there are some writers of more temperate judgment who, while they reject the Temple theory, still claim for the Third degree an antiquity of no certain date, but much anterior to the time of the organization of the Grand Lodge in the beginning of the 18th century.

Thus, Bro. Hyde Clark, in an article in the London Freemasons' Magazine, says that "the ritual of the Third degree is peculiar and suggestive of its containing matter from the old body of Masonry," whence he concludes that it is older than the time of the so-called Revival in 1717, and he advances a theory that the First degree was in that olden time conferred on minors, while the Second and Third were restricted to adults.[119] This view of the origin of the degrees can only be received as a bare assumption, for there is not a particle of authentic evidence to show that it has an historical foundation. No old document has been yet discovered which gives support to the hypothesis that there were ceremonies or esoteric instructions before the year 1719 which were conferred upon a peculiar class. All the testimony of the Old Records and manuscript Constitutions is to the effect that there was but one reception for the Craftsmen, to which all, from the youngest to the oldest Mason, were admitted.

It is true that one of the Old Records, known as the Sloane MS. 3329, mentions different modes of recognition, one of which was peculiar to Masters, and is called in the manuscript "their Master's gripe," and another is called "their gripe for fellowcrafts."

---

[118] "Orthodoxie Maconnique," par J. M. Ragon, Paris, 1853, p. 29.
[119] "Old Freemasonry before Grand Lodges," by Hyde Clark, in the London Freemasons' Magazine, No. 534.

Of the many Masonic manuscripts which, within the last few years have been discovered and published, this is perhaps one of the most important and interesting. Findel first inserted a small portion of it in his History of Freemasonry, but the whole of it in an unmutilated form was subsequently published by Bro. Woodford in 1872, and also by Hughan in the same year in the Voice of Masonry. It was discovered among the papers of Sir Hans Sloane which were deposited in the British Museum, and there is numbered 3329. Bro. Hughan supposes that the date of this manuscript is between 1640 and 1700; Messrs. Bond and Sims, of the British Museum, think that the date is "probably of the beginning of the 18th century." Findel thinks that it was originally in the possession of Dr. Plot, and that it was one of the sources whence he derived his views on Freemasonry. He places its date at about the end of the 17th century. Bro. Woodford cites the authority of Mr. Wallbran for fixing its date in the early part of that century, in which opinion he coincides. The paper-mark of the manuscript in the British Museum appears to have been a copy of an older one, for Bro. Woodford states that though the paper-mark is of the early part of the 18th century, experts will not deny that the language is that of the 17th. He believes, and very reasonably, that it represents the ceremonial through which Ashmole passed in 1646.

As this is the only Old Record in which a single passage is to be found which, by the most liberal exegesis, can be construed even into an allusion to the existence of a Third degree with a separate ritual before the end of the second decade of the 18th century, it may be well to quote such passages of the manuscript as appear to have any bearing on the question.

The methods of recognition for Fellow-Crafts and Masters is thus described in the Sloane MS.:

"Their gripe for fellow craftes is grasping their right hands in each other, thrusting their thumb naile upon the third joynt of each others first Fing'r; their masters gripe is grasping their right hands in each other; placing their four fingers nailes hard upon the carpus or end of others wrists, and their thumb nailes thrust hard directly between the second joynt of the thumb and the third joynt of the first Finger; but some say the mast'rs grip is the same I last described, only each of their middle Fing'rs must reach an inch or three barley corns length higher to touch upon a vein y't comes from the heart."

No indication is to be found in this passage of the existence at the time of three degrees and three separate rituals. All that it tells us is that the Fellow-Crafts were provided with one form of salutation and the

Masters with another, and we are left in uncertainty whether these forms used by one class were unknown to the other, or whether the forms were openly used only to distinguish one class from the other, as the number of stripes on the arm distinguish the grades of non-commissioned officers in the army.

That the latter was the use would appear evident from the fact that the close of the passage leaves it uncertain that the "gripes" were not identical, or at least with a very minute difference. "Some say," adds the writer, "the Master's grip is the same" as the FellowCraft's - "only" - and then he gives the hardly appreciable variation.

Here is another passage which appears to show that no value was attached to the use of the grip as marking a degree, though it might be employed to distinguish a rank or class.

"Another salutation," says the manuscript, "is giving the Masters or fellows grip, saying the right worshipful the mast'rs and fellows in that right worshipful lodge from whence we last came, greet you, greet you, greet you well, then he will reply, God's good greeting to you, dear brother."

Here I take it that all that is meant is that the Masters saluted with the grip peculiar to their class, and the Fellows that peculiar to theirs. But what has become of the Apprentices? Did they salute with the grip of the Fellows or that of the Masters? If so, they must have been acquainted with one or both, and then the secret instruction incidental to the condition of degrees and a distinct ritual must be abandoned, or the Apprentices were not admitted to the privileges of the Craft, and were debarred from a recognition as members of a lodge.

Let the following questions and answers decide that point. They are contained in the manuscript, and there called "a private discourse by way of question and answer."

"Q. Where were you made a mason?
"A. In a just and perfect or just and lawful lodge.
"Q. What is a perfect or just and lawful lodge?
"A. A just and perfect lodge is two Interprintices two fellow crafts, and two Mast'rs, more or fewer, the more the merrier, the fewer the better chear, but if need require five will serve, that is, two Interprintices, two fellow crafted and one Mast'r on the highest hill or the lowest valley of the world without the crow of a cock or the bark of a dog."

This was no lodge of Master Masons, nor of Fellow-Crafts, nor of Entered Apprentices, as they have been distinguished since the establishment of degrees. It was simply a lodge of Freemasons to legalize and perfect whose character it was necessary that representatives of all the classes should be present. The Apprentices forming a part of the lodge must have been privy to all its secrets; and this idea is sustained by all the Old Constitutions and "Charges" in which the Apprentices are enjoined to keep the secrets of the lodge.

The manuscript speaks of two words, "the Mast'r Word" and "the Mason word." The latter is said to have been given in a certain form, which is described. It is possible that the former may have been communicated to Masters as a privilege attached to their rank, while the latter was communicated to the whole Craft. In a later ritual it has been seen that there were two words, "the Jerusalem Word" and "the universal word," but both were known to the whole Fraternity. The Sloane MS. does not positively state that the two words used in its ritual were like these two, or that the Master's was confined to one class. It is, however, likely that this Word was a privileged mark of distinction to be used only by the Masters, though possibly known to the rest of the Fraternity. How else could it be given in the lodge where the three classes were present ? Bro. Lyon has arrived at the same conclusion. He says: " It is our opinion that in primitive times there were no secrots communicated by Lodges to either fellows or craft or master's that were not known to apprentices, seeing that members of the latter grade were necessary to the legal constitution of communications for the admission of masters or fellows."[120] The argument, indeed, appears to be unanswerable.

The Word might, however, as has been suggested, have been whispered by the Master communicating it to the one to whom it was communicated. If this were so, it supplies us with the origin of the modern Past Master's degree. But even then it could only be considered as a privileged mark of a rank or class of the Crafts men and not as the evidence of a degree.

I will merely suggest, but I will not press the argument, that it is not impossible that by a clerical mistake, or through some confusion in the mind of the writer, "Mast'r Word" may have been written for "Mason Word," an expression which has been made familiar to us in the minutes of the Scottish lodges, and which is the only word the secrecy of which is required by the oath that is contained in the manuscript. On the other hand, " Master Word " is a phrase not met with in any other manuscript, Scotch or English.

The "Oath," which forms a part of the Sloane MS., supplies itself the strongest proof that, during the period in which it formed a

---

[120] "History of the Lodge of Edinburgh," p. 23.

part of the ritual, that ritual must have been one common to the three classes; in other words, there could have been but one degree, because there was but one obligation of secrecy imposed, and the secrets, whatever they were, must have been known to all Freemasons, to the Apprentices as well as on to the Master. The "Oath" is in the following words:

"The Mason Word and everything therein contained you shall keep secret, you shall never put it in writing directly or indirectly; you shall keep all that we or your attenders shall bid you keep secret from man, woman or child, stock or stone, and never reveal it but to a brother or in a Lodge of Freemasons, and truly observe the charges in the Constitution; all this you promise and swear faithfully to keep and observe, without any manner of equivocation or mental reservation, directly or indirectly; so help you God and the contents of this Book."

The "Mason Word," with the secrets connected with it, formed a very prominent part of the ritual of the Scotch Freemasons, though there is no reference to it in any of the English manuscripts except in the Sloane.

In fact, so important was this word considered as to be sometimes figuratively employed to designate the whole body of the Fraternity. Thus, in a record of the Musselburgh Lodge, in December, 1700, where complaint is made of the great disorders into which the lodge had fallen, it is said, among other evils, that the practice of Fellow Grafts encouraging Apprentices to take work as journeymen, " at last, by degrees, will bring all law and order and consequently the Mason Word to contempt "[121] - where, evidently by a figure of speech, it is meant that the Fraternity or Craft of Masonry will be brought to contempt.

In the Lodge of Edinburgh, which was the principal Lodge of Scotland, and whose records have been best preserved, the Masons or employers were, up to the beginning of the 18th century, the dominant power, and seldom called the Fellows or Craftsmen of an inferior class, who were only journeymen, into their counsel.

The controversy between the Masters and journeymen, which led, in 1712, to the establishment of a new lodge, are faithfully de scribed by Bro. Lyon from the original records.[122] It is sufficient here to say that one of the principal grievances complained of by the latter was in respect to the giving of the Mason Word, with the secrets connected with it and the fees arising from it. The Masters claimed the right to confer it and to dispose of the fee, so to speak, of initiation.

---

[121] "History of the Lodge of Edinburgh," p. 175.
[122] Ibid., p. 140

Finally, the controversy was partially ended by arbitration. The "Decreet- Arbitral," as is the Scottish legal phrase, or award of the arbitrators made on January 17, 1715, has been recorded, and has been published by Bro. Lyon. The only point of importance to the present subject is that the arbitrators decreed that the journeymen Masons, that is, the Fellow- Crafts, should be allowed "to meet together by themselves, as a Society for giving the Mason Word and to receive dues therefor."

From this fact it is clearly evident that the knowledge of the "Mason Word" and the secrets pertaining to it formed no part of a degree exclusively confined to the Masters, but that all esoteric knowledge in connection with this subject was also the property of the Fellow-Crafts, and of the Apprentices, too, because it has been shown that they were required to be present at all lodge meetings.

The expression, "Mason Word," which is common in the Scottish lodge records, has been, so far, found only in one English manuscript, the Sloane 3329. But as the theory is now generally accepted as having been proved, that the Scottish Freemasons derived their secrets from their English brethren, there can hardly be a doubt that the regulations relative to this Word must have been nearly the same in both countries.

That this was the case after the organization of the Grand Lodge of England, there can be no doubt. It is proved by the visit of Dr. Desaguliers to Edinburgh in 1721, and long before. Bro. Lyon was aware of that visit.

He had, from other considerations, expressed the opinion " that the system of Masonic degrees which for nearly a century and a half has been known in Scotland as Freemasonry, was an importation from England."[123]

What this "Mason Word" was, either in England or Scotland, we have, at this day, no means of knowing. But we do know from the records of the 17th century, which have been preserved, that it was the most important, and in Scotland perhaps the only, secret that was communicated to the Craft.

"The Word," says Bro. Lyon, "is the only secret that is even alluded to in the minutes of Mary's Chapel, or in those of Kilwinning, Acheson's Haven, or Dunblane, or any other that we have examined of a date prior to the erection of the Grand Lodge."[124]

---

[123] "History of the Lodge of Edinburgh," p. 153
[124] Ibid., p. 22.

We know also that in England, in Scotland, and in Germany, the giving of the Word was accompanied by a grip and by the communication of other secrets.

But we know also, positively, that this Word and these secrets were bestowed upon Fellows as well as Masters, and also, as we have every reason to infer, upon Apprentices.

Besides the proofs that we derive from old Masonic records, we have a right to draw our inferences from the prevalence of similar customs among other crafts.

Thus, the carpenters, wrights, joiners, slaters, and other crafts who were connected in the art of building with the Masons, were called in Scotland "Squaremen," and they had a secret word which was called the "Squaremen Word." This word, with a grip and sign, was communicated to both journeymen and apprentices in a ceremony called the "brithering." A portion of this ceremony which was performed in a closely guarded apartment of a public-house was the investiture with a leather apron.[125]

I can not doubt that the communication of the "Mason Word and the secrets pertaining to it" was accompanied by similar ceremonies in Scotland, and by a parity of reasoning also in England.

The final conclusion to which we must arrive from the proofs which have been adduced, is that as there was no such system as that of degrees known to the mediaeval Operative Freemasons, that no such system was practiced by the Speculative Freemasons who in 1717 instituted the Grand Lodge of England, until at least two years after its organization; that in 1719 the two degrees of Entered Apprentice and Fellow-Craft were invented; and that subsequently the present system of symbolic or ancient Craft degrees was perfected by the fabrication of a new degree, now recognized as the Third or Master Mason's degree.

At what precise time and under what circumstances this Third degree was invented and introduced into the Grand Lodge system of modern Freemasonry, is the next subject that must engage our attention.

---

[125] Lyon's "History of the Lodge of Edinburgh," p. 23.

CHAPTER XXXVI

THE INVENTION OF THE THIRD OR MASTER MASON'S DEGREE

WE have seen that up to the year 1719 the Masonic ritualistic system consisted of but one degree, which was common to the whole, and the secrets of which were communicated to the Apprentice at his initiation, or as it was, perhaps, more properly called, in reference to the paucity of ceremonies, his admission. At that time Desaguliers and his collaborators originated a Second degree, to be appropriated to the Fellow-Crafts. To do this it was necessary, or, at least, it was deemed expedient, to disintegrate the primitive degree and out of it to make two degrees, those of Entered Apprentice and Fellow-Craft.

For a short time - how long is to be hereafter seen - the Masonic system consisted of two degrees, and the summit of the system was the Fellow- Craft's degree.

From this time the Fellow-Crafts began to take a prominent place in the business of Masonry, and the Apprentice lost some of the importance he had obtained in early times as a component part of the Craft and an equal participant with Masters and Fellows in its secrets. He was permitted, it is true, to be present at the meetings of the lodge, and to take his share in its business (except, of course, where candidates were to be "passed "), and even to vote in the Grand Lodge on the question of an alteration of the "General Regulations," but the offices were to be held and the lodge represented in the Grand Lodge by Fellow-Crafts only. Of this there is abundant evidence in contemporary documents.

The first edition of Anderson's Constitutions contains "the Charges of a Free-mason, extracted from the Records of Lodges beyond

Sea." The exact date when these "Charges" were compiled is not known. It must have been after 1718, for they distinctly refer to the Fellow-Craft's degree, and it must have been before the beginning of 1723, for that is the year of their publication. It is, however, certain from their phraseology that when they were compiled for the use of the lodges, the Fellow-Craft's degree had been instituted, but the Master's degree was not yet known. For this reason I am inclined to place the date between 1718, in which year Anderson tells us that "several old copies of the Gothic Constitutions were produced and collated," and 1721, when he submitted his manuscript, including the "Charges" and "Regulations" to the Grand Lodge. There is no date prefixed to the "Charges," but I think it not improbable that they were constructed by Payne in 1720, at the same time that he compiled the "General Regulations." It is certain that they must have been in existence on December 27, 1721, when a committee was appointed by the Grand Lodge to examine them and the Constitutions. And this date sufficiently accounts for the fact that there are no allusions in them to the Master's degree.

These "Charges," therefore, give us a very good idea of the status of Apprentices and Fellow-Crafts in English Masonry at the time when the system consisted of two degrees, and the "part of Master" had not yet been composed.

In Charge IV. it is said that if the Apprentice has learned his art, he then may in due time be made a Fellow-Craft, and then if otherwise qualified may become a Warden and successively Master of his lodge, the Grand Warden, and at length the Grand Master.

Here we see that at that time the Fellow-Craft was at the summit of the Fraternity so far as degrees and qualifications for promotions in rank were concerned. Nothing is said of the degree of Master; it was still simply as in primitive times - a gradation of rank.

In the same Charge we are told that "no Brother can be a Warden until he has passed the part of a Fellow-Craft, nor a Master[126] until he has acted as a Warden; nor Grand Warden until he has been Master of a lodge; nor Grand Master unless he has been a Fellow Craft before his election."

It is very evident that at this time there could be no degree higher than that of the Fellow-Craft. If there had been, that higher degree would have been made the necessary qualification for these high offices. We are not without the proof of how these

---

[126] That is, Master of a Lodge, as the context shows.

"Charges" would have been made to read had the degree of Master Mason been in existence at the time of their compilation.

Notwithstanding that Speculative Freemasonry owes much to Dr. Anderson, we are forced to reluctantly admit that, as an historian, he was inexact and inaccurate, and that while he often substituted the inventions of tradition for the facts of history, he also often modified the phraseology of old documents to suit his own views.

In 1738 he published a second edition of the Book of Constitutions, a work which, although at first perhaps carelessly approved, was subsequently condemned by the Grand Lodge. In this work he inserted a copy of these "Charges." But now the Master's degree had been long recognized and practiced by the lodges as the summit of the ritual.

Now let us see how these "Charges" were modified by Dr. Anderson in this second edition, so as to meet the altered condition of the Masonic system. The Apprentice is no longer admonished, as he was in the first edition, that his ambition should be to become a Fellow-Craft and in time a Warden, a Master of a Lodge, a Grand Warden, and even a Grand Master. But in the copy of 1738 he is told that "when of age and expert he may become an Entered Prentice, or a Free-Mason of the lowest degree, and upon his due improvement a Fellow-Craft and a Master Mason."

Again, in the "Charges" of 1720,[127] it is said that is "no brother can be a Warden until he has passed the part of a Fellow-Craft."

In the "Charges" of 1738, it is said that "the Wardens are chosen from among the Master Masons."

In Charge V. of 1720 it is directed that "the most expert of the Fellow Crafts shall be chosen or appointed the Master or Overseer of the Lord's Work."

In the same Charge, published in 1738, it is prescribed that "a Master Mason only must be the Surveyor or Master of Work."

Now, what else can be inferred from this collation of the two editions (which, if deemed necessary, could have been much further extended), except that in 1720 the Fellow-Craft was the highest degree, and that after that year and long before 1738 the Master's degree had been invented.

But let us try to get a little nearer to the exact date of the introduction of the Third degree into the Masonic system.

---

[127] I assume this date for convenience of reference, and because, as I have already shown, it is probably correct.

The Constitutions of the Free-Masons, commonly called the Book of Constitutions, was ordered by the Grand Lodge, on March 25, 1722, to be printed and was actually printed in that year, for it was presented by Dr. Anderson to the Grand Lodge "in print" on January 17, 1723. So that although the work bears on its title-page the imprint of 1723, it must really be considered as having been controlled in its composition by the opinions and the condition of things that existed in the year 1722.

Now, in the body of this book there is no reference to the degree of Master Mason. It is true that on page 33 the author speaks of is such as were admitted Master Masons or Masters of the Work," by which expression he evidently meant not those who had received a higher degree, but those who in the "Charges" contained in the same book were said to be "chosen or appointed the Master or Overseer of the Lord's Work," and who the same Charge declares should be "the most expert of the Fellow-Craftsmen."[128]

On the contrary, when speaking of the laws, forms, and usages practiced in the early lodges by the Saxon and Scottish kings, he says: Neither what was conveyed nor the manner how, can be communicated by writing; as no man can indeed understand it without the key of a Fellow- Craft."[129]

So that in 1722, when this note was written, there was no higher degree than that of Fellow-Craft, because the Fellow-Crafts were, as being at the summit of the ritual, in possession of the key to all the oral and esoteric instructions of the Craft.

Guided by the spirit of the "General Regulations," printed in the first edition of Anderson's Constitutions, I am induced to place the invention of the Third degree in the year 1722, although, as will be hereafter seen, it did not get into general use until a later period. The investigations which have led me to this conviction were pursued in the following train, and I trust that the reader, if he will follow the same train of investigation with me, will arrive at the same conclusion. In pursuing this train of argument, it will be unavoidably necessary to repeat some of what has been said before. But the subject is so important that a needful repetition will be surely excused for the sake of explicitness in the reasoning.

---

[128] Its preparation by Dr. Anderson had been previously directed on September 29, 1721. This and the date of its publication in January, 1723, lead us irresistibly to the conclusion that the work was written in 1722.

[129] Anderson's "Constitutions," 1st edition, p. 29, note.

The "General Regulations" were published in the first edition of the Book of Constitutions, edited by Anderson. This edition bears the imprint of 1723, but Anderson himself tells us that the work was " in print " and produced before the Grand Lodge on the 17th of January in that year. Hence, it is evident that although the work was published in 1723, it was actually printed in 1722. Whatever, therefore, is contained in the body of that work must refer to the condition of things in that year, unless Anderson may (as I shall endeavor to show he has done) have made some slight alteration or interpolation, toward the end of 1722 or the very beginning of 1723, while the book was passing through the press.

I have shown by the sold Charges," whose assumed date is 1720, that at that time the degree of Fellow-Craft was the highest recognized or known in Speculative Freemasonry, and I shall now attempt to prove from the "General Regulations" that the same condition existed in 1722, the year in which those "Regulations" were printed.

The "General Regulations" consist of thirty-nine articles, and throughout the whole composition, except in one instance, which I believe to be an interpolation, there is not one word said of Master Masons, but the only words used are Brethren and Fellow-Crafts - Brethren being a generic term which includes both Fellows and Apprentices.

Thus it is said (art. vi.), that "no man can be entered a Brother in any particular Lodge or admitted to be a Member thereof without the unanimous consent of all the members."

That is, no man can be made an Entered Apprentice, nor having been made elsewhere, be affiliated in that particular lodge.

Again (art. vii.), "every new Brother, at his making, is decently to cloath the Lodge." That is, every Apprentice at his making, etc.

The word "Brother," although a generic term, has in these instances a specific signification which is determined by the context of the sentence.

The making of a Brother was the entering of an Apprentice, a term we still use when speaking of the making of a Mason. The Fellow-Craft was admitted, or, as Ashmole says in his Diary, "admitted into the Fellowship of Freemasons."

Lyon,' referring to the nomenclature of the Scottish lodges "of the olden time," says, that the words "made" and "accepted" were frequently used as indicating the admission of Fellow-Crafts, but he adds that the former was sometimes, though rarely, used to denote the entry of Apprentices. He states, however, that toward the end of the 17th century these words gave way to the expression "passed," to indicate the reception of a Fellow-Craft, and that the Lodge of Mary's Chapel, at about that time, used the word "accepted" as equivalent to the making or passing of a Fellow Craft. But the Schaw statutes of 1598, which are among the very oldest of the Scottish records extant, employs the word "entered" in reference to the making of an Apprentice, and received or "admitted" in reference to the making of a Fellow-Craft.

I think, however, that in the English lodges, or at least in the "General Regulations" of 1720, the words "making a Brother" meant, as it does in the present day, the initiation of an Entered Apprentice, and that Fellow- Crafts were "admitted." The word 'passed" soon afterward came into use.

With this explanation of certain technical terms which appeared to be necessary in this place, let us proceed to examine from the document itself what was the status of Fellow-Crafts at the time of the compilation of the "General Regulations" by Grand Master Payne, in 1720, and their adoption in 1722 by the Grand Lodge. From this examination I contend that it will be found that at that period there was in Freemasonry only two degrees, those of Entered Apprentice and Fellow-Craft.

It will be admitted that in a secret society no one has such opportunities of undetected "eavesdropping" as the guardian of the portal, and hence, the modern ritual of Freemasonry requires that the Tiler shall be in possession of the highest degree worked by the body which he tiles.

Now the 13th General Regulation prescribes that a Brother "who must be a Fellow-Craft should be appointed to look after the door of the Grand Lodge."[130]

But it may be argued that the Grand Lodge always met and worked in the Entered Apprentices' degree, and that Apprentices as well as Fellow- Crafts were present at its communications.

I admit the fact, and acknowledge that from this point of view my argument would be untenable. But why was not the office of Tiler entrusted to an Entered Apprentice ? Because, if there were three degrees at the time, it would have been manifestly improper to have bestowed this trustworthy and responsible office on one who was in possession of only the lowest. And if it was prudent and proper, as I suppose will be admitted, that it should have been bestowed on one of the highest

---

[130] "History of the Lodge of Edinburgh," p. 76.

degree, why was it not given to a Master Mason ? Simply, I reply, because there were no Master Masons, as a degree class, from whom the selection could be made. As the laws of every lodge at the present day prescribe that the Tiler must be a Master Mason, because the Third degree is the highest one known to or practiced in the lodge, so the laws of the Grand Lodge in 1723, or the "General Regulations," required the Tiler to be a Fellow-Craft because the Second degree was the highest one known to or practiced in the Grand Lodge at that time. It would seem hardly to need an argument to prove that if the Third degree had been in practical existence when these "Regulations" were approved by the Grand Lodge, they would have directed that the guardian of the door should be in possession of that degree.

Another clause in this 13th Regulation is very significant. The Treasurer and Secretary of the Grand Lodge are permitted to have, each, a clerk, and it is directed that he "must be a Brother and Fellow-Craft." Again, and for a silnilar reason, the officer is selected from the highest degree. Had the Third degree been known at that time, these assistants would surely have been chosen from among the Master Masons; for if not, theywould have had to be sometimes entrusted with the records of the transactions of a degree of which they had no right to possess a knowledge.

In the 14th Regulation it is prescribed that in the absence of the Grand Wardens the Grand Master may order private Wardens, that is, the Wardens of a subordinate lodge, to act as Grand Wardens pro fempore, and then, that the representation of that lodge in the Grand Lodge may be preserved, the lodge is to supply their place, not by two Master Masons, but "by two Fellow-Crafts of the same lodge, called forth to act or sent thither by the particular Master thereof."

The fact that the second was the highest degree known in the early part of the year 1723 is confirmed by the formula inserted in the first edition of the Book of Constitutions, and which is there entitled "the Manner of Constituting a New Lodge, as practiced by his Grace the Duke of Wharton, the present Right Worshipful Grand Master, according to the ancient usages of Masons." It was, according to Anderson's record in the second edition, presented to the Grand Lodge and approved on January 17, 1723. It is therefore a fair testimony as to the condition of the degree question at that date.

In this formula it is said that 'the new Master and Wardens being yet among the Fellow-Craft" the Grand Master shall ask his Deputy if he has examined them and finds the Candidate well skilled, etc. And this being answered in the affirmative, he is duly installed, after which the new Master, "calling forth two Fellow-Craft, presents them to the Grand Master for his approbation," after which they are installed as Wardens of the lodge.[131]

This, I think, is conclusive evidence that the degree of Fellow Craft was then the highest known or used. In January, 1723, it did not require a Mason to be more than a Fellow-Craft to prove himself, as Wharton's form of Constitution has it, " well skilled in the noble science and the Royal Art, and duly instructed in our mysteries, and competent to preside as Master over a lodge."

In the 25th of these "General Regulations" it is directed that a committee shall be formed at the time of the Grand Feast, to examine every person bringing a ticket, "to discourse him, if they think fit, in order to admit or debar him as they shall see cause." It was, in fact, an examining committee, to inquire into the qualifications of applicants for admission to the annual meeting of the Grand Lodge. The members of such a committee must necessarily have been in possession of the highest degree practiced by the Grand Lodge. It is very evident that a Fellow-Craft was not competent to examine into the qualifications and attainments of a Master Mason. Yet the Regulation prescribes that to compose such a committee "the Masters of lodges shall each appoint one experienced and discreet Fellow-Craft of his lodge."

But there is evidence in these "Regulations," not only that Fellow-Crafts were in 1723 appointed to the responsible offices of Tilers, Wardens, and Committees of Examination, but that they were competent to fill the next to the highest office in the Craft. The 17th Regulation says that " if the Deputy Grand Master be sick, or necessarily absent, the Grand Master may chuse any Fellow-Craft he pleases to be his Deputy pro tempore."

This, I think, is as conclusive proof as legitimate logical deduction can produce, that at the beginning of the year 1723, which was the date of the publication of these "Regulations" for the governrnent of the Grand Lodge, the degree of Fellow-Craft was the highest practiced by the Grand Lodge, and that the degree of Master Mason was not then known or recognized in the system of Speculative Freemasonry. A Fellow-Craft presiding over Master Masons would indeed be a Masonic anomaly of which it would require something more than a blind reverence for the claims of antiquity to extort belief.

The citations that I have made seem to me to leave no doubt on the mind. The whole spirit and tenor of these "General Regulations," as

---

[131] Anderson's "Constitutions," edition of 1723, pp. 71, 72.

well as the "Form of Constituting a new Lodge," which is so closely appended to them as to make, as it were, a part of them, go to prove that at the time they were approved by the Grand Lodge, which was on January 17, 1723, there were but two degrees recognized in Speculative Freemasonry, namely, those of Entered Apprentice and Fellow-Craft; and that at that time the degree of Master Mason constituted no part of the system.

That Anderson himself placed the same interpretation on these passages, and was perfectly aware of the deduction to be made from them, is evident from the fact that when he next published these "General Regulations," which was in the second edition of the Book of Constitutions, in 1738, at which time there is no doubt of the existence of the Master's degree, he almost invariably changed the words "Fellow-Craft" to "Master Mason."

And, accordingly, we find that in 1738 the Wardens, the Tiler, and the Assistant Treasurer and Secretary were required to be Master Masons. The change had taken place, and the Third degree had been adopted between the years 1723 and 1738.

But those who deny this theory and contend that the Third degree is of greater antiquity, and was known and practiced long before the beginning of the 18th century, would quote against my argument the words contained in the 13th Regulation, which words are as follows:

Apprentices must be admitted Masters and Fellow-Craft only here (in the Grand Lodge) unless by a dispensation."

I candidly admit that if this passage be proved to be a genuine part of the original "General Regulations," compiled in 1720 by Grand Master Payne and approved in 1723 by the Grand Lodge, the question would be decided at once and we could no longer doubt that the Third degree was in existence not only in 1723, but three years before, that is, in 1720.

But I do not hesitate to assert that this passage is an interpolation by Anderson and Desaguliers, made for a certain purpose, and I think that this assertion is capable of critical proof.

In criticism there are two methods of determining whether a suspected passage in an ancient work or an old document is genuine or spurious.

The first method is by the collation of other editions or manuscripts. If, in the examination of an ancient manuscript, a certain passage is found which is not met with in any other manuscripts of an anterior or a contemporary date, it is deduced from this collation that the passage is an interpolation by the writer of that particular manuscript, because if it were genuine and a part of the original writing it would have been found in all the older manuscripts, from one of which it must have been copied.

It is by this method of reasoning that the most eminent Biblical critics have arrived at the conclusion that the celebrated passage in the First Epistle General of St. John (v. 7) is an interpolation. Since it is not found in any of the earlier Greek manuscripts of the Epistle, it must, they argue, have been subsequently inserted, perhaps from a marginal commentary, either carelessly or designedly, by some later copyist whose error has been followed by all succeeding scribes. This is criticism from external evidence.

But there are other instances in which it is not possible to collate the book or manuscript which contains the suspected passage with others of an earlier date. Where there is but one copy extant there can, of course, be no comparison. In such cases it becomes necessary to determine whether the passage be genuine or spurious by what the critics call the method by internal evidence.

If the suspected passage is found to contain the expression of opinions which, we are led to believe from the known character of the author, he could not have uttered; or, if the statements which it sets forth are plainly in conflict with other statements made in the same work; or if it be found in a part of the work where it does not harmonize with the preceding and following portions of the context; or, in short, if the whole spirit and tenor of the other writings of the same author are in unmistaken opposition to the spirit and tenor of the passage under review; and, above all, if a reasonable motive can be suggested which may have given occasion to the interpolation, then the critic, guided by all or most of these reasons, will not hesitate to declare that the suspected passage is spurious; that it formed no part of the original book or manuscript, and that it is an interpolation made subsequent to the original composition. This is criticism from internal evidence.

It is by this method that the critics have been led to the conclusion that a certain passage in the Antiquities of Flavius Josephus, in which he eulogizes Jesus, was not written, and could not have been written, by the Jewish historian. Not only does its insertion very awkwardly interrupt the continuity of the narrative in which the author was engaged at the time, but the sentiments of the passage are wholly irreconcilable with the character of Josephus. As a Pharisee, at least professedly, he was influenced by all the prejudices of his sect and his nation against the new sect of Christians and its founder. Such a man never could have vouched, as the writer of this passage does, for the Messiahship, the miraculous powers, and the resurrection of Jesus.

Hence it is now believed by nearly all scholars that the passage was interpolated as a "pious fraud" by some early Christian who was anxious to enlist in favor of his religion the authority of one of the most eminent of its adversaries.

It is now my purpose to apply these principles to an investigation of the only passage in the "General Regulations" which furnishes any evidence of the existence of the Third degree at the time when they were compiled.

As the copy of the "General Regulations" contained in Anderson's Constitutions of 1723 is the first edition; as the original manuscript copy is lost; and as there were no previously printed copies, it is impossible, through comparison and collation, to prove from external evidence that the passage referring to the Third degree is spurious.

We must then have recourse to the second method of critical investigation, that is, by internal evidence.

And submitted to this test, the suspected passage fails, I think, to maintain a claim to genuineness.

Although the first edition of the Constitutions is now readily accessible in consequence of its numerous reprints, still, for the sake of convenience to the reader, in the discussion I shall copy the whole of the paragraph in which the suspected passage is contained, marking that passage by italics.

The passage will be found in the first paragraph of Article XIII. of the "General Regulations," and is in these words:

"At the said Quarterly Communications, all Matters that concern the Fraternity in general, or particular Lodges or single Brothers, are quietly, sedately, and maturely to be discours'd of and transacted: *Apprentices must be admitted Masters and FellowCraft only here unless by a Dispensatson.* Here also all Differences that can not be made up and accommodated privately, nor by a particular Lodge, are to be seriously considered and decided; And if any Brother thinks himself aggrieved by the decision of this Board, he may appeal to the annual Grand Lodge next coming, and leave his Appeal in Writing, with the Grand Master or his Deputy, or the Grand Wardens."

Anyone not prepossessed with the theory of the antiquity of the Third degree who will look at this paragraph will, I think, be struck with the suspicious incongruity of the clause in italics in relation to the parts that precede and follow it. I will endeavor to demonstrate this point as follows:

The 13th Article of the "General Regulations" is divided into eight paragraphs. Each of these paragraphs is wholly independent and homogeneous in respect to its subject-matter. Each is devoted to the consideration of one subject only, to the exclusion of all others.

Thus the first paragraph relates to matters that concern lodges and private brethren, such as differences that can not be settled otherwise than by the Grand Lodge. The second paragraph relates to the returns of lodges and the mode and manner of making them. The third relates to the charity fund and the most effectual method of collecting and disposing of money for that purpose. The fourth to the appointment of a Treasurer and a Secretary for the Grand Lodge, and to their duties. The fifth to the appointment of a clerk for each of those officers. The sixth to the mode of inspecting their books and accounts. The seventh to the appointment of a Tiler to look after the door of the Grand Lodge. And the eighth provides for the making of a new regulation for the government of these officers whenever it may be deemed expedient.

Thus it will be seen, from this synopsis, that each of these paragraphs embraces but one subject. Whatever is begun to be treated at the opening of a paragraph is continued without interruption and without the admission of any other matter to its close.

This methodical arrangement has, in fact, been preserved throughout the whole of the thirty-nine "Regulations." No Regulation will be found which embodies the consideration of two different and irrelevant subjects.

So uniformly is this rule observed that it may properly be called a peculiar characteristic of the style of the writer, and a deviation from it becomes, according to the axioms of criticism, at once suspicious.

Now this deviation occurs only in the first paragraph of the 13th Article, the one which has been printed above.

That paragraph, as originally written, related to the disputes and difference which might arise between particular lodges and between single brethren, and prescribed the mode in which they should be settled when they could not "be made up and accommodated privately." Leaving out the lines which I have printed in italics, we will find that the paragraph is divided into three clauses, each separated from the other by a colon.

The first clause directs that all matters that concern the Fraternity in general, particular lodges or single brethren, "are quietly, sedately, and maturely to be discoursed of and transacted" in the Grand Lodge. It is to questions that might arise between lodges and brethren - questions which in modern phraseology are called grievances - that the clause evidently refers. And in the Grand Lodge only are such questions to be discussed, because it is only there that they can be definitely settled.

The second clause continues the same subject, and extends it to those differences of brethren which can not be accommodated privately by the lodges of which they are members.

And the third clause provides that if the decision made by the Grand Lodge at its Quarterly Communication is not satisfactory to the parties interested, it may be carried up, by appeal, to the Grand Lodge in its Annual Communication.

Now, it is evident that this whole paragraph is intended to explain the duties of the Quarterly Communication as a Board of Inquiry in respect to matters in dispute between lodges and between the Craft, and the paragraph itself calls the decision of the Grand Lodge on these occasions the "Decision of this Board."

Viewed in this way, this first paragraph of the 13th Article is entirely congruous in all its parts, refers to but one subject, and is a perfect specimen of the style adopted by the compiler and pursued by him in all the other portions of the "Regulations" without a single exception - a style plain, simple, and methodical, yet as marked and isolated from other styles as is the Doric roughness of Carlyle or the diffusiveness of De Quincey from the manner of composition of other authors in a more elevated class of literature.

But if we insert the passage printed in italics between the first and second clauses, we will at once see the incongruity which is introduced by the interpolation.

Placed as it is between the first and second clauses, it breaks the continuity of the subject. A regulation which refers to the differences and disputes among the Craft, and the mode of settling them, is disjointed and interrupted by another one relating to an entirely different subject - namely, the initiation of Master Masons and Fellow-Crafts.

What has the subject of initiation to do with that of fraternal or lodge disputes? Why should a regulation relating to degrees be mixed up with another of a totally distinct and different character?

Judging, as we are not only authorized but compelled, as critical observers, to do, from the style of the compiler of the "Regulations" and the uniform custom pursued by him, we feel certain that if this passage formed a genuine part of the "Regulations," he would have placed it in an independent paragraph. That this has not been done affords a strong presumption that the passage is an interpolation, and that it formed no part of the "Regulations" when compiled about the year 1720, most probably by Grand Master Payne, at the same time that he compiled the "Charges" printed in the same volume.

Still more suspicious is the fact that except in this passage there is not in the "General Regulations" the slightest allusion to Master Masons or to the Master's degree. As has already been shown, the whole spirit and tenor of the "Regulations" is to the effect that the highest grade in Freemasonry at that time, and the one from which all officers were to be selected, was that of Fellow-Craft. It is impossible to believe that if, at the time of the preparation of the "Regulations" and their approval by the Grand Lodge, the degree of Master Mason was in existence, it would have been passed over in such complete silence, and all important matters referred to a subordinate degree.

Hence I again deduce the conclusion that at the time of the compiling of these "Regulations" and their approval by the Grand Lodge, the Third degree was not in existence as a part of Speculative Masonry.

And then I assume as a logical deduction from these premises that the clause in the first paragraph of the 13th General Regulation is an interpolation inserted in those "Regulations" between the time of their being approved and the time of their final passage through the press.

It is barely possible that the suspected clause may have been inserted in the copy presented to the Grand Lodge on March 25, 1722, for examination and approval, and have escaped the attention of the reviewers from the fact that it was obscurely placed in the center of a paragraph relating to an entirely different subject. Or the Committee may have concurred with Desaguliers and Anderson in the policy of anticipating the control of the degree when it should be presented to the Craft, by an ante factum regulation.

Be that as it may, the passage formed neither then nor at any time thereafter a genuine part of the "General Regulations," although from its appearance in the printed copies it was as a mere matter of course accepted as a part of the law. It was, however, soon afterward repealed and a regulation was adopted on November 22, 1725, which remitted to the Master and Wardens, with a competent number of the lodge, the power of making Masters and Fellows at discretion.

The questions next arise, by whom, at what time, and for what purpose was this interpolation inserted?

By whom ? I answer, by Anderson at the instigation of Desaguliers, under whose direction and with whose assistance the former had compiled the first edition of the Book of Constitutions.[132]

At what time ? This question is more difficult to answer than the preceding one. At the communication of the Grand Lodge, September 29, 1721, Anderson was ordered to prepare the Book of Constitutions. On December 27, 1721, the manuscript was presented to the Grand Lodge and referred to a committee. On March 25, 1722, the Committee reported and the work was ordered to be printed. On January 17, 1723, Anderson produced the new Book of Constitutions, which was again approved, "with the addition of the Ancient manner of constituting a lodge."

Now, between September, 1721, when the book was ordered to be prepared, and March, 1722, when the work was approved and ordered to be printed, the passage could not have existed as a regulation, because, in the first place, it was directly antagonistic to the body of the work, in which there is no mention of the Third degree;[133] but, on the contrary, it is distinctly stated that the FellowCrafts were in possession of all the secrets, and they alone could understand them.[134] And, secondly, any such regulation would come in direct conflict with the "Manner of Constituting a Lodge" approved at the same time, and which, completely ignoring the Master's degree, directed the Master and Wardens to be selected from among the Fellow-Crafts of the lodge. The Master's degree could not have been known at that time as a part of the system of Freemasonry, and no regulation in reference to it was therefore necessary.

---

[132] This edition is dedicated to the Duke of Montague, not by Anderson, but by Desaguliers, with an air of patronage to the author, as if it were a work accomplished by his direction.

[133] In describing the Temple of Solomon, Anderson, it is true, enumerates among the workmen " 3,600 Princes or Master Masons, to conduct the work according to Solomon's directions." (Page 10.) But it is very clear that these were simply "Masters of the Work" - the "Magistri Operis" of the old Operative Freemasons - skilled Craftsmen appointed to superintend the bands or lodges of workmen engaged in the construction of the building.

[134] In a note on a page of the "Book of Constitutions," Anderson says: "No man can indeed understand it (Masonry) without the key of a Fellow- Craft." Certainly, he at that time knew nothing of a higher degree. This passage was probably written in 1721, when he was directed by the Grand Lodge to compile a "Book of Constitutions." Much of the proposed work was then in manuscript.

Anderson has by implication admitted the soundness of this reasoning, because when he published the second edition of the Constitution in 1738, the Third degree being then a recognized part of the system, he changed the words "Fellow Crafts" whereever they occurred in the "Charges," as indicating the highest degree in the "Regulations," and in the "Manner of Constituting a Lodge," to the words "Master Mason."

I think, therefore, that the suspected clause was inserted in the 13th Regulation at the beginning of the year 1723, just before the work was issued from the press. There was neither time nor opportunity to make any other changes in the book and its appendices, and therefore this clause stands in reference to all the other parts of the Constitutions, Regulations, etc., in all the incongruity which I have endeavored to demonstrate.

For what purpose? The reply to this question will involve the determination of the time at which the Third degree was introduced into the ritual of Freemasonry. The theory which I present on this subject is as follows:

If the suspected clause which has been under consideration be admitted to be no genuine part of the Book of Constitutions, then it must follow that there is not the slightest evidence of the existence of the Third degree in the Ritual of Speculative Masonry up to the year 1723.

It is now very generally admitted that the arrangement of Freemasonry into the present system of three degrees was the work of Dr. Desaguliers, assisted by Anderson, Payne, and perhaps some other collaborators. The perfecting of this system was of very slow growth. At first there was but the one degree, which had been derived from the Operative Masons of preceding centuries. This was the degree practiced in 1717, when the so- called "Revival" took place. It was no doubt improved by Desaguliers, who was Grand Master in 1719, and who probably about that time began his ritualistic experiments. The fact that Payne, in 1718, "desired any brethren to bring to the Grand Lodge any old writings and records concerning Masons and Masonry in order to shew the usages of antient times,"[135] exhibits a disposition and preparation for improvement.

The First and Second degrees had been modeled out of the one primitive degree about the year 1719. The "Charges" compiled in 1720 by Grand Master Payne recognize the Fellow-Craft as the leading degree and the one from which the officers of lodges and of the Grand Lodge

---

[135] "Book of Constitutions," 2d edition, 1738.

were to be selected. The same recognition is found in the "General Regulations," and in the Constitutions which were printed in 1723.

Up to this time we find no notice of the Third degree. The "particular lodges " conferred only the First degree. Admission or initiation into the Second degree was done in the Grand Lodge. This was perhaps owing to the fact that Desaguliers and the inventors of the new degree were unwilling to place it out of their immediate control, lest improper persons might be admitted or the ceremonies be imperfectly performed.

In 1722 I imagine that Desaguliers and his collaborators had directed their attention to a further and more complete organization.

The Operative Masons had always had three different ranks or classes of workmen, but not degrees in the modern Masonic sense of that word. These were the Masters, who undertook the work and superintended it; the Fellow-Crafts or Journeymen, who did the manual labor; and the Apprentices, who were engaged in acquiring a knowledge of their handicraft.

After the "Revival," in 1717 (I use the term under protest), Desaguliers had divided the one degree which had been common to the three classes into two, making the degrees of Entered Apprentice and Fellow-Craft. It is not to be supposed that this was a mere division of the esoteric instruction into two parts. All is here, of course, mere guesswork. The rituals were oral, and there is no memorial of them left except what we can learn from The Grand Mystery and the Sloane MS. 3329. But we may believe that taking the primitive degree of the Operatives as a foundation, there was built upon it an enlarged superstructure of ceremonies and lectures. The catechism of the degree was probably changed and improved, and the "Mason Word," as the Operatives had called it, with the secrets connected with it, was transferred to the Second degrees to be afterward again transferred to the Third degree.

After this, Desaguliers continued to exercise his inventive genius, and consummated the series of degrees by adding one to be appropriated to the highest class, or that of the Masters. But not having thoroughly perfected the ritual of the degree until after the time of publication of the Book of Constitutions, it was not probably disseminated among the Craft until the year 1723.

The Second degree, as we have seen, had been invented in the year 1719. Its ritual had been completed, but the Masters of the lodges had not yet become so well acquainted with its forms and ceremonies as to be capable of managing an initiation.

The lodges, therefore, between 1719 and 1723, did not confer the Second degree. They were not restricted from so doing by any regulation, for there were no regulations on the subject enacted until the approval of the Book of Constitutions by the Grand Lodge in January, 1723. Besides, if there had been any law restricting the conferring of the Second degree lo the Grand Lodge, Desaguliers would not have violated the law, which was of his own making, by conferring it in 1721 in a lodge in Edinburgh.

The fact undoubtedly is, that the lodges did not confer the Second degree in consequence of a usage derived from necessity. Dr. Desaguliers and his collaborators were the only persons in possession of the ritual, and therefore qualified to confer the degree, which they always did in the Grand Lodge, for two reasons: first, for their own convenience, and secondly, because they feared that if the ceremony of initiation was intrusted to the officers of the lodges who were inexperienced and unskillful, it might be mutilated or unsatisfactorily performed.

In the meantime Desaguliers had extended his labors as a ritualmaker, and had invented a supplementary or Third degree. But as is said of a cardinal whose appointment the Pope has made but has not yet announced to the college of Cardinals, the degree was still in petto. The knowledge of it was confined to Dr. Desaguliers and a few of his friends.

It is absolutely impossible that the degree could have been known generally to the members of the Grand Lodge. For with the knowledge that the establishment of such a degree was even in contemplation, they would not have approved a series of regulations which recognized throughout the Second or Fellow-Craft as the highest degree in Speculative Freemasonry, and the one from which Grand Masters were in future to be selected.

But a code of laws was about to be established for the government of the Craft - a code expressly appropriated to the new system of Speculative Freemasonry, which by this time had completely dissevered itself from the Operative institution.

This code was to be published for the information of the Fraternity, so that every Freemason might know what was to be henceforth his duties and his rights. Law was now to become paramount to usage, and if there were no positive regulation which restricted the conferring of the Second degree to the Grand Lodge, it would, if permanently adopted as a part of the new system, fall into the hands of the Masters of the particular lodges.

This was an evil which, for the reason already assigned, was, if possible, to be avoided. It would also apply to the Third degree, which, though not yet in practical existence, was, soon after the adoption of the "General Regulations," to be presented to the Grand Lodge and put in working order.

Therefore, anticipating the dissemination of the Third degree, and being desirous to restrict it as well as the Second, by a positive law, to the Grand Lodge, he, with Anderson, interpolated, at the last moment, into the 13th of the "General Regulations" the words, "Apprentices must be admitted Masters and Fellow-Craft only here, unless by dispensation."

This is a serious charge to make against any writer of good reputation, and it would be an act of great temerity to do so, unless there were ample proof to sustain it. But I think the arguments I have advanced, though only based on legitimate inferences and the internal evidence afforded by the document itself, have shown that this passage could never have formed a part of the "Regulations" as originally compiled by Payne and afterward approved and adopted by the Grand Lodge.

But while we pay all due respect to the memory of Dr. Anderson, and hold in grateful remembrance his zeal and devotion in the foundation and advancement of Speculative Freemasonry, it is impossible to concede to him the possession of those virtues of accuracy and truthfulness which are essential to the character of an historian.

The motive of Desaguliers and Anderson for inserting the interpolated clause into the "General Regulations" was to prevent the two new degrees from falling into the hands of unskilled Masters of lodges, until by future experience they should become qualified to confer them.

THE
CONSTITUTIONS
OF THE FREE-MASONS.
CONTAINING THE
History, Charges, Regulations, &c. of that most Ancient and Right
Worshipful FRATERNITY
For the Use of the LODGES.
LONDON: Printed by WILLIAM HUNTER, for JOHN SENEX at the
Globe, and JOHN
HOOKE at the Flower-de-luce over-against St. Dunstan's Church, in
Fleet-Street.
In the Year of Masonry 5723 Anno Domini
1723
THE
CONSTITUTION.
History, Laws, Charges, Orders, Regulations, and Usages,
OF THE Right Worshipful FRATERNITY of
Accepted Free MASONS;
COLLECTED From their general RECORDS, and their faithful
TRADITIONS of many Ages.
TO BE READ
At the Admission of a NEW BROTHER, when the Master or Warden shall begin, or order some other Brother to read as follows:

ADAM, our first Parent, created after the Image of God, the great Architect of the Universe, must have had the Liberal Sciences, particularly Geometry, written on his Heart; for even since the Fall, we find the Principles of it in the Hearts of his Offspring, and which, in process of time, have been drawn forth into con

THE CHARGES OF A
FREE-MASON,
EXTRACTED FROM The ancient RECORDS of LODGES beyond Sea, and of those in England, Scotland, and Ireland, for the use of the Lodges in LONDON:
TO BE READ
At the making of NEW BRETHREN, or when the MASTER shall order it.

The General Reads, viz.
I. Of GOD and RELIGION
II. Of the CIVIL MAGISTRATE Supreme and Subordinate.
III. Of LODGES.
IV. Of MASTERS, Wardens, Fellows, and Apprentices.

V. Of the Management of the Craft in working
VI. Of BEHAVIOUR, viz.
1. In the Lodge while constituted.
2. After the Lodge is over and the Brethren not gone.
3. When Brethren meet without Strangers, but not in a Lodge
4. In Presence of Strangers not Masons.
5. At Home, and in the Neighbourhood
6. Towards a strange Brother,

I Concerning GOD and RELIGION.

A Mason is oblig'd, by his Tenure, to obey the moral Law; and if he rightly understands the Art, he will never be a stupid Atheist nor an irreligious Libertine. But though in ancient Times Masons were charg'd in every Country to be of the Religion of that Country or Nation, whatever it was, yet 'tis now thought more expedient only to oblige them to that Religion in which all Men agree, leaving their particular Opinions to themselves; that is, to be good Men and true, or Men of Honour and Honesty, by whatever Denominations or Persuasions they may be-distinguish'd; whereby Masonry becomes the Center of Union, and the Means of conciliating true Friendship among Persons that must have remain'd at a perpetual Distance.

II. Of the CIVIL MAGISTRATE Supreme and Subordinate.

A Mason is a peaceable Subject to the Civil Powers, wherever he resides or works, and is never to be concern'd in Plots and Conspiracies against the Peace and Welfare of the Nation, nor to behave himself undutifully to inferior Magistrates; for as Masonry hath been always injured by War, Bloodshed, and Confusion, so ancient Kings and Princes have been much dispos'd to encourage the Craftsmen, because of their Peaceableness and Loyalty, whereby they practically answer'd the Cavils of their Adversaries, and promoted the Honour of the Fraternity, who ever flourish'd in Times of Peace. So that if a Brother should be a Rebel against the State, he is not to be countenanc'd in his Rebellion, however he may be pitied as an unhappy Man; and, if convicted of no other Crime, though the loyal Brotherhood must and ought to disown his Rebellion, and give no Umbrage or Ground of political Jealousy to the Government for the time being; they cannot expel him from the Lodge, and his Relation to it remains indefeasible.

III. Of LODGES.

A LODGE is Place where Masons assemble and work: Hence that Assembly, or duly organizd Society of Masons, is call'd a Lodge, and every Brother ought to belong to one, and to be subject to its By-Laws and the GENERAL REGULATIONS. It is either particular or general, and will be left understood by attending it, and by the Regulations of the General or Grand Lodge hereunto annex'd. In ancient Times, no Master or Fellow could be absent from it, especially when warn'd to appear at it, without incurring a severe Censure, until it appear'd to the Master and Wardens, that pure Necessity hinder'd him.

The Persons admitted Members of a Lodge must be good and free Men, free-born, and of mature and discreet Age, no Bondmen, no Women, no immoral or scandalous Men, but of good Report.

IV Of MASTERS, WARDENS, FELLOWS, and Apprentices.

All Preferment among Masons is grounded upon real Worth and personal Merit only; that so the Lords may be well served, the Brethren not put to Shame, nor the Royal Craft despis'd: Therefore no Master or Warden is chosen by Seniority, but for his Merit. It is impossible to describe these things in writing, and every Brother must attend in his Place, and learn them in a way peculiar to this Fraternity: Only Candidates may know, that no Master should take an Apprentice, unless he has sufficient Employment for him, and unless he be a perfect Youth, having no Maim or Defect in his Body, that may render him uncapable of learning the Art, of Serving his Master's LORD, and of being made a Brother, and then a Fellow-Craft in due time, even after he has served such a Term of Years as the Custom of the Country directs; and that be should be descended of honest Parents; that so, when otherwise qualify'd he may arrive to the Honour of being the WARDEN, and then the Master of the Lodge, the Grand Warden, and at length GRAND MASTER of all the Lodges according to his Merit.

No Brother can be a WARDEN until he has passd the part of a Fellow- Craft; nor a MASTER until he has acted as a Warden, nor a GRAND-WARDEN until he has been Master of a Lodge, nor Grand Master unless he has been a Fellow-Craft before his Election, who is also to be nobly born, or a Gentleman of the best Fashion, or some eminent Scholar, or some curious Architect, or other Artist, descended of honest Parents, and who is of singular great Merit in the Opinion of the Lodges. And for the better, and easier, and more by honourable Discharge of his

Office, the Grand-Master has a Power to chuse his own DEPUTY GRAND-MASTER, who must be then, or must have been formerly, the Master of a particular Lodge, and has the Privilege of acting whatever the GRAND-MASTER, his Principal, should act, unless the said Principal be Present, or interpose his Authority by a Letter.

These Rulers and Governors, Supreme and Subordinate, of the ancient Lodge, are to be obey'd in their respective Stations by all the Brethren, according to the old Charges and Regulations, with all Humility, Reverance, Love, and Alacrity.

V. Of the Management of the CRAFT in working

All Masons shall work honestly on working Days, that they may live creditably on holy Day; and the time appointed by the Law of the Land, or confirm'd by Custom, shall be observ'd;

The most expert of the Fellow-Craftsmen shall be chosen or appointed the Master, or Overseer of the Lord's Work; who is to be call'd MASTER by those that work under him. The Craftsman are to avoid all ill Language, and to call each other by no disobliging Name, but Brother or Fellow; and to behave themselves courteously within and without the Lodge.

The Master, knowing himself to be able of Cunning, shall undertake the Lord's Work as reasonably as possible, and truly dispend his Goods as if they were his.own; nor to give more Wages to any Brother or Apprentice than he really may deserve.

Both the Master and the Masons receiving their Wages justly, shall be faithful to the Lord, and honesty finish their Work, whether Task or Journey, nor put the Work to Task that hath been acoustom'd to Journey.

None shall discover Envy at the Prosperity of a Brother, nor supplant him, or put him out of his Work, if he be capable to finish the fame; for no Man can finish another's Work so much to the Lord's Profit, unless he be thoroughly acquainted with the Designs and Draughts of him that began it.

When a Fellow-Craftsman is chosen Warden of the Work under the Master, he shall be true both to Master and Fellows, shall carefully oversee the Work in the Masters Absence to the Lord's Profit; and his Brethren shall obey him.

All Masons employ'd, shall meekly receive their Wages without Murmuring or Mutiny, and not desert the Master till the Work is finish'd.

A younger Brother shall be instructed in working, to prevent spoiling the Materials for want of Judgment, and for encreasing and continuing of Brotherly Love.

All the Tools used in working shall be approved by the Grand Lodge.

No Labourer shall be employ'd in the proper Work of Masonry; nor shall Free Masons work with those that are not free, without an urgent Necessity; nor shall they teach Labourers and unaccepted Masons, as they should teach a Brother or Fellow.

VI. Of BEHAVIOUR, VIZ.

1. In the Lodge while constituted.

You are not to hold private Committees, or Separate Conversation, without Leave from the Master, nor to talk of anything impertinent or unseemly, nor interrupt the Master or Wardens, or any Brother speaking to the Master: Nor behave yourself ludicrously or priestingly while the Lodge is engaged in what is serious and solemn; nor use any unbecoming Language upon any Pretence whatsoever; but to pay due Reverence to your Master, Wardens and Fellows, and put them to worship

If any Complaint be brought, the Brother find guilty shall stand to the Award and Determination of the Lodge, who are the proper and competent Judges of all such Controversies, (unless you carry it by Appeal to the GRAND LODGE) and to whom they ought to be referr'd, unless a Lord's Work be hinder'd the mean while, in which Cafe a particular Reference may be made; but you must never go to Law about what concerneth Masonry, without an absolute Necessity apparent to the Lodge.

2. Behaviour after the LODGE is over and the Brethren not gone.

You may enjoy yourselves with innocent Mirth, treating one another according to Ability, but avoiding all Excess, or forcing any brother to eat or drink beyond his Inclinations or hindering him from going when his Occasions call him, or doing or saying anything offensive, or that may forbid an easy and free Conversation; for that would blast our Harmony, and defeat our laudable purposes. Therefore no Private Piques or Quarrels must be brought within the Door of the Lodge, far less any Quarrels about Religion, or Nations, or State Policy, we being only, as Masons, of the Catholick Religion above-mention'd; we are also of all Nations, Tongues, Kindreds, and Languages, and are resolv'd against all politicks, as what never yet conduc'd to the Welfare of the Lodge, nor ever will. This Charge has been always strictly enjoin'd and observ'd; but especially ever since the Reformation in BRITAIN, or the Different and Secession of these Nations from the Communion of ROME.

3. Behaviour when Brethren meet without Strangers, but not in a Lodge form'd

You are to salute one another in a courteous manner, as you will be instructed, calling each other Brother, freely giving mutual Instruction as shall be thought expedient, without being overseen or over heard, and without encroaching upon each other, or derogating from that respect which is due to any brother, were he not a Mason: For though all Masons are as Brethren upon the same Level, yet Masonry takes no Honour from a Man that he had before; nay rather it adds to his Honour, especially if he has deferv'd well of the Brotherhood, who must give Honour to whom it is due, and avoid ill Manners.

4. Behaviour in Presence of STRANGERS not Masons.

You shall be cautious in your Words and Carriage, that the most penetrating stranger shall not be able to discover or find out what is not proper to be intimated; and sometimes you shall divert a Discourse, and manage it prudently for the Honour of the worshipful Fraternity.

5. Behaviour at HOME, and in your Neighbourhood.

You are to act as becomes a moral and wise Man; particularly, not to let your Family, Friends and Neighbours know the Concerns of the Lodge, &c. but wisely to consult your own Honour, and that of the ancient Brotherbood, for Reasons not to be mention'd here. You must also consult your Health, by not continuing together too late, or too long from home, after Lodge Hours are past; and by avoiding of Gluttony or Drunkenness, that your Families be not neglected or injured, nor you disabled from working.

6. Behaviour towards a strange Brother

You are cautiously to examine him, in such a Method as Prudence shall direct you, that you may not be impos'd upon by an ignorant false Pretender, whom you are to reject with Contempt and Derision, and beware of giving him any Hints of Knowledge.

But if you discover him to be a true and genuine Brother, you are to respect him accordingly; and if he is in want, you must relieve him if you can, or else direct him how he may be reliev'd: You must employ him some Days, or else recommend him to be employ'd. But you are not charged to do beyond your Ability, only to prefer a poor Brother, that is a good Man and true, before any other poor People in the same Circumstances.

FINALLLY, All these Charges you are to observe, and also those that shall be communicated to you in another way; cultivating BROTHERLY LOVE, the Foundation and Cape-stone, the Cement and Glory of this ancient Fraternity, avoiding all wrangling and Quarrelling, all Slander and Backbiting, nor permitting others to slander any honest Brother, but defending his Character, and doing him all good Offices, as far as is confident with your Honour and Safety, and no farther. And if any of them do you Injury, you must apply to your own or his lodge; and from thence you may appeal to the GRAND LODGE at the Quarterly Communications and from thence to the annual GRAND LODGE, as has been the ancient laudable Conduct of our forefathers in every Nation; never taking a legal Course but when the Case cannot be otherwise decided, and patiently listening to the honest and friendly Advice of Master and Fellows, when they would prevent your going to Law with Strangers, or would excite you to put a speedy Period to all Law-Suits, that so you may mind the Affair of MASONRY with the more Alacrity and Success; but with respect to Brother or Fellows at Law, the Master and Brethren should kindly offer their Mediation, which ought to be thankfully submitted to by the contending Brethren; and if that Submission is impracticable, they must however carry on their Process, or Law-Suit, without Wrath and Rancor (not in the common way) saying or doing nothing which may hinder Brotherly Love, and good Offices to be renew'd and continu'd; that all may see the benign Influence of MASONRY, as all true Masons have done from the Beginning of the World, and will do to the End of Time.

Amen so mote it be.

They were not long, it appears, in becoming qualified, or at least the doubts of their qualification were soon dispelled, for we find that on the 22d of November, 1725, less than three years after its appearance in the Book of Constitutions, the Regulation was rescinded, and it was ordered by the Grand Lodge that "the Master of a lodge, with his Wardens and a competent number of the lodge assembled in due form, can make Masters and Fellows at discretion."[136]

It might be argued that although the words "Master Mason" may be an interpolation, the rule regulating the conferring of the Second degree might well have formed a part of the original "Regulations," seeing that they were not compiled until after the invention of the Second degree.

But the argument founded on the incongruity of subjects and the awkward interruption of their continuity in the paragraph occasioned by the insertion of the suspected words, is applicable to the whole passage. If the internal evidence advanced is effective against a single word of the passage on these grounds, it is effective against all.

But Bro. Lyon, in his History of the Lodge of Edinburgh,[137] has supplied us with an authentic document, which presents the strongest presumptive evidence of three facts. 1. That the Second degree had been invented before the year 1721, and at that time constituted a part of the

---

[136] Anderson's "Constitutions," 2d edition, p. 161.
[137] "History of the Lodge of Edinburgh," p. 151.

new Speculative system. 2. That in the English lodges there was no positive law forbidding the conferring of it by them, but only a recognized usage. 3. That in the year 1721 the Third degree had not been invented.

In the year 1721 Dr. Desaguliers paid a visit to Edinburgh and placed himself in communication with the Freemasons of that city.

A record of the most important Masonic event that occurred during that visit is preserved in the minutes of the Lodge of Edinburgh for the 24th and 25th of August, 1721. This record has been published by Bro. Lyon in his history of that lodge. It is in the following words:

"Att Maries chapped the 24 of August, 1721 years, James Wattson, present deacon of the Masons of Edinbr., Preses. The which day Doctor John Theophilus Desaguliers, fellow of the Royall Societie, and chaplain in Ordinary to his Grace, James, Duke of Chandois. late Generall Master of the Mason Lodges in England, being in town and desirous to have a conference with the Deacon, Warden, and Master Masons of Edinbr., which was accordingly granted, and finding him duly qualified in all points of Masonry, they received him as a Brother into their Societie."

"Likeas, upon the 25th day of the sd. moneth the Deacon, Wardens, Masters, and several other members of the Societie, together with the sd. Doctor Desaguliers, haveing mett att Maries Chapell, there was a supplication presented to them by John Campbell, Esqr., Lord Provost of Edinbr., George Preston and Hugh Hathorn, Baillies; James Nimo, the asurer; William Livingston, Deacon-convener of the Trades thereof, and George Irving, Clerk to the Dean of Guild Court, and humbly craving to be admitted members of the sd. Societie; which being considered by them, they granted the desire thereof, and the saids honourable persons were admitted and receaved Entered Apprentices and Fellow-Crafts accordingly."

"And sicklike upon the 28th day of the said moneth there was another petition given in by Sr. Duncan Campbell of Lochnell, Barronet; Robert Wightman, Esqr., present Dean of Gild of Edr.; George Drummond, Esq., late Theasurer thereof; Archibald M'Aulay, late Bailly there; and Patrick Lindsay, merchant there, craving the like benefit, which was also granted, and they were receaved as members of the societie as the other persons above mentioned. The same day James Key and Thomas Aikman, servants to James Wattson, deacon of the masons, were admitted and receaved entered apprentices, and payed to James Mack, Warden, the ordinary dues as such. Ro. Alison, Clerk."

I agree with Bro. Lyon that "there can be but one opinion as to the nature and object of Dr. Desaguliers's visit to the Lodge of Edinburgh." And that was the introduction into Scotland of the new system of Masonry recently fabricated by himself for the lodges of London. That he conferred only the First and Second degrees is to me satisfactory proof that the Third had not been arranged.

Lyon says "it is more than probable that on both occasions (the two meetings of the Lodge recorded above) the ceremony of entering and passing would, as far as the circumstances of the lodges would permit, be conducted by Desaguliers himself in accordance with the ritual he xvas anxious to introduce." [138]This is undoubtedly true; but why did he not complete the instruction by conferring the Third degree ? Bro. Lyon's explanation here is wholly untenable:

"It was not," he says, "till 1722-23 that the English regulation restricting the conferring of the Third Degree to Grand Lodge was repealed. This may account for the Doctor confining himself to the two lesser degrees."

Bro. Lyon, usually so accurate, has here unaccountably fallen into two important errors.

First, the regulation alluded to was not repealed in 1723 but was only promulgated in that year. The repeal took place in 1725.

His next error is that the restriction was confined to the Third degree, while in fact, if we accept the passage in the "General Regulations" as genuine, it restricted, as we have seen, the conferring of both the Second and Third degrees to the Grand Lodge.

Therefore, if Desaguliers had considered himself as governed by this regulation (which, however, was impossible, seeing that it had not been enacted until after his visit to Edinburgh), he would have been restrained from conferring the Second as well as the Third degree.

That he conferred the Second degree in a lodge of Edinburgh, notwithstanding the usage in London of conferring it only in the Grand Lodge, may be accounted for on the very reasonable supposition that he did not consider that the English usage was binding on Scottish Masons.

Besides, there was, at that time, no Grand Lodge in Scotland, and if he had not conferred the degree in a lodge, the object of his visit would have been frustrated, and that was to introduce into the sister kingdom the new system of Speculative Freemasonry which he had invented and which had been just adopted in England or rather in London.

---

[138] "History of the Lodge of Edinburgh," p. 153.

But that he should have taken a long and arduous journey to Edinburgh (a journey far more arduous than it is in the present day of railroads) for the purpose of introducing into the Scotch lodges the ritual invented by him for English Freemasonry, and yet have left the task uncompleted by omitting to communicate the most important part of the degree which was at the summit, is incomprehensible, unless we suppose that the Third degree had not, at that time, been invented.

For if the language of the "General Regulations" receives the only interpretation of which they are capable, it is evident that in the beginning of the year 1723, when they were published in the Book of Constitutions, the degree of Fellow-Craft was the highest degree known to the Freemasons of London.

It is the belief of all Masonic scholars, except a few who still cling with more or less tenacity to the old legends and traditions, that the Third degree can not be historically traced to a period earlier than the second decade of the 18th century. It has not, however, been hitherto attempted by anyone, so far as I am aware, to indicate the precise time of its invention.

The general opinion seems to have been that it was first introduced into the ritual of Speculative Freemasonry a very short time after the organization of the Grand Lodge in London, in the year 1717. But I think that I have conclusively and satisfactorily proved that the actual period of its introduction as a working degree was not until six years afterward, namely, in the year 1723, and after the publication of the first edition of the Book of Constitutions, and that the only passage referring to it in that work or in the "General Regulations" appended to it, was surreptitiously inserted in anticipation of its intended introduction.

The first writer who questioned the antiquity of the Third degree as conferred under the Grand Lodge was Laurence Dermott, the Grand Secretary, and afterward the Deputy Grand Master of that body of Freemasons which, in the year 1753, seceded from the legal Grand Lodge of England and constituted what is known in Masonic history as the "Grand Lodge of Ancients," the members thus distinguishing themselves from the constitutional Grand Lodge, which they stigmatized as "Moderns." In the second edition of the Ahiman Rezon, published in 1764, he has, in the part called "A Philacteria," the following statement in reference to the Third degree:[139]

---

[139] This statement is not contained in the 1st edition, published in 1756.

"About the year 1717 some joyous companions who had passed the degree of a craft (though very rusty) resolved to form a lodge for themselves, in order (by conversation) to recollect what had been formerly dictated to them, or, if that should be found impracticable, to substitute something new, which might for the future pass for Masonry amongst themselves. At this meeting the question was asked, whether any person in the assembly knew the Master's part, and being answered in the negative, it was resolved that the deficiency should be made up with a new composition, and what fragments of the old order found amongst them, should be immediately reformed and made more pliable to the humours of the people."

I should be unwilling to cite the unsupported testimony of Dermott for anything in reference to the "Modern" because of his excessive partisan spirit. But the extract just given may be considered simply as confirming all the evidence heretofore produced, that after the year 1717 a "Master's part" or Third degree had been fabricated. Dermott's details, which were intended as a sneer upon the Constitution Grand Lodge, should pass for nothing.

As for Dermott's assertion that the true Master's degree, as it existed before the Revival, was in the possession of the Grand Lodge of the Ancients, as it was called, it is not only false, but absolutely absurd, for if the Ancients were in possession of a Third degree which had been in existence before the year 1717, and the Moderns were not, where did the former get it, since they sprang out of the latter and carried with them only the knowledge which they possessed as a part of that Grand Lodge?

Dr. Oliver, notwithstanding his excessive credulity in respect to the myths and legends of Freemasonry, has from time to time in his various writings expressed his doubts as to "the extreme antiquity of the present arrangement of the three degrees."[140] In one of his latest works[141] he admits that Desaguliers and Anderson were accused of the fabrication of the Hiramic legend and of the manufacture of the degree by their seceding contemporaries, which accusation, he says, they did not deny.[142]

---

[140] State of Freemasonry in the 18th Century. Introduction to his edition of Hutchinson.
[141] "The Freemason's Treasury," Spencer, 1863.
[142] This is an example of the carelessness with which Masonic writers were accustomed to make their statements. The "seceding contemporaries" of Oliver consisted simply of Laurence Dermott, who first made the accusation, and when he made it, both Desaguliers and Anderson were dead.

Findel says: "Originally, it seems, there was but one degree ot initiation in the year 1717. . . . The introduction of the degrees of Fellow-Craft and Master Mason took place in so imperceptible a manner, that we do not know the accurate date. No mention is made of them before 1720, even not yet in the Book of Constitutions of 1722.[143]

I do not, however, concur with this learned German writer in his hypothesis that the Third degree originated as a reward for Masonic merits, especially to be conferred on all the brethren who had passed the chair from 1717 to 1720. Doubtless, as soon as it was invented it was conferred on all who were or had been Masters of lodges, but Findel places too low an estimate on the design of the degree. I think rather that it was intended by Desaguliers to develop the religious and philosophic sentiment in Speculative Freemasonry which it was his intention to establish. It is probable that the "eloquent Oration about Masons and Masonry," which Anderson tells us he delivered before the Grand Lodge in 1721, but which is unfortunately lost, contained a foreshadowing of hls views on this subject.

Bro. Hughan, who is of the very highest authority on all points of the documentary history of English Masonry, settles the question in the following remarks:[144]

"The sublime degree of a Master Mason, alias the 'Third degree,' may be very ancient, but, so far, the evidence respecting its history goes no farther back than the early part of the last century. Few writers on the subject appear to base their observations on facts, but prefer the 'traditions' (so called) derived from old Masons. We, however, give the preference to the minutes and bylaws of lodges, as all of which we have either seen, traced, or obtained copies of, unequivocally prove the degree of Master Mason to be an early introduction of the Revivalists of A.D. 1717. No record prior to the second decade of the last century ever mentions Masonic degrees, and all the MSS. preserved decidedly confirm us in the belief that in the mere Operative (although partly speculative) career of Freemasonry the ceremony of reception was of a most unpretentious and simple character, mainly for the communication of certain lyrics and secrets, and for the conservation of ancient customs of the craft."

Hughan cites a MS. (No. 23,202) in the British Museum showing that the rules of a Musical and Architectural Society formed in February, 1724, in London, required its members to be Master Masons.

---

[143] "History of Freemasonry," Lyon's Translation, p. 150.
[144] See Voice of Masonry for August, 1873.

This might be, and yet the degree not have been fabricated until January, 1723.

He also cites the minutes of a lodge held at Lincoln (England). From these minutes it appears that in December, 1734, the body of the lodge consisted of Fellow-Crafts; and when the "two new Wardens, as well as several other Brothers of the lodge, well qualified and worthy of the degree of Master had not been called thereto," the Master directed a lodge of Masters to be held for the purpose of admitting these candidates to the Third degree.

Hence, as Bro. Hughan says, the lodge at that time worked the degree only at intervals. And he concludes, I think, correctly, that as there was a rule prescribing the fee when a "Brother made in another lodge shall be passed Master in this," that "all lodges had not authority or did not work the degree in question." I suppose they had the authority but not the ability.

All this shows that the Third degree in 1734 was yet in its infancy.

The provision contained in the "General Regulations," which restricted the conferring of the Second and Third degrees to the Grand Lodge was rescinded on November 22, 1725, and yet we see that nine years afterward the Third degree was not conferred in all the lodges.

It is a singular circumstance that in 1731, when the Duke of Lorraine was made a Mason in a special lodge held at the Hague, notwithstanding that Desaguliers presided over it, he received only the First and Second degrees, and came afterward to England to have the Third conferred upon him.

The first evidence of the Third degree being conferred in Scotland is in the minutes of Canongate Kilwinning Lodge in a minute dated March 31, 1735.[145]

The degree is first referred to in the minutes of St. Mary's Chapel Lodge under the date of November 1, 1738, when George Drummond, Esq., an Entered Apprentice, "was past a Fellow-Craft and also raised as a Master Mason in due form."[146]

According to Bro. Lyon, possession of the Third degree was not at this period a necessary qualification to a seat in the Grand Lodge of Scotland. For thirty years after its introduction into Mary's Chapel it conferred no rights in the management of the lodge that were not possessed by Fellow-Crafts.

---

[145] Lyon, "History of the Lodge of Edinburgh," p. 213.
[146] Ibid., p. 212.

It was not, in fact, until the year 1765 that Master Masons alone were qualified to hold office.

Continental Speculative Masonry having derived its organized existence from the Grand Lodge of England, must necessarily have borrowed its forms and ceremonies and ritual from the same source, and consequently received the Third degree at a still later period.

From all that has been said, I think that we are fairly entitled to deduce the following conclusions:

1. When the four old Lodges of London met on June 24, 1717, at the "Goose and Gridiron Tavern" and organized the Grand Lodge of England, there was but one degree known to the Craft, to the esoteric instructions of which all Freemasons were entitled.

2. Between 1717 and 1720, in which latter year the "Charges" and probably the "General Regulations" were compiled by Grand Master Payne, a severance of this primitive degree into two parts was effected, and the Second or Fellow-Craft's degree was fabricated, the necessary result being that what was left of the primitive degree, with doubtless some modifications and even additions, was constituted as the Entered Apprentice's degree.

3. A Third degree, called that of the Master Mason, was subsequently fabricated so as to complete the series of three degrees of Speculative Masonry as it now exists.

4. The Third degree, as an accomplished fact, was not fabricated before the close of the year 1722, and was not made known to the Craft, or worked as a degree of the new system, until the beginning of 1723.

5. The inventor or fabricator of this series of degrees was Dr. John Theophilus Desaguliers, assisted by Anderson and probably a few other collaborators, among whom I certainly would not omit the learned antiquary, George Payne, who had twice been Grand Master.

In coming to these conclusions I omit all reference to the Legend of the Third Degree as to the time or place when it was concocted, and whether it was derived by Desaguliers, as has been asserted, from certain Jewish rabbinical writers, or whether its earliest form is to be found in certain traditions of the mediaeval Stonemasons.

CHAPTER XXXVII

THE DEATH OF OPERATIVE AND THE BIRTH OF SPECULATIVE FREEMASONRY

GROWTH, says Dr. South, "is progress, and all progress designs, and tends to the acquisition of something, which the growing thing or person is not yet possessed of."

This apothegm of the learned divine is peculiarly applicable to the history of that system of Speculative Freemasonry which, springing into existence at the "Apple Tree tavern," in London, at the close of the second decade of the 18th century, made such progress in the acquisition of new knowledge as to completely change its character soon after the beginning of the third decade.

We have seen that it was derived from an older institution whose objects were altogether practical, and whose members were always engaged in the building of public edifices. But there were other members of the guild who were not Operative Masons, but who had been admitted to the privileges of membership for the sake of the prestige and influence which the Fraternity expected to obtain from their learning, their wealth, or their rank.

These unprofessional brethren, who were at first called Theoretic Masons or Honorary members, but who afterward assumed the title of Speculative Freemasons, began even in the very outset of what they were pleased, most inaccurately, to call a Revival, to exercise an unexpected and detrimental influence on the Operative Guild.

This influence was so exerted that Operative Freemasonry was gradually extruded from the important place which it had so long occupied, and finally, in and after the year 1723, ceased entirely to exist.

The gradual transformation from Operative to Speculative Free masonry is one of the most interesting points in the history of the institution, and is well worth our careful consideration.

Hardly more wonderful is the change from the insignificant acorn to the majestic oak, than was this expansion of a guild of workingmen, limited in their design and their numbers, into a Fraternity of moralists and philosophers, whose object was the elevation of their fellow-men, and whose influence has extended into every quarter of the civilized world.

Operative Freemasonry, which flourished in the Middle Ages and long after as an association of skillful builders who were in the possession of architectural secrets unknown to the ruder workmen of the same craft, and who were bound to each other by a fraternal tie, no longer exists. Like the massive cathedrals which it constructed, it has crumbled into decay.

But Speculative Freemasonry, erected on its ruins, lives and will always live, a perpetual memorial in its symbols and its technical language of the source whence it sprang.

Let us inquire how the one died and how the other was born.

When on the 24th day of June in the year 1717 certain Freemasons of London met at the "Goose and Gridiron Tavern" and carried into effect the arrangement made in the previous February, by organizing a Grand Lodge, it is not to be presumed that any other idea had at that time entered their minds than that of consolidating the four Operative Lodges of which they were members into one body. The motives that actuated them were to produce a stronger union among the Craft than had previously existed, each lodge having hitherto been independent and isolated, and also to enlarge their numbers and to increase their influence, by throwing the door more widely open to the admission of gentlemen who were not otherwise connected with the Craft.

The fact is that the fashion then prevailed to a remarkable extent in London for men of like sentiments or of the same occupation to form themselves into clubs. The Freemasons, both Operative and Theoretic, in thus uniting, were doing nothing else than following the fashion, and were really instituting a club of a more elevated character and under a different name.

Hence the consolidation of the four Lodges was called a Grand Lodge, a title and an organization which had previously been unknown to English Freemasonry.[147]

There was no thought, at that early period, by those who were engaged in the organization, of changing to any greater extent the character of the society. It was still to be a Guild of Operative Freemasons, but consisting more largely in proportion than ever before of members who were not professional workmen.

"At the revival in 1717," says Dr. Oliver, "the philosophy of the Order was seldom considered, and our facetious brethren did not think it worth their while to raise any question respecting the validity of our legends; nor did they concern themselves much about the truth of our traditions. Their principal object was pass a pleasant hour in company with a select assemblage of brethren; and that purpose being attained, they waived all inquiry into the truth or probability of either the one or the other."[148]

The scanty records of the transaction, which Dr. Anderson, our only authority, has supplied, make no mention of those distinguished persons who afterward took a prominent part in affecting the transmutation of Operative into Speculative Freemasonry, and who were indeed the founders of the latter system.

It is said, though I know not on what authentic authority, that Dr. Desaguliers, the corypheus of the band of reformers, had been admitted five years before into the honorary membership of the Lodge which met at the sign of the "Rummer and Grapes," and which was one of the four that united in the formation of a Grand Lodge.

If this be true, and there are good reasons for believing it, it can not be doubted that he was present at the organization of the Grand Lodge, and that he took an active part in the proceedings of the meetings both in February and in June, 1717.

Neither the names of Payne nor of Anderson, who subsequently became the collaborators of Desaguliers in the formation of Speculative Freemasonry, are mentioned in the brief records of those meetings. If they were present or connected with the organization, the fact is not recorded. Payne first appears in June, 1718, when he was elected Grand Master; Desaguliers in 1719, when he was elected to the same office. This would tend to show that both had been for some years

---

[147] It is not worth while to repeat the argument so often advanced, and by which Masonic scholars have satisfied themselves that no Grand Lodge ever existed in England before the year 1717.

[148] "Discrepancies of Freemasonry," p. 13.

in the Fraternity, since new-comers would hardly have been chosen for those positions.

It is not so certain that Anderson was a Freemason in 1717. It is not improbable that he was soon afterward admitted, for in September, 1721, he acquired such a reputation in the society as to have been selected by the Duke of Montagu, who was then the Grand Master, to digest the old Gothic Constitutions, a task of great importance.

Of one thing, however, there can be no doubt, that no one of these three persons, who were afterward so distinguished for their services in Speculative Freemasonry, had in 1717 been prominently placed before the Craft. In the selection of an officer to preside over the newly established Grand Lodge, the choice fell, not on one of them, but on a comparatively insignificant person, Mr. Anthony Sayer. Of his subsequent Masonic career, we only know that he was appointed by Desaguliers one of the Grand Wardens. He is also recorded as having been the Senior Warden at one of the four original Lodges after he had passed the Grand Mastership. He afterward fell into financial difficulties, and having received relief from the Grand Lodge, we hear no more of him in the history of Freemasonry.

It is to Desaguliers, to Payne, and to Anderson that we are to attribute the creation of that change in the organization of the system of English Freemasonry which gradually led to the dissolution of the Operative element, and the substitution in its place of one that was purely Speculative. The three were members of the same lodge, were men of education,[149] were interested in the institution, as is shown by their regular attendance on the meetings of the Grand Lodge until near the middle of the century, and were all zealously engaged in the investigation of the old records of the institution, so as to fit them for the prosecution of the peaceful revolution which they were seeking to accomplish.

Among the multitudinous books contributed by Dr. Oliver to the literature of Freemasonry, is one entitled The Reversions of a Square, which contains much information concerning the condition of

---

[149] John Robison, a professor of Natural Philosophy in Edinburgh, wrote and published in 1797 an anti-masonic work entitled "Proofs of a Conspiracy against all the Religions and Government in Europe," etc., the falsehoods in which, unfortunately for the author's reputation, were extended by French and Dutch translations. In this book he says of Anderson and Desaguliers that they were "two persons of little education and of low manners, who had aimed at little more than making a pretext, not altogether contemptible, for a convivial meeting." (P. 71.) This is a fair specimen of Robison's knowledge and judgment.

the ritual and the progress of the institution during the early period now under consideration. Unfortunately, there is such a blending of truth and fiction in this work that it is difficult, on many occasions, to separate the one from the other.

It is but fair, however, to admit the author's claim that his statements are not to be accounted fabulous and without authority because its contents are communicated through an imaginary medium," for, as he avers, he is in possession of authentic vouchers for every transaction.

These vouchers consisted principally of the contents of a masonic diary kept by his father, who had been initiated in 1784, and was acquainted with a distinguished Freemason who had been a contemporary of Desaguliers. With this brother the elder Oliver had held many conversations, as well as with others of the 18th century. The substance of these conversations he had committed to his diary, and this came into the possession of his son, and is the basis on which he composed his Revelations of a Square.

If Dr. Oliver had given in marginal notes or otherwise special references to the diary and to other sources which he used as authorities for his statements, I do not hesitate to say that The Revelations of a Square would, by these proofs of authenticity, be the most valuable of all his historical works.

Still, I am disposed to accept generally the statements of the work as authentic, and if there be sometimes an appearance of the fabulous, it can not be doubted that beneath the fiction there is always a considerable substratum of truth.

According to Oliver, Desaguliers had at that early period determined to renovate the Order, which was falling into decay, and had enlisted several active and zealous brethren in the support of his plans. Among these were Sayer and Payne, the firsf and second Grand Masters, and Elliott and Lamball, the first two Wardens, with several others whose names have not elsewhere been transmitted to posterity.[150]

There is nothing unreasonable nor improbable in this statement. It is very likely that Desaguliers and a few of his friends had seen and deplored the decaying condition of the four lodges in London.

It is also likely that their first thought was that a greater degree of success and prosperity might be secured if the lodges would abandon to some extent the independence and isolation of their condition, and

---

[150] "Revelations of a Square," ch. i., p. 5.

would establish a bond of union by their consolidation under a common head.

Whatever views might have been secretly entertained by Desaguliers and a few friends in his confidence, he could not have openly expressed to the Craft any intention to dissolve the Operative guild and to establish a Speculative society in its place. Had such an intention been even suspected by the purely Operative Freemasons who composed part of the membership of the four lodges, it can not well be doubted that they would have declined to support a scheme which looked eventually to the destruction of their Craft, and consequently the organization of a Grand Lodge would never have been attempted.

But I am not willing to charge Desaguliers with such duplicity. He was honest in his desire to renovate the institution of Operative freemasonry, and he believed that the first step toward that renovation would be the consolidation of the lodges. He expected that an imperfect code of laws would be improved, and perhaps that a rude and unpolished ritual might be expanded and refined.

Farther, he was not, it may be supposed, prepared at that time to go.

Whatever modifications he subsequently made by the invention of degrees which at once established a new system were the results of afterthoughts suggested to his mind by a sequence of circumstances.

That the change from Operative to Speculative Freemasonry was of gradual growth, we know from the authentic records that are before us.

In the year 1717 we find an Operative guild presenting itself in cold simplicity of organization as a body of practical workmen to whom were joined some honorary members, who were not Craftsmen; with an imperfect and almost obsolete system of by-laws; with but one form of admission; with secrets common to all classes, and which were of little or no importance, for the architectural and geometrical secrets of the medieval Craft had been lost; and finally with an insignificant and unpolished ritual, a mere catechism for wandering brethren to test their right to the privileges and the hospitality of the Fraternity.

Six years after, in 1723, this association of workmen has disappeared, and in its place we find a new society which has been erected on the foundations of that edifice which has crumbled into ruins; a society that has repudiated all necessary knowledge of the art of building; to which workmen may be admitted, not because they are workmen, but because they are men of good character and of exemplary conduct; with a well- framed code of laws for its government; with three degrees, with three forms of initiation, and with secrets exclusively appropriated to each; and with rituals which, produced by cultured minds, present the germs of a science of symbolism.

Operative Freemasonry no longer wields the scepter; it has descended from its throne into its grave, and Speculative Freemasonry, as a living form, has assumed the vacant seat.

That the transmutation was gradually accomplished we know, for six years were occupied in its accomplishment, and the records of that period, brief and scanty as they are, unerringly indicate the steps of its gentle progress.

From June, 1717, to June, 1718, under the administration of Anthony Sayer, Gentleman, as Grand Master, there are no signs of a contemplated change. He was not, if negative evidence may be accepted as the index of his character, the man to inaugurate so bold an enterprise.

His efforts seem to have been directed solely to the strengthening and confirming of the union of the Operative lodges by consulting at stated periods with their officers.

From June, 1718, to June, 1719, George Payne presided over the Craft.

Now we discover the first traces of a sentiment tending toward the improvement of the institution. Old manuscripts and records were anxiously sought for that the ancient usages of the Craft might be learned. In preparing for the future it was expedient to know something of the past.

The result of this collation of old documents was the compilation of the "Charges of a Freemason," appended to the first edition of the Book of Constitutions. The composition of this code is generally attributed to Anderson. Without positive testimony on this point, I am inclined to assign the authorship to Payne. He was a noted antiquary, and well fitted by the turn of his mind to labors of that kind.

Desaguliers was Grand Master from June, 1719, to June, 1720, His administration is made memorable by the first great change in the system.

An examination of the old manuscripts which had been collected by Payne must have shown that the body of the Craft had always been divided into two classes, Apprentices and Fellows, who were distinguished by the possession of certain privileges as workmen peculiar to each.

In the lodge they assembled together and partook equally of its counsels. But the prominence of the Fellows in rank as a class of workmen and in numbers as constituting the principal membership of the four old Lodges, very probably suggested to the mind of Desaguliers the advantages that would result from a more distinct separation of the Fellows from the Apprentices, not by a recognition of the higher rank of the former as workmen, because if a Speculative system was to be established, a qualification derived from skill in the practical labors of the Craft would cease to be of avail; but a separation by granting to each class a peculiar form of initiation, with its accompanying secrets.

The fact, also, that in some of the old manuscripts, which were then called the "Gothic Constitutions," copies of which had been produced as the result of the call of Grand Master Payne, there were two distinct sets of "Charges," one for the Masters and Fellows and one for the Apprentices, would have strengthened the notion that there should be a positive and distinct separation of the two classes as the first preparatory step toward the development of the new system.

This step was taken by Desaguliers soon after his installation as Grand Master. Accordingly, in 1719, he modified the one degree or form of initiation or admission which had been hitherto common to all ranks of Craftsmen.

One part of the degree (but the word is not precisely correct) he confined to the Apprentices, and made it the working degree of the lodge. Another part he enlarged and improved, transferred to it the most important secret, the MASON WORD, and made it a degree to be conferred only on Fellow-Crafts in the Grand Lodge; while the degree of the Apprentices thus modified continued as of old to be conferred on new candidates in the lodge.

Thus it was that in the year 1719 the first alteration in the old Operative system took place, and two degrees, the First and Second, were created.

The Entered Apprentice now ceased to be a youth bound for a certain number of years to a Master for the purpose of learning the mysteries of the trade. The term henceforth denoted one who had been initiated into the secrets of the First degree of Speculative Freemasonry, a meaning which it has ever since retained.

In former times, under the purely Operative system, the Masters of the Work, those appointed to rule over the migratory lodges and to superintend the Craftsmen in their hours of labor, were necessarily selected from the Fellows, because of their greater skill, acquired from experience and their freedom from servitude.

But when the Theoretic Freemasons, the Honorary members, began to be the dominant party, in consequence of their increased number, their higher social position, and their superior education, it was plainly seen that any claim to privileges which was derived from greater skill in the practical art of building, from the expiration of indentures and from the acquisition of independence and the right to go and come at will, would soon be abolished.

The Operative members only could maintain a distinction between themselves founded on such claims. The Theoretic members were, so far as regarded skill in building or freedom from the servitude of indentures, on an equal footing, everyone with all the others.

But Desaguliers and his collaborators were anxious to retain as many as they could of the old usages of the Craft. They were not prepared nor willing to obliterate all marks of identity between the old and the new system. Nor could they afford, in the infancy of their enterprise, to excite the opposition of the Operative members by an open attack on the ancient customs of the Craft.

Hence they determined to retain the distinction which had always existed between Fellows and Apprentices, but to found that distinction, not on the possession of superior skill in the art of building, but in the possession of peculiar secrets.

The Second degree having been thus established, it became necessary to secure the privileges of the Fellows. These in the old system had inured to them by usage and the natural workings of the trade; they were now to be perpetuated and maintained in the new system by positive law.

Accordingly, in the following year, Payne made that compilation or code of laws for the government of the new society which is known as the "General Regulations," and which having been approved by the Grand Lodge, was inserted in the Book of Constitutions.

It has been already abundantly shown that the whole tenor of these "Regulations" was to make the Fellow-Crafts the possessors of the highest degree then known, and to constitute them the sole legislators of the society (except in the alteration of the "Regulations") and the body from which its officers were to be chosen.

Thus the first step in the separation of Speculative from Operative Freemasonry was accomplished by the establishment of two degrees of initiation instead of one, and by making the Fellow-Crafts distinct from and superior to the Apprentices, not by a higher skill in an Operative art, but by their attainment to greater knowledge in a Speculative science.

For four years this new system prevailed, and Speculative Freemasonry in England was divided into two degrees. The system, in fact, existed up to the very day of the final approval, in January, 1723, of the Book of Constitutions.

The First degree was appropriated to the initiation of candidates in the particular, or, as we now call them, the subordinate lodges.

The Second degree conferred in the Grand Lodge was given to those few who felt the aspiration for higher knowledge, or who had been elected as Masters of lodges or as officers in the Grand Lodge.

The Operative members submitted to the change, and continued to take an interest in the new society, receiving in proportion to their numbers a fair share of the offices in the Grand Lodge.

But the progress of change and innovation was not to cease at this point. The inventive genius of Desaguliers was not at rest, and urged onward, not only by his ritualistic taste and his desire to elevate the institution into a higher plane than would result by the force of surrounding circumstances, he contemplated a further advance.

"Circumstances," says Goethe, in his Wilhelm Meister, "move backward and forward before us and ceaselessly finish the web, which we ourselves have in part spun and put upon the loom."

Desaguliers, with the co-operation of other Theoretic Freemasons. had united the four Operative Lodges into a Grand Lodge, a body until then unknown to the Craft; he had established a form of government with which they were equally unfamiliar; he had abolished the old degree, and inventedtwo new ones; and yet it appears that he did not consider the system perfect.

He contemplated a further development of the ritual by the addition of another degree. In this design he was probably, to some extent, controlled by surrounding circumstances.

The Fellow-Crafts had been invested with important privileges not granted to the Entered Apprentices, and the possession of these privileges was accompanied by the acquisition of a higher esoteric knowledge.

Among the privileges which had been acquired by the Fellow Crafts were those of election to office in the Grand Lodge and of Mastership in a subordinate lodge.

It is not unreasonable to suppose that the Fellows who had been elevated to these positions in consequence of their possession of a new degree were desirous, especially the Master of the lodges, to be farther distinguished from both the Apprentices and the Fellow Crafts by the acquisition of a still higher grade.

Besides this motive, the existence of which, though not attested by any positive authority, is nevertheless very presumable, another and a more philosophic one must have actuated Desaguliers in the further development of his system of degrees.

He had seen that the old Operative Craft was divided into three classes or ranks of workmen. To the first and secede of these classes he had appropriated a degree peculiar to each. But the third and highest class was still without one. Thus was his system made incongruous and incomplete.

To give it perfection it was necessary that a Third degree should be invented, to be the property of the third class, or the Masters.

It is possible that Desaguliers had, in his original plan, contemplated the composition of three degrees, or it may have been that the willing acceptance of the First and Second by the Craft had suggested the invention of a Third degree.

Be this as it may, for it is all a matter of mere surmise and not of great importance, it is very certain that the invention and composition of the ritual of so philosophic a degree could not have been the labor of a day or a week or any brief period of time.

It involved much thought, and months must have beer occupied in the mental labor of completing it. It could not have been finished before the close of the year 1722. If it had, it would have been presented to the Grand Lodge before the final approval of the Book of Constitutions, and would then have received that prominent place in Speculative Freemasonry which in that book and in the "General Regulations" is assigned to the degree of Fellow-Craft.

But at that time the degree was so far completed as to make it certain that it would be ready for presentation to the Grand Lodge and to the Craft in the course of the following year.

But as the Book of Constitutions was finally approved in January, 1723, and immediately afterward printed and published, Desaguliers being desirous of keeping the new degree under his own control for a brief period, until its ritual should be well understood and properly worked, anticipated the enactment of a law on the subject, and interpolated the passage in the "General Regulations" which required the Second and Third degrees to be conferred in the Grand Lodge only.

Logical inferences and documentary evidence bring us unavoidably to the conclusion that the following was the sequence of events which led to the establishment of the present ritual of three degrees.

In 1717 the Grand Lodge, at its organization, received the one comprehensive degree or ritual which had been common to all classes of the Operative Freemasons.

This they continued to use, with no modification, for the space of two years.

In 1719 the ritual of this degree was disintegrated and divided into two parts. One part was appropriated to the Entered Apprentices; the other, with some augmentations, to the Fellow-Craft.

From that time until the year 1723 the system of Speculative Freemasonry, which was practiced by the Grand Lodge, consisted of two degrees. That of Fellow-Craft was deemed the summit of Freemasonry, and there was nothing esoteric beyond it.

On this system of two degrees the Book of Constitutions, the "General Regulations," and the "Manner of Constituting a new Lodge" were framed. When these were published the Craft knew nothing of a Third degree.

In the year 1723 Dr. Desaguliers perfected the system by presenting the Grand Lodge with the Third degree, which he had recently invented.

This degree was accepted by the Grand Lodge, and being introduced into the ritual, from that time forth Ancient Craft Masonry, as it has since been called, has consisted of these three degrees. [151]

There can be little doubt that this radical change from the old system was not pleasing to the purely Operative Freemasons who were members of the Grand Lodge. Innovation has always been repugnant to the Masonic mind. Then, as now, changes in the ritual and the introduction of new degrees must have met with much opposition from those who were attached traditionally to former usages and were unwilling to abandon the old paths.

From 1717 to 1722 we find, by Anderson's records, that the Operatives must have taken an active part in the transactions of the Grand Lodge, for during that period they received a fair proportion of the offices. No one of them, however, had been elected to the chief post of Grand Master, which was always bestowed upon a Speculative.

But from the year 1723, when, as it has been shown, the Speculative system had been perfected, we lose all sight of the Operatives in any further proceedings of the society. It is impossible to determine whether this was the result of their voluntary withdrawal or whether the Speculatives no longer desired their co-operation. But the evidence is

---

[151] The dismemberment of the Third degree, which is said to have subsequently taken place to form a fourth degree, has nothing to do with this discussion.

ample that from the year 1723 Speculative Freemasonry has become the dominant, and, indeed, the only feature of the Grand Lodge.

Bro. Robert Freeke Gould, who has written an elaborate sketch of the history of those times, makes on this point the following remark, which sustains the present views:

"In 1723, however, a struggle for supremacy, between the Operatives and the Speculatives, had set in, and the former, from that time, could justly complain of their total supercession in the offices of the Society." [152]

It is, then, in the year 1723 that we must place the birth of Speculative Freemasonry. Operative Masonry, the mere art of building, that which was practiced by the "Rough Layers" of England and the wall builders or Murer of Germany, still remains and will always remain as one of the useful arts.

But Operative Freemasonry, the descendant and the representative of the mediaeval guilds, ceased then and forever to exist.

It died, but it left its sign in the implements of the Craft which were still preserved in the new system, but applied to spiritual uses; in the technical terms of the art which gave rise to a symbolic language; and in the ineffaceable memorials which show that the new association of Speculative Freemasonry has been erected on the foundations of a purely Operative Society.

---

[152] "History of the Four Old Lodges," p. 34.

CHAPTER XXXVIII

INTRODUCTION OF SPECULATIVE FREEMASONRY INTO FRANCE

SPECULATIVE Freemasonry having been firmly established in London and its environs (for it did not immediately extend into the other parts of England), it will now be proper to direct our attention to its progress in other countries, and in the first place into the neighboring kingdom of France.

The unauthentic and unconfirmed statements of Masonic scholars, until a very recent period, had thrown a cloud of uncertainty over the early history of Freemasonry in France, which entirely obscured the true era of its introduction into that country.

Moreover, the accounts of the origin of Freemasonry in France made by different writers are of so conflicting a nature that it is utterly impossible to reconcile them with historical accuracy. The web of confusion thus constructed has only been recently disentangled by the investigations of some English writers, conspicuous among whom is Bro. William James Hughan.

Before proceeding to avail ourselves of the result of these inquiries into the time of the constitution of the first lodge in France, it will be interesting to present the views of the various authors who had previously written on the subject.

In the year 1745 a pamphlet, purporting to be an exposition of Freemasonry, was published in Paris, entitled Le Sceau Rompu, ou la Loge ouverte aux profanes. In this work it is stated that the earliest introduction of Freemasonry into France is to be traced to the year 1718. This work is, however, of no authority, and it is only quoted to show the recklessness with which statements of Masonic history are too frequently made.

The Abbe Robin, who in 1776 published his Researches on the Ancient and Modern Initiations,[153] says that at the time of his writing Thory, in 1815, in his Acta Latomorum, gives the story as follows,[154] having borrowed it from Lalande, the great astronomer, who had previously published it in 1786, in his article on Freemasonry in that immense work, the Encyclopedie Methodique.

"The year 1725 is indicated as the epoch of the introduction of Freemasonry into Paris. Lord Derwentwater, the Chevalier Maskelyne, M. d'Henquelty, and some other Englishmen, established a lodge at the house of Hure, the keeper of an ordinary in the Rue des Boucheries. This lodge acquired a great reputation, and attracted five or six hundred brethren to Masonry in the space of ten years. It worked under the auspices and according to the usages of the Grand Lodge at London.

"It has left no historical monument of its existence, a fact which throws much confusion over the first labors of Freemasonry in Paris."

In his record of the year 1736, he says that "four lodges then existed at Paris, which united and elected the Earl of Harnouester, who thus succeeded Lord Derwentwater, whom the brethren had chosen at the epoch of the introduction of Freemasonry into Paris. At this meeting the Chevalier Ramsay acted as Orator."[155]

T. B. Clavel, in his Histoire Pittoresque de la Franc-Maconnerie,[156] says that according to certain English and German historians, among others Robison and the aulic counsellor Bode, Freemasonry was introduced into France by the Irish followers of King James II., after the English revolution in 1688, and the first lodge was established at the Chateau de Saint Germain, the residence of the dethroned monarch, whence the Masonic association was propagated in the rest of the kingdom, in Germany and Italy.

---

[153] "Recherches sur les initiations anciennes et modernes," par l'Abbe Rxxx. The work, though printed anonymously, was openly attributed to Robin, by the publisher. no memorial of the origin of Freemasonry in France remained, and that all that has been found does not go farther back than the year 1720, when it seems to have come from England. But of the date thus ascribed he gives no authentic evidence. It is with him but a surmise.

[154] "Acta Latomorum, ou chronologie de l'Histoire de la Franc-Masonnerie Francaise et Etrangire," p. 21.

[155] Ibid., p 51

[156] Chapter III., p. 107.

Clavel acknowledges that he does not know on what documentary evidence these writers support this opinion; he does not, however, think it altogether destitute of probability.

Robison, to whom Clavel has referred, says that when King James, with many of his most zealous adherents, had fled into France, "they took Freemasonry with them to the continent, where it was immediately received by the French, and was cultivated with great zeal, and in a manner suited to the tastes and habits of that highly polished people."[157]

Leaving this wholly apocryphal statement without discussion, I proceed to give Clavel's account, which he claims to be historical, of the introduction of Freemasonry from England into France.

The first lodge, he says, whose establishment in France is historically proved, is the one which the Grand Lodge of England instituted at Dunkirk in the year 1721, under the title of Amitie et Fraternite. The second, the name of which has not been preserved, was founded at Paris in 1725 by Lord Derwentwater, the Chevalier Maskelyne, Brother d'Heguerty, and some other followers of the Pretender. It met at the house of Hure, an English tavern-keeper or restaurateur in the Rue des Boucheries in the Faubourg Saint Germain. A brother Gaustand, an English lapidary, about the same time created a third lodge at Paris. A fourth one was established in 1726, under the name of St. Thomas. The Grand Lodge of England constituted two others in 1729; the name of the first was Au Louis d'Argent, and a brother Lebreton was its Master; the other was called A Sainte Marguerite; of this lodge we know nothing but its name, which was reported in the Registry of the year 1765. Finally there was a fourth lodge formed in Paris in the year 1732, at the house of Laudelle, a tavern-keeper in the Rue de Bussy. At first it took its name from that of the street in which it was situated, afterward it was called the Lodge d'Aumont, because the Duke of Aumont had been initiated in it.[158]

Ragon, in his Orthodoxie Maconnique, asserts that Freemasonry made its first appearance in France in 1721, when on October 13th the Lodge l'Amidie et Fraternite was instituted at Dunkirk. It appeared in Paris in 1725; in Bordeaux in 1732, by the establishment

---

[157] "Proofs of a Conspiracy," p. 27.

[158] A review of the Report made in 1838 and 1839 to the Grand Orient of France by a Committee, which is contained in the French journal La Globe (tome I., p. 324), states that "cette loge fut regulierment constituee par la Grande Loge d'Angleterre, le 7 Mas, 1729, sous le titre distinctif de Saint-Thomas au Louis d'Argent."

of the Lodge l'Anolaise No. 204; and on January 1, 1732, the Lodge of la Parfaits Union was instituted at Valenciennes.[159]

Two other French authorities, not, however, Masonic, have given similar but briefer statements.

In the Dictionnaire de la conversation et de Za Lecture it is said that Freemasonry was introduced into France in 1720 by Lord Derwentwater and the English. The Grand Masters who succeeded him were Lord d'Arnold-Esler and the Duc d'Autin, the Comte de Clermont-Tonnerre and the Duc d'Orleans. In 1736 there were still only four lodges in Paris; in 1742 there were twenty-two, and two hundred in the provinces.[160]

Larousse, in his Grand Universal Dictionary of the Nineteenth Century,[161] simply repeats this statement as to dates, simply stating that the first lodge in France was founded at Dunkirk in 1721, and the second at Paris in 1725, by Lord Derwentwater.

Rebold has written, in his Histoire des Trois Grandes Loges, a more detailed statement of the events connected with the introduction of Freemasonry into France. His narrative is as follows:

"It was not until 1725 that a lodge was for the first time founded at Paris by Lord Derwentwater and two other Englishmen, under the title of St. Thomas. It was constituted by them in the name of the Grand Lodge of London, on the 12th of June, 1720. Its members, to the number of five or six hundred, met at the house of Hure, a tavern-keeper in the Rue des Boucheries-Saint Germain. Through the exertions of the same English gentlemen a second lodge was established on the 7th of June, 1729, under the name of Louis d'Argent. Its members met at the tavern of the same name, kept by one Lebreton. On the 11th of December of the same year a third lodge was instituted, under the title of Arts Sainte Marguerite. Its meetings were held at the house of an Englishman named Gaustand. Finally, on the 29th of November, 1732, a fourth lodge was founded, which was called Buci,[162] from the name of the tavern in which it held its meetings, which was situated in the Rue de Buci, and was kept by one Laudelle. This lodge, after having initiated the Duke d'Aumont, took the name of the Lodge d'Aumont.

"Lord Deroventwater, who, in 1725, had received from the Grand Lodge of London plenary powers to constitute lodges in France,

---

[159] "Orthodoxie Maconnique," p. 35.
[160] "Dictionnaire de la Conversation," art. Franc-Maconnerie, vol. xxviii., p. 136.
[161] "Grand Dictionnaire Universal du XIXme Siecle," par M. Pierre Larousse. Paris, 1872.
[162] This is evidently a mistake of Rebold for Bussy.

was, in 1735, invested by the same Grand Lodge with the functions of Provincial Grand Master. When he left France (in 1745) to return to England, where he soon after perished on the scaffold, a victim to his attachment for the House of Stuart, he transferred the full powers which he possessed to his friend Lord Harnouester, who was empowered to represent him as Provincial Grand Master during his absence.

"The four lodges then existing at Paris resolved to found a Provisional Grand Lodge of England, to which the lodges to be thereafter constituted in France might directly address themselves as the representative of the Grand Lodge at London. This resolution was put into effect after the departure of Lord Derwentwater. This Grand Lodge was regularly and legally constituted in 1736 under the Grand Mastership of Lord Harnouester."[163]

Such is the story of the introduction of Speculative Freemasonry into France, which, first published by the astronomer Lalande, has been since repeated and believed by all French Masonic historians. That a portion of this story is true is without doubt; but it is equally doubtless that a portion of it is false. It will be a task of some difficulty, but an absolutely necessary one, to unravel the web and to distinguish and separate what is true from what is false.

The names of three of the four founders of the first lodge in Paris present a hitherto insurmountable obstacle in the way of any identification of them with historical personages of that period. The unfortunate propensity of French writers and printers to distort English names in spelling them, makes it impossible to trace the names of Lord Harnouester and M. Hugety to any probable source. I have made the most diligent researches on the subject, and have been unable to find either of them in any works relating to the events of the beginning of the 18th century, which have been within my reach.

Lord Derwent-Waters, as the title is printed, was undoubtedly Charles Radcliffe, the brother of James, the third Earl of Derwentwater who had been beheaded in 1715 for his connection with the rebellion in that year, excited by the Old Pretender, or, as he styled himself, James III. Charles Radcliffe had also been convicted of complicity in the rebellion and sentenced to be beheaded. He, however, made his escape and fled to the continent. At first he repaired to Rome, where the Pretender then held his court, but afterward removed to France, where he married the widow of Lord Newburghe and remained in that city until the year 1733. He then went for a short time to England, where he

---

[163] "Histoire des Trois Grandes Loges," par Em. Rebold, p. 44.

appeared openly, but afterward returned to Paris and continued there until 1745. In that year the Young Pretender landed in Scotland and invaded England in the attempt, as Regent, to recover the throne of his ancestors and to place his father upon it.

Charles Radcliffe, who had assumed the title of the Earl of Derwentwater on the demise of his nephew, who died in 1731, sailed on November 21, 1745, for Montrose in Scotland, in the French privateer Soleil, for the purpose of joining the Pretender. He was accompanied by a large number of Irish, Scotch, and French offiers and men. On the passage the privateer was captured by the English ship-of-war Sheerness, and carried, with its crew and passengers, to England.

On December 8th in the following year Radcliffe was beheaded, in pursuance of his former sentence, which had been suspended for thirty years.

Of Lord Harnouester, who is said by the French writers to have succeeded the titular Earl of Derwentwater as the second Grand Master, I have been unable to find a trace in any of the genealogical, heraldic, or historical works which I have consulted. The name is undoubtedly spelled wrongly, and might have been Arnester, Harnester, or Harnevester. The change made by the Dictionnaire de la Conversation, which converts it into "d'Arnold-Esler," only adds more confusion to that which was already abundantly confounded.

Maskelyne is an English name. It was that of a family in Wiltshire, from which Nevil Maskelyne, the distinguished Astronomer Royal, born in 1734, was descended. But I am unable to identify the Chevalier Maskelyne, of the French writers, with any person of distinction or of notoriety at that period.

I am equally at a loss as to M. Hugetty, a name which has been variously spelt as Heguetty and Heguelly. The name does not, in either of these forms, indicate the nationality of the owner, and the probable transformation from the original forbids the hope of a successful investigation.

One fact alone appears to be certain, and fortunately that is of some importance in determining the genuineness of the history.

The titular Earl of Derwentwater was a Jacobite, devoted to the interests of the fallen family of Stuart, and the English, Irish, and Scotch residents of Paris, with whom he was on terms of intimacy, must have been Jacobites or adherents of the Stuarts also. The political jealousy of the British Government at that time made it unpleasantly suspicious for any loyal subject to maintain intimate relations with the Jacobites who were living in exile at Paris and elsewhere.

This fact will be an important element in determining the genuineness of the authority claimed to have been given to Lord Derwentwater by the Grand Lodge at London.

The German historians have generally borrowed their authority from the French writers, and on this occasion have not shown their usual thoroughness of investigation.

Lenning simply states that the first lodge of France was founded at Paris in 1725, and that it was soon followed by others.[164]

Gadicke had previously said that Freemasonry was introduced into France from England and Scotland in the year 1660, but while it flourished in England it soon almost entirely disappeared in France. Afterwards in the year 1725, England again planted it in France, for in that year three Englishmen founded a lodge in Paris which was called the English Grand Lodge of France.[165]

Findel is a little more particular in his details, but affords us nothing new.

He says that "it is impossible to determine with any certainty the period of the introduction of Freemasonry into France, as the accounts handed down to us are very contradictory, varying from the years 1721, 1725, 1727, to 1732. In an historical notice of the Grand Lodge of France, addressed to her subordinate lodges, there is a statement specifying that Lord Derwentwater, Squire Maskelyne, a lord of Heguerty and some other English noblemen, established a lodge in Paris in 1725, at Hure's Tavern.

Lord Derwentwater is supposed to have been the first who received a Warrant from the Grand Lodge of England. It is recorded that other lodges were established by these same authorities, and amongst others the Lodge d'Aumont (au Louis d'Argent) in 1729, in la Rue Bussy at Laudelle's tavern, the documents bearing the date of 1732 as that of their foundation."[166]

Kloss, who has written a special work on the history of Freemasonry in France, supported as he says by reliable documents,[167] adopts the statements made originally by Lalande in the Encyclopedie Methodique, and which were repeated by successive French writers.

So, on the whole, we get nothing more from the German historians than what we already had from the French.

---

[164] "Encyclopadie der Freimaurerei."
[165] "Freimaurer-Lexicon."
[166] "Geschichte der Freimaurerei," Lyon's Translation, p. 200.
[167] "Geschichte der Freimaurerei in Frankreich, aus achten Urkunden dargestellt," von Georg Kloss. Darmstadt, 1852.

We come next to the English writers, whose information must have been better than that of either the French or German, as they possessed a written history of the contemporary events of that period. Therefore it is that on them we are compelled to lean in any attempt to solve the riddle involved in the introduction of the Speculative institution into the neighboring kingdom. Still we are not to receive as incontestable all that has been said on this subject by the earlier English writers on Freemasonry. Their wonted remissness here, as well as elsewhere in respect to dates and authorities, leaves us, at last, to depend for a great part on rational conjecture and logical inferences.

Dr. Oliver, the most recent author to whom I shall refer, accepts the French narrative of the institution of a lodge at Paris in 1725, and adds that it existed "under the sanction of the Grand Lodge of England by virtue of a charter granted to Lord Derwentwater, Maskelyne, Higuetty and some other Englishmen."[168]

Elsewhere he asserts that the Freemasonry which was practiced in France between 1700 and 1725 was only by some English residents, without a charter or any formal warrant.[169] In this opinion he is sustained by the Committee of the Grand Orient already alluded to, in whose report it is stated that "most impartial historians assert The author of an article in the London Freemasons' Quarterly Review,[170] under the title of "Freemasonry in Europe During the Past Century," says that "the settlement in France of the abdicated king of England, James II., in the Jesuitical Convent of Clermont, seems to have been the introduction of Freemasonry into Paris, and here it was (as far as we can trace) the first lodge in France was formed, anno 1725." The writer evidently connects in his mind the establishment of Freemasonry in France with the Jacobites or party of the Pretender who were then in exile in that kingdom, a supposed connection which will, hereafter, be worth our consideration.

Laurie (or rather Sir David Brewster, who wrote the book for him) has, in his History of Freemasonry, when referring to this subject, indulged in that spirit of romantic speculation which distinct guishes the earlier portion of the work and makes it an extravagant admixture of history and fable.

He makes no allusion to the events of the year 1725, or to the lodge said to have been created by the titular Earl of Derwentwater, but

---

[168] "Historical Landmarks," vol. ii., p. 32.
[169] "Origin of the Royal Arch," p. 27. that from 1720 to 1725 Freemasonry was clandestinely introduced into France by some English Masons."
[170] New Series, anno 1844, p. 156.

thinks "it is almost certain that the French borrowed from the Scots the idea of their Masonic tribunal, as well as Freemasonry itself."[171] And he places the time of its introduction at "about the middle of the 16th century, during the minority of Queen Mary."[172]

After all that has hitherto been said about the origin of Speculative Freemasonry, it will not be necessary to waste time in the refutation of this untenable theory or of the fallacious argument by which it is sought to support it. It is enough to say that the author entirely confounds Operative and Speculative Freemasonry, and that he supposes that the French soldiers who were sent to the assistance of Scotland were initiated into the Scotch lodges of Operative Masons, and then brought the system back with them to France.

Preston passes the subject with but few words. He says that in 1732 Lord Montagu, who was then Grand Master, granted a deputation for constituting a lodge at Valenciennes in French Flanders, and another for opening a new lodge at the Hotel de Bussy, in Paris."[173]

The word "new" might be supposed to intimate that there was already an older lodge in Paris. But Preston nowhere makes any reference to the Derwentwater lodge of 1725, or to any other, except this of 1732. We learn nothing more of the origin of Freemasonry in France from this generally reliable author.

We now approach an earlier class of authorities, which, however, consists only of Dr. Anderson and the contemporary records of the Grand Lodge at London.

In 1738 Dr. Anderson published the second edition of the Book of Constitutions. In the body of the work, which contains a record, frequently very brief, of the proceedings of the Grand Lodge from 1717 to June, 1738, there is no mention of the constitution of a lodge at Paris, or in any other part of France.

In a "List of the lodges in and about London and Westminster," appended to the work,[174] he records that there was a "French lodge," which met at the "Swan Tavern" in Long Acre, and which received its warrant June 12, 1723. In the list its number is 18.

This fact is only important as showing that Frenchmen were at that early period taking an interest in the new society, and it may or may not be connected with the appearance, not long afterward, of a lodge at Paris.

---

[171] "History of Freemasonry " p. x 10.
[172] Ibid., p. 109.
[173] "Illustrations," Jones's edition, p. 212.
[174] "Constitutions," 2d edition, p. 186.

In the list of "Deputations sent beyond Sea"[175] it is recorded that in 1732 Viscount Montagu, Grand Master, granted a Deputation for constituting a lodge at Valenciennes, in France, and another for constituting a lodge at the Hotel de Bussy, in Paris.

According to the same authority, Lord Weymouth, Grand Master in 1735, granted a Deputation to the Duke of Richmond "to hold a lodge at his castle d'Aubigny, in France." [176]He adds, referring to these and to other lodges instituted in different countries, that "all these foreign lodges are under the patronage of our Grand Master of England."[177]

This is all that Anderson says about the introduction of Freemasonry into France. It will be remarked that he makes no mention of a lodge constituted at Dunkirk in 1721, nor of the lodge in Paris instituted in 1725. His silence is significant.

Entick, who succeeded Anderson as editor of the Book of Constitutions, the third edition of which he published in 1756, says no more than his predecessor, of Freemasonry in France. In fact, he says less, for in his lists of "Deputations for Provincial Grand Masters,"[178] he omits those granted by Lords Montagu and Weymouth. But in a "List of Regular Lodges, according to their Seniority and Constitution, by order of the Grand Master,"[179] he inserts a lodge held at La Ville de Tonnerre, Rue des Boucheries, at Paris, constituted April 3, 1732, another at Valenciennes, in French Flanders, constituted in 1733, and a third at the Castle of Aubigny in France, constituted August 12, 1735. He thus confirms what Anderson had previously stated, but, like him, Entick is altogether silent in respect to the Dunkirk lodge of 1721, or that of Paris in 1725.

Northouck, who edited the fourth edition of the Book of Constitutions, appears to have been as ignorant as his predecessors of the existence of any lodge in France before the year 1732. From him, however, we gather two facts. The first of these is that in the year 1768 letters were received from the Grand Lodge of France expressing a desire to open a correspondence with the Grand Lodge of England. The

---

[175] Ibid., p. 194.
[176] Ibid., p. 195
[177] Ibid., p. 196.
[178] "Constitutions," by Entick, p. 333.
[179] Ibid., p. 335. This list bears some resemblance to Cole's engraved list for 1756, but the two are not identical.

overture was accepted, and a Book of Constitutions, a list of lodges, and a form of deputation were presented to the Grand Lodge of France.

The second fact is somewhat singular. Notwithstanding the recognized existence of a Grand Lodge of France it seems that in that very year there were lodges in that country which the Grand Lodge of England claimed as constituents, owing it their allegiance; for Northouck tells us that in 1768 two lodges in France, "having ceased to meet or neglected to conform to the laws of this society, were erazed out of the list."

It may be that these were among the lodges which, in former times, had been created in France by the Grand Lodge of England, and that they had transferred their allegiance to the Grand Lodge of their own country, but had omitted to give due notice of the act to the Grand Lodge which had originally created them.

Our next source of information must be the engraved lists of lodges published, from 1723 to 1778, by authority of the Grand Lodge of England. Their history will be hereafter given. It is enough now to say, that being official documents, and taken for the most part from the Minute Book of the Grand Lodge, they are invested with historical authority.

The earliest of the engraved lists, that for 1723, contains the designations[180] of fifty-one lodges. All of them were situated in London and Westminster. There is no reference to any lodge in France.

The list for 1725 contains the titles of sixty-four lodges. The Society was extending in the kingdom, and the cities of Bath, Bristol, Norwich, Chichester, and Chester are recorded as places where lodges had been constituted. But no lodge is recorded as having been created in France.

In the list of lodges returned in 1730 (in number one hundred and two), which is contained in the Minute Book of the Grand Lodge,[181] a lodge is recorded as being at Madrid in Spain, the number 50 being attached, and the place of meeting the "French Arms," which would seem almost to imply, but not certainly, that most of its members were Frenchmen.[182] Lodge No. 90 is said to be held at the "King's Head,

---

[180] At that time lodges were not distinguished by names, but by the signs of the taverns at which they met, as the "King's Arms," the "Bull and Gate," etc.

[181] The list is given in Bro. GouldÆs "Four Old Lodges," p. 50.

[182] This lodge met on Sunday, a custom still practiced by many French lodges, though never, as far as I know, by English or American lodges. Le Candeur, an old lodge of French members, in Charleston, S. C., which had its warrant

Paris." This is the first mention in any of the lists of a lodge in Paris. The name of the tavern at which it was held is singular for a French city. But as it is said by Bro. Gould to be copied from "the Minute Book of the Grand Lodge," it must be considered as authoritative.

We next find an historical record of the institution of lodges in France by the Grand Lodge of England in Pine's engraved list for 1734.[183] Bro. Hughan has said that the first historical constitution of a lodge at Paris is that referred to in Pine's list of 1734; but the lodge No. 90 at the "King's Head," recorded as has just been shown in the Grand Lodge list of 1730, seems to have escaped his attention.

Pine's list for 1734 contains the names of two lodges in France: No. 90 at the Louis d'Argent, in the Rue des Boucheries, at Paris, which was constituted on April 3, 1732, and No. 127 at Valenciennes in French Flanders, the date of whose Warrant of Constitution is not given.

In Pine's list for 1736 these lodges are again inserted, with a change as to the first, which still numbers as 90, is said to meet at the "Hotel de Bussy, Rue de Bussy." The sameness of the number and of the date of Constitution identify this lodge with the one named ln the list for 1734, which met at the Louis d'Argent, in the Rue des Boucheries.

The list for 1736 contains a third lodge in France, recorded as No. 133, which met at "Castle Aubigny," and was constituted August 22, 1735.

In Pine's list for 1740 the three lodges in France are again recorded as before, one in Paris, one at Valenciennes, and one at Castle d'Aubigny,[184] but the first of them, formerly No. 90, is now said to meet

---

originally from the brand Orient of France, always met on Sunday, nor did it change the custom after uniting with the Grand Lodge of South Carolina.

[183] A transcript of Pine's list for 1734, copied by Bro. Newton of Bolton from the original owned by Bro Tunnen, Provincial Grand Secretary of East Lancashire. This transcript was presented by Bro. Newton to Bro. W.J. Hughan, who published it in the "Masonic Magazine for November, 1876. He also republished it in pamphlet form, and to his kindness I am indebted for a copy. This list had been long missing from the archives of the Grand Lodge.

[184] The date of the Constitution of this lodge in the list for 1736 is August 22d. In the present and in subsequent lists the date is August 12th. The former date is undoubtedly a typographical error, It was the custom of the Grand Lodge to issue annually an engraved list of the lodges under its jurisdiction. The first was printed by Eman Bowen in 1723; afterward the engraver was John Pine, who printed them from 1725 to 1741, and perhaps to 1743, as the lists for that and the preceding year are missing. The list for 1744 was printed by Eman Bowen;

as No. 78, at the Ville de Tonnerre, in the same Rue des Boucheries. This was apparently a change of name and number and not of locality. It was the same lodge that had been first described as meeting as No. 90 at the Louis d'Argent.

In Benjamin Cole's list for 1756 the lodge's number is changed from 78 to 49, but under the same old warrant of April 3, 1732, it continues to meet at "la Ville de Tonnerre," in the Rue des Boucheries.

It is unnecessary to extend this investigation to subsequent lists or to those to be found in various works which have been mainly copied from the engraved lists of Pine and Cole. Enough has been cited to exhibit incontestable evidence of certain facts respecting the origin of Speculative Freemasonry in France. This evidence is incontestable, because it is derived from and based on the official records of the Grand Lodge of England.

The engraved lists," says Gould, "were renewed annually, certainly from 1738, and probably from the commencement of the series. Latterly, indeed, frequent editions were issued in a single year, which are not always found to harmonize with one another."[185]

The want of harmony consisted principally in the change of numbers and in the omission of lodges. This arose from the erasures made in consequence of the discontinuance of lodges, or their failure to make returns. It is not to be supposed that in an official document, published by authority and for the information of the Craft, the name of any lodge would be inserted which did not exist at the time, or which had not existed at some previous time.

We can not, therefore, unless we might reject the authority of these official lists as authoritative documents, and thus cast a slur on the honesty of the Grand Lodge which issued them, refuse to accept them as giving a truthful statement of what lodges there were, at the time of their publication, in France, acting under warrants from the Grand Lodge at London.

Bro. Hughan asserts that the first historical record of the Constitution of a lodge at Paris is to be referred to the one mentioned in Pine's list for 1734, as having been held au Louis d'Argent in the Rue des Boucheries, and the date of whose Constitution is April 3, 1732.

It is true that Anderson's first mention of a deputation to constitute a lodge in Paris is that granted in 1732 by Viscount Montagu as Grand Master, and I presume that there is no earlier record in the

---

from 1745 to 1766 Benjamin Cole was the printer, who was followed by William Cole, until 1788, which is the date of the latest engraved list.
[185] "Four Old Lodges," p. 16.

Minutes of the Grand Lodge, for if there were, I am very sure that Bro. Hughan would have stated it.

But how are we to reconcile this view with the fact that in the list of lodges for 1730 a lodge is said to be in existence in that year in Paris? This list, as printed by Bro. Gould in his interesting work on the Four Old Lodges,[186] is now lying before me. It is taken from the earliest Minute Book of the Grand Lodge, and is thus headed, "List of the names of the Members of all the lodges as they were returned in the year 1730."

Now if this heading were absolutely correct, one could not avoid the inference that there was a "regular lodge " in Paris in the year 1730, two years before the Constitution of the lodge recorded in Pine's list for 1734, for among the lodges named in this 1730 list is "90. King's Head at Paris."

For a Parisian hotel, the name is unusual and therefore suspicious. But the list is authentic and authoritative, and the number agrees with that of the lodge referred to in the 1734 list as meeting at the Louis d'Argent, in the Rue des Boucheries.

Indeed, there can be no doubt that the lodge recorded in the list for 1730 is the same as that recorded in the list for 1734. The number is sufficient for identification.

Bro. Gould relieves us from the tangled maze into which this difference of dates had led us. He says of the list, which in his book is No. 11, and which he calls a List of lodges, 1730 - 32," that this List seems to have been continued from 1730 to 1732."

The list comprises 102 lodges; the lodge No. 90, at the "King's Head, Paris," is the fifteenth from the end, and was, as we may fairly conclude, inserted in and upon the original list in 1732, after the lodge at the Rue des Boucheries had been constituted.

So that, notwithstanding the apparent statement that there was a regular lodge, that is, a lodge duly warranted by the London Grand Lodge in 1730, it is evident that Bro. Hughan is right in the conclusion at which he has arrived that the first lodge constituted by the Grand Lodge of England in Paris, was that known as No. 90, and which at the time of its constitution, on April 3, 1732, met at the Tavern called Louis d'Argent, in the Rue des Boucheries. Its number was subsequently changed to 78, and then to 49. It and the lodge at Valenciennes are both omitted in the list for 1770, and these were probably the two lodges in France recorded by Northouck as having been erased from the roll of the Grand Lodge of England in 1768. With their erasure passed away all

---

[186] Page 50.

jurisdiction of the English Grand Lodge over any of the lodges in France. In the same year it entered into fraternal relations with the Grand Lodge of France. The lodge at Castle d'Aubigny is also omitted from the list of 1770, and if not erased, had probably voluntarily surrendered its warrant.

Thus we date the legal introduction of lodges into France at the year 1732.

But it does not necessarily follow that Speculative Freemasonry on the English plan had not made its appearance there at an earlier period.

The history of the origin of Freemasonry in France, according to all French historians, from the astronomer Lalande to the most recent writers, is very different from that which it has been contended is the genuine one, according to the English records.

It has been shown, in a preceding part of this chapter, that the Abbe Robin said that Freemasonry had been traced in France as far back as 1720, and that it appeared to have been brought from England.

Rebold has been more definite in his account. His statement in substance is as follows, and although it has been already quoted I repeat it here, for the purpose of comment.

Speaking of the transformation of Freemasonry from a corporation of Operatives to a purely philosophic institution, which took place in London in 1717, he proceeds to say, that the first cities on the Continent where this changed system had been carried from London were Dunkirk and Mons, both in Flanders, but then forming a part of the kingdom of France. The lodge at Mons does not seem to have attracted the attention of subsequent writers, but Rebold says of it that a it was constituted by the Grand Lodge of England on June 4, 1721, under the name of Parfaite Union. It was, at a later period, erected into the English Grand Lodge of the Austrian Netherlands, and from 1730 constituted lodges of its own.[187]

This narrative must be rejected as being unsupported by the English records. There may have been, as I shall presently show, an irregular lodge at Mons, organized in 1721, but there is no proof that it had any legal connection with the Grand Lodge of England.

Of the lodge at Dunkirk, Rebold says that it assumed the name of Amitie et Fraternite, and that in 1756 it was reconstituted by the Grand Lodge of France. Of the constitution of this lodge by the Grand Lodge at London, in 1721, we have no more proof than we have of the

---

[187] See "Histoire des Trois Grandes Loges," p. 43.

Constitution of that at Mons, and yet it has been accepted as a fact by Dr. Oliver and some other English authors. Rebold, however, is the only French historian who positively recognizes its existence.

He then tells us the story as it has been quoted on a preceding page of the foundation of the lodge of St. Thomas in 1725 at Paris by Lord Derwentwater and two other Englishmen, and of its constitution by the Grand Lodge at London on June 12, 1726.

Now the fact is, that while we are compelled to reject the statement that the Grand Lodge at London had constituted this lodge in the Rue des Boucheries in 1726, because we have distinct testimony in the records of the Grand Lodge that it was not constituted until 1732, yet we find it equally difficult to repudiate the concurrent authority of all the French historians that there was in 1725 a lodge in the city of Paris, established by Englishmen, who were all apparently Jacobites or adherents of the exiled family of Stuart.

Paris at that time was the favorite resort of English subjects who were disloyal to the Hanoverian dynasty, which was then reigning, as they believed, by usurpation in their native country.

Clavel tells us that one Hurre or Hure was an English tavernkeeper, and that his tavern was situated in the Rue des Boucheries. It is natural to suppose that his house was the resort of his exiled countrymen. That Charles Radcliffe and his friends were among his guests would be a strong indication that he was also a Jacobite.

Radcliffe, himself, could not have been initiated into the new system of Speculative Freemasonry in London, because he had made his escape from England two years before the organization of the Grand Lodge. But there might have been, among the frequenters of Hure's tavern, certain Freemasons who had been Theoretic members of some of the old Operative lodges, or even taken a share in the organization of the new Speculative system.

There was nothing to prevent these Theoretic Freemasons from opening a lodge according to the old system, which did not require a Warrant of Constitution. The Grand Lodge which had been organized in 1717 did not claim any jurisdiction beyond London and its precincts, and there were at that time and long afterward many lodges in England which paid no allegiance to the Grand Lodge and continued to work under the old Operative regulations.

It can not be denied that the Grand Lodge which was established in 1717 did not expect to extend its jurisdiction or to enforce its regulations beyond the city of London and its suburbs. This is evident from a statute enacted November 25, 1723, when it was agreed that no new lodge in or near London, without it be regularly constituted, be countenanced by the Grand Lodge nor the Master or Wardens admitted to Grand Lodge."[188]

Gould, who quotes this passage, says: "It admits of little doubt, that in its inception, the Grand Lodge of England was intended merely as a governing body for the Masons of the Metropolis.[189] Even as late as 1735 complaint was made of the existence of irregular lodges not working by the authority or dispensation of the Grand Master.[190]

What was there then to prevent the creation of such a lodge in Paris by English Freemasons who had left their country? A lodge would not only be, as Anderson has called it, "a safe and pleasant relaxation from intense study or the hurry of business," but it would be to these exiles for a common cause a center of union. Politics and party, which were forbidden topics in an English lodge at home, would here constitute important factors in the first selection of members.

It was in fact a lodge of Jacobites. These men paid no respect to acts of attainder, and to them Charles Radcliffe, as the heir presumptive to the title of Earl of Derwentwater, was a prominent personage, and he was, therefore, chosen as the head of the new lodge. [191]

The tavern in which they met was kept by Hure or Hurre, or some name like it, who, according to the statement of Clavel and others, was an Englishman. His house very naturally became the resort of his countrymen in Paris. As it was also the Locate of the Jacobite lodge, it may be safely presumed that Hure was himself a Jacobite. Thus it came to pass that to signify that his hostelry was an English one, he adopted an English sign, and to show that he was friendly to the cause of the Stuarts he made that sign the "King's Head," meaning, of course, not the head of George I., who in 1725 was the lawful King of England, but of James III., whom the Jacobites claimed to be the rightful king, and who had been recognized as such by the French monarch and the French people.

Thus it happens that we find, in the engraved list for 1730, the record that Lodge No. 90 was held at the " King's Head, in Paris."

---

[188] From the Grand Lodge Minutes.
[189] "The Four Old Lodges," p. 19.
[190] See New Regulations in Anderson, 2d edition, p. 156.
[191] The French writers and the English who have followed them are all wrong in saying that Lord Derwentwater was Master of the lodge in 1725. At that time Lord Derwentwater, the only son of the decapitated Earl, was a youth. On his death in 1731, without issue, his uncle, Charles Radcliffe, as next heir assumed the title, though, of course, it was not recognized by the English law.

It may be said that all this is mere inference. But it must be remembered that the carelessness or reticence of our early Masonic historians compels us, in a large number of instances, to infer certain facts which they have not recorded from others which they have. And if we pursue the true logical method, and show the absolutely necessary and consequent connection of the one with the other, our deduction will fall very little short of a demonstration.

Thus, we know, from documentary evidence, that in a list of "regular lodges" begun in 1730, and apparently continued until 1732, there was a lodge held in Paris at a tavern whose sign was the "King's Head," and whose number was 90. We know from the same kind of evidence that in 1732 there was a lodge bearing the same number and held in the Rue des Boucheries.

All the French historians tell us that a lodge was instituted in that street in 1725, at a tavern kept by an Englishman, the founders of which were Englishmen. The leader we know was a Jacobite, and we may fairly conclude that his companions were of the same political complexion.

Now we need not accept as true all the incidents connected with this lodge which are stated by the French writers, such as the statement of Rebold that it was constituted by the Grand Lodge of England in 1726. But unless we are ready to charge all of these historians, from Lalande in 1786 onward to the present day, with historical falsehood, we are compelled to admit the naked fact, that there was an English lodge in Paris in 1725. There is no evidence that this lodge was at that date or very soon afterward constituted by the Grand Lodge at London, and, therefore, I conclude, as a just inference, that it was established as all lodges previous to the year 1717 had been established in London, and for many years afterward in other places by the spontaneous action of its founders. It derived its authority to meet and "make Masons," as did the four primitive Lodges which united in forming the Grand Lodge at London in 1717, from the "immemorial usage" of the Craft.

As to the two lodges which are said to have been established in 1721 at Dunkirk and at Mons, the French generally concur in the assertion of their existence. Ragon alone, by his silence, seems to refuse or to withhold his assent.

There is, however, nothing of impossibility in the fact, if we suppose that these two lodges had been formed, like that of Paris, by Freemasons coming from England, who had availed themselves of the ancient privilege, and formed their lodges without a warrant and according to "immemorial usage."

What has been said of the original institution of the Paris lodge is equally applicable to these two.

It would appear that a Masonic spirit had arisen in French Flanders, where both these lodges were situated, which was not readily extinguished, but which led in 1733 to the Constitution by the English Grand Lodge of a lodge at Valenciennes, a middle point between the two, in the same part of France, and distant not more than thirty miles from Mons and about double that distance from Dunkirk.

Rebold says that the lodge at Dunkirk was re-constituted by the Grand Lodge of France in 1756, and he speaks as if he were leaning upon documentary authority. He also asserts that the lodge at Mons was, in 1730, erected into a Grand Lodge of the Australian Netherlands. He does not support this statement by any evidence, beyond his own assertion, and in the absence of proofs, we need not, when treating of the origin of Freemasonry in France, discuss the question of the organization of a Grand Lodge in another country.

Before closing this discussion, a few words may be necessary respecting the connection of the titular Earl of Derwentwater with the English lodge. A writer in the London Freemason of February 17, 1877, has said, when referring to the statement that the lodge at Hure's Tavern had received in the year 1726 a warrant from the Grand Lodge at London, "of this statement no evidence exists, and owing to the political questions of the day much doubt is thrown upon it, especially as to whether the English Grand Lodge would have given a Warrant to no Jacobites and to a person who was not Lord Derwentwater, according to English law."

But there was no political reason in 1726, certainly not in 1732, why a Warrant should not have been granted by the English Grand Lodge for a Lodge in Paris of which a leading Jacobite should be a member or even the head.

Toward Charles Radcliffe, who, when he was quite young, had been led into complicity with the rebellion of 1715 by the influence of his elder brother, the Earl of Derwentwater, and who had been sentenced to be beheaded therefor, the government was not vindictive.

It is even said by contemporary writers that if he had not prematurely made his escape from prison, he would have been pardoned After his retirement to France, he remained at least inactive, married the widow of a loyal English nobleman, and in 1833, two years after he had assumed, when his nephew died without issue, the title of Earl of

Derwentwater, he visited London and remained there for some time unmolested by the government. It was not until 1745 that he became obnoxious by taking a part in the ill-advised and unsuccessful invasion of England by the Young Pretender, and for this Radcliffe paid the penalty of his life.

The Grand Lodge at London had abjured all questions of partisan politics or of sectarian religion; some of its own members are supposed to have secretly entertained proclivities toward the exiled family of Stuarts, and there does not seem to be really any serious reason why a Warrant should not have been granted to a lodge in Paris, though many of its members may have been Jacobites.

I do not, however, believe that a warrant of constitution was granted by the Grand Lodge of England to the lodge at Paris in 1726. The French historians have only mistaken the date, and confounded the year 1726 with the year 1732. Both Thory and Ragon tell us that the lodge has left no historical monument of its existence, and that thus much obscurity has been cast over the earliest labors of Freemasonry in Paris.[192]

One more point in this history requires a notice and an explanation.

Rebold says that in the year 1732 there were four lodges at Paris: 1. The lodge of St. Thomas, founded in 1725 by Lord Derwentwater and held at Hure's Tavern. 2, A lodge established in May, 1729, by the same Englishmen who had founded the first, and which met at the Louis d'Argent, a tavern kept by one Lebreton. 3. A lodge constituted in December of the same year under the name of Arts-Sainte Marguerite.[193] Its meetings were held at the house of one Gaustand, an Englishman. 4. A lodge established in November, 1732, called de Buci, from the name of the tavern kept by one Laudelle in the Rue de Buci. This lodge afterward took the name of the Lodge d'Aumont, when the Duke of Aumont had been initiated in it.

It will not be difficult to reduce these four lodges to two by the assistance of the English lists. The first lodge, which was founded by Radcliffe, improperly called Lord Derwentwater, is undoubtedly the same as that mentioned in the 1730 list under the designation of No. 90

---

[192] Thory, in the "Histoire de la Fondation de Grand Orient of France p. 20, and Rayon in the "Acta Latomorum," p. 22.
[193] Clavel ("Histoire Pittoresque," p. 108) calls it A Sainte Marguerite, which is probably the correct name. The Arts in Rebold may be viewed as a typographical error.

at the "King's Head." Rebold, Clavel, and the other French authorities tell us that it was held in the Rue des Boucheries

Now the list for 1734 gives us the same No. 90, as designating a lodge which met in the same street but at the sign of the Louis d'Argent. This was undoubtedly the same lodge which had formerly met at the "King's Head." The tavern may have been changed, but I think it more likely that the change was only in the sign, made by the new proprietor, for Hure, it seems, had given way to Lebreton, who might have been less of a Jacobite than his predecessor, or no Jacobite at all, and might have therefore discarded the head of the putative king, James. The first and second in this list of Rebold's were evidently to be applied to the same lodge.

The fourth lodge was held at the Hotel de Buci. Here, again, Rebold is wrong in his orthography. He should have spelt it Bussy. There was then a lodge held in the year 1732 at the Hotel de Bussy. Now Anderson tells us, in his second edition, that Viscount Montagu granted a deputation "for constituting a lodge at the Hotel de Bussy in Paris." But the lists for 1732, 1734, 1740, and 1756 give only one Parisian lodge which was constituted on April 3, 1732, and they always assign the same locality in the Rue des Boucheries, but change the number, making, however, the change from 90 to 78, and then to 49, and change also the sign, from the "King's Head" in 1732 to the Louis d'Argent in 1734, and to the Ville de Tonnerre in 1740 and 1746. But it is important to remark that while the Engraved List for 1734 says that No. 90 met at the Louis d'Argent in the Rue de Boucheries, the list for 1736 says that No. 90 met at the Hotel de Bussy, in the Rue de Bussy, and each of these lists gives the same date of constitution, namely, April 3, 1732.

I am constrained, therefore, to believe that the lodge at the Hotel de Bussy was the same as the one held first at Hure's Tavern in 1725 as an independent lodge and which, in 1732, was legally constituted by the Grand Lodge of England, and which afterward met either at the same tavern with a change of sign or at three different taverns.

The first, second, and fourth lodges mentioned by Rebold, therefore, are resolved into one lodge, the only one which the English records say was legally constituted by the deputation granted in 1732 by Lord Montagu.

As to the third lodge on Rebold's list, which he calls Arts-Sainte Marguerite, but which Clavel more correctly styles A Sainte Marguerite, there is no reference to it, either in the English engraved lists or in the Book of Constitutions. It is said to have been founded at the close of the year 1729 and to have held its meetings at the house or tavern of an Englishman named Gaustand.

I can not deny its existence in the face of the positive assertions of the French historians. I prefer to believe that it was an offshoot of the lodge instituted in 1725 at Hure's, that that lodge had so increased in numbers as to well afford to send off a colony, and that, like its predecessor, the lodge A Saints Marguerite had been formed independently and under the sanction of "immemorial usage."

Hence, I think it is demonstrated that between the years 1725 and 1732 there were but two lodges in Paris and not four, as some of the French writers have asserted. Bro. Hughan is inclined to hold the same opinion, and the writer in the London Freemason, who has previously been referred to, says that he thinks it "just possible." The possibility is, I imagine, now resolved into something more than a probability.

Having thus reconciled, as I trust I have, the doubts and contradictions which have hitherto given so fabulous a character to the history of the introduction of Speculative Freemasonry into France, I venture to present the following narrative as a consistent and truthful account of the introduction of the English system of Speculative Freemasonry into France. It is divested of every feature of romance and is rendered authentic, partly by official documents of unquestionable character and partly by strictly logical conclusions, which can not fairly be refuted.

It was not very long after the foundation of purely Speculative Freemasonry in London by the disseverance of the Theoretic Masons from their Operative associates and the establishment of a Grand Lodge, that a similar system was attempted to be introduced into the neighboring kingdom of France.

Freemasons coming from England, either members of some of the old Operative lodges or who had taken a part in the organization of the London Grand Lodge, having passed over into France. founded in the year 1721 two independent lodges which adopted the characteristics of the new Speculative system, so far as it had then been completed, but claimed the right, according to the ancient usage of Operative Freemasons, to form lodges spontaneously without the authority of a Warrant of Constitution.

These lodges were situated respectively at Dunkirk and at Mons, two cities in French Flanders, and which were at that time within the territory of the French Empire.

Four years after, namely, in 1725, a similar lodge was founded in Paris, at the sign of the "King's Head," a tavern which was kept in the

Rue des Boucheries by an Englishman named Hure or Turret or some other name approximating nearly to it. French historians inform us that the name of the lodge was St. Thomas, but this name is not recognized in any of the English engraved lists. Then and for some time afterward English lodges were known only by the name or sign of the tavern where their meetings were held. But there is no reason for disbelieving the assertion of the French writers. The number and the place of meeting were the only necessary designations to be inserted in the Warrant when it was granted. Of the one hundred and twenty-eight lodges recorded in Pine's list for 1734, not one is otherwise designated than by its number and the sign of the tavern. So that the fact that the lodge is not marked in the English lists as "the Lodge of St. Thomas," is no proof whatever that its founders did not bestow upon it that title.

The founders of this lodge were Charles Radcliffe, the younger brother of the former Earl of Derwentwater, Whose title he six years afterward assumed, and three other Englishmen, of whose previous or subsequent history we know nothing, but who are said by the French writers to have been Lord Harnouester, the Chevalier Maskelyne, and Mr. Heguetty.

These men were, it is supposed, Jacobites or adherents, passively at least, of the exiled family of Stuarts, represented at that time by the son of the late James II., and who was known in France and by his followers as James III. From this fact, and from the character of the tavern where they met, which was indicated by its sign, it is presumed that the lodge was originally formed as a resort for persons of those peculiar political sentiments.

If so, it did not long retain that feature in its composition. The institution of Speculative Freemasonry became in Paris, as it had previously become in London, extremely popular. In a short time the lodge received from French and English residents of Paris an accession of members which amounted to several hundreds.

In December, 1729, another independent lodge was formed under the name of A Sainte Marguerite, which was held at the tavern of an Englishman named Gaustand. It was probably formed by members of the other lodge whose number had, from the popularity of the institution, become unwieldy. Of the subsequent career of this lodge we have no information. The records do not show that it was ever legally constituted by the Grand Lodge of England.

In 1732 Lord Montagu, the Grand Master of the Grand Lodge at London, granted a deputation for the Constitution of the original lodge in Paris, which was then holding its meetings at the Hotel de

Bussy, in the Rue de Bussy. It was accordingly constituted on April 3, 1732. But at the time of the Constitution it appears to have returned to its old locality, as it is recorded in the first part of the lists in which it is mentioned as meeting in the Rue des Boucheries at the " King's Head Tavern," and in the second list at the Louis d'Argent, which, as I have already said, I take to be the same house with a change of sign.

Thus the fact is established that the new system of Speculative Freemasonry was introduced into France from England, but not by authority of the English Grand Lodge, in the year 1721 by the founding of two independent lodges in French Flanders, and into Paris by the founding of a similar lodge in 1725.

In 1732 the Grand Lodge of London extended its jurisdiction over the French territory and issued two deputations, one for the constitution of the lodge in Paris, and the other for the constitution of a lodge in French Flanders at the city of Valenciennes. The former was constituted in 1732, in the month of April, and the latter in the following year.

The further action of the English Grand Lodge in the constitution of other lodges, and the future history of the institution which resulted in the formation of a Grand Lodge in France, must be reserved for consideration in a future chapter.

CHAPTER XXXIX

THE GRAND LODGE OF ALL ENGLAND, OR THE GRAND LODGE OF YORK

THE pretension, so stoutly maintained by many Freemasons who have not thoroughly investigated the subject, that there was a General Assembly of Masons held, and a Grand Lodge established, at the city of York in the year 926, by Prince Edwin, the brother of King Athelstan, is a tradition derived from the old Legend of the Craft. As such it has already been freely discussed in the preceding division of this work, and will not be further considered at this time.

The object of the present chapter will be to inquire into the time when, and the circumstances under which, the modern Theoretic Freemasons of York separated from the Operative association and, following the example of their antecessors in London, established a purely Speculative society to which they, too, gave the name of a Grand Lodge.

To distinguish it from the Grand Lodge which had been established eight years before in London, they applied to that body the title of the "Grand Lodge of England," while in a somewhat arrogant spirit they assumed for themselves the more imposing title of the "Grand Lodge of all England," epithets which were first employed by Drake in his speech at York in 1726.[194]

---

[194] There is not the slightest evidence that the Grand Lodge in London ever accepted this distinction of titles, involving, as it did, an acknowledgment of the supremacy of its rival. Neither Anderson, Entick, nor Northouck have used in their successive editions of the "Book of Constitutions" these epithets. In these editions the body in London is always called simply Athe Grand Lodge." It is not until 1775 that we meet with a more distinctive name. In the Latin inscription

This distinction was suggested by the ecclesiastical usage of the kingdom, which, dividing the government of the church between two Archbishops, calls the Archbishop of York the APrimate of England," while his brother, the Archbishop of Canterbury, of somewhat more elevated rank and more extensive jurisdiction, is dignified as the APrimate of All England."

Angliae and totius Angliae are the distinctions between the two Archbishops, and so, also, they became the distinctions between the two Grand Lodges.

Operative Freemasonry was established with great vigor and maintained with strict discipline at York during the building of the Cathedral in the 14th century. Of this fact we have the most undoubted evidence in the Fabric Rolls of York Minster, which were published several years ago by the ASurtees Society."[195]

These ARolls," extending from 1350 to 1639, were made up during the progress of the work. They consist of accounts of contracts at different periods and regulations adopted from time to time for the government of the workmen. A fragment remaining of one of the Rolls, with the date of 1350, records that the Masons and the Carpenters who at that time were employed on the building were respectively under the control of William de Hoton, as the Master Mason, and Philip de Lincoln as the Master Carpenter. As Bro. Hughan very correctly remarks, AWithout doubt the Master Mason thus referred to was simply the chief among the Masons, the others being Apprentices and Craftsmen."

One of the Rolls contains a code of rules which had been agreed upon in 1370. It is entitled Oridinacio Cementariorum. This is interesting, as it shows what was the internal government of the Craft at that period.

These regulations were made by the Chapter of the Church of St. Peter's at York, under whose direction the Minster was being built. They did not emanate from any General Assembly or Grand Lodge, nor

---

on the corner-stone of the Freemasons' Hall, which was laid in that year, Lord Petre is designated as "Summus Latomorum Angliae Magister," or chief Master of Masons of England, while the Grand Lodge is called ASummus Angliae Conventus," or Chief Assembly of England.

[195] The existence of these Rolls was discovered by Mr. John Browne, who based upon them his "History of the Metropolitan Church of St. Peter, York." They were printed at Durham in 1859 by the Surtees Society, and edited by Mr. James Raine, Jr., the Secretary of the Society, who has enriched the work with valuable notes, an Appendix, and a Glossary.

even from a private lodge, but were derived from the ecclesiastical authority with which in that age Freemasonry was closely connected. Whether these Masons were acquainted with the old manuscripts which Anderson called the Gothic Constitutions it is impossible to say. We have no copies of any which date before the end of the 15th century, except the Halliwell MS., and the date of that is supposed to be 1390, which is twenty years after the adoption of the regulations by the Chapter of the Cathedral for the government of the Freemasons of York.

It is, however, almost, if not absolutely, demonstrable that the Halliwell MS. is a copy and a combination of two distinct poems, and it is, therefore, not unlikely that the York Masons, as a guild, were familiar with and even governed by its " points and articles."

The rules preserved in the Fabric Rolls were only intended for the direction of the Masons in their hours of labor and of refreshment, and contain no Legend of the Craft. A faithful copy of the Ordinacio Cementariorum, or Constitution of the Masons, translated into modern and more intelligible English,[196] will be interesting and useful as showing the guild organization of the Craft at York in the 14th century. This Ordinacio runs as follows: "It is ordained by the Chapter of the Church of Saint Peter of York that all the masons that shall work in the works of the same Church of Saint Peter shall, from Michaelmas day to the first Sunday of Lent, be each day in the morning at their work in the lodge, which is provided for the masons at work within the enclosure at the side of the aforesaid church,[197] at as early an hour as they can clearly see by daylight to work; and they shall stand there faithfully working at their work all day after, as long as they can clearly see to work, if it be an all work day; otherwise until high noon is struck by the clock, when a holiday falls at noon, except within the aforesaid time between Michaelmas and Lent; and at all other times of the year they may dine before noon if they will, and also eat at noon where they like, so that they shall not remain from their work in the aforesaid lodge, at no time of the year, at dinner time more than so short a time that no reasonable man shall find fault with their remaining away; and in time of eating at

---

[196] The earlier Rolls are written in the Low Latin of the Middle Ages. The later ones from 1544 are in the vernacular tongue of the times. The one about to be quoted is in a northern dialect, and is, as Mr. Raine observes, remarkable on account of its language as well as its contents.

[197] This confirms the statement made in the "Parentalia" that the Traveling Freemasons, when about to commence the erection of a religious edifice, built huts, or, as they were called, Alodges," in the vicinity in which they resided for the sake of economy as well as convenience.

noon they shall, at no time of the year, be absent from the lodges nor from their work aforesaid over the space of an hour; and after noon they may drink in the lodge, and for their drinking time, between Michaelmas and Lent, they shall not cease nor leave their work beyond the space of time that one can walk half a mile; and from the first Sunday of Lent until Michaelmas they shall be in the aforesaid lodge at their work at sunrise and remain there truly and carefully working upon the aforesaid work of the church, all day, until there shall be no more space than the time that one can walk a mile,[198] before sunset, if it be a work day, otherwise until the time of noon, as was said before; except that they shall, between the first Sunday of Lent and Michaelmas, dine and eat as beforesaid, after noon in the aforesaid lodge; nor shall they cease nor leave their work in sleeping time exceeding the time in which one can walk a mile, nor in drinking time after noon beyond the same time. And they shall not sleep after noon at any time except between Saint Elemnes and Lammas; and if any man remain away from the lodge and from the work aforesaid, or commit offense at any time of the year against this aforesaid ordinance, he shall be punished by an abatement of his wages, upon the inspection and judgment of the master mason; and all their times and hours shall be governed by a bell established therefor. It is also ordained that no mason shall be received at work on the work of the aforesaid church unless he be first tried for a week or more as to his good work; and if after this he is found competent for the work, he may be received by the common assent of the master and keepers of the work and of the master mason, and he must swear upon the book that he will truly and carefully, according to his power, without any kind of guile, treachery, or deceit, maintain and keep holy all the points of this aforesaid ordinance in all things that affect or may affect him, from the time that he is received in the aforesaid work, as long as he shall remain a hired mason at the work on the aforesaid work of the church of Saint Peter, and that he will not go away from that aforesaid work unless the masters give him permission to depart from the aforesaid work; and let him whosoever goes against this ordinance and breaks it against the will of the aforesaid chapter have God's malison and Saint Peter's."

---

[198] Time of a mileway. A common method at that period of computing time. "Way. The time in which a certain space can be passed over. Two mileway, the time in which two miles could be passed over, etc." - Halliwell, "Dictionary of Archaic and Provincial Words." We had Ahalf a mileway" above.

We learn from this ordinance, and others of the same import contained in these Fabric Rolls, that the Masons who wrought at the building of the York Cathedral in the 14th century were an entirely Operative guild, like their brethren who, at about the same time, were engaged in the construction of the Cathedrals of Cologne and Strasburg.

They confirm the statement made in Wren's Parentalia that the lodge was a building contiguous to the edifice they were constructing, and that in it they not only worked, cutting and otherwise preparing the stones, but also ate and slept there. Over them there was a superintendent of their work who was called the Master Mason.

What were the duties of the Magister Cementarius or Master Mason may be learned from an indenture between the Chapter and William de Hoton in the year 1351, a copy of which will be found at page 166 of the Fabric Rolls.

While overlooking other works, which shows that he might have different contracts at the same time, he was not to neglect the work of the Minster.

If he became affected with blindness or other incurable disease so that he should be unable to work, he was to employ and pay an assistant- subcementarius - who was to be the Second or Deputy Master of the Masons - Magister Secundarius Cementariorum.

He was to oversee the building and to receive a salary of ten pounds of silver annually, and to be furnished with a dwelling-house within the inclosure of the Cathedral.[199]

But while the Master Mason had the direct supervision of the workmen, there was an officer above him who was called the Magister Operis, or Master of the Work. This is shown by another agreement with Robert de Patrington in 1368, wherein it is said that his salary is to be paid to him "by the hands of the Master of the work of our said church" - per manus Magistri operis dicta ecclesiae rostra.

---

[199] From the "Fabric Rolls" the following list of Master Masons, who superintended the work from its beginning to its close, has been obtained by Mr. Raine:
1351, William de Hoton and William de Hoton, junior, probably the son of the first; 1368, Robert de Patrington; 1399-1401, Hugh de Hedon; 1415, William Colchester; 1421, John Long; 1433, Thomas Pak; 1442-43, John Bowde; 1445-47, John Barton; 1456, John Porter; 1466, Robert Spyllesby; 1472, William Hyndeley; 1505, Christian Horner; 1526, John Forman. In the lists of workmen many names foreign to Yorkshire will be found, and the names of foreigners also occur, such as Begon Baious and James Dum. - Preface to "Fabric Rolls"

Now, this Magistri Operis, or Master of the Work, sometimes called the Operarius, was not a member of the body of Masons, but, according to Ducange, an officer in Monasteries and Chapters of Canons, whose duty it was to have charge over the public works.

When the Cathedral was finished, the occupation of these Operative Masons ceased. But there were other religious edifices in the province on which they were subsequently employed, so that there was a continuous existence of Operative lodges during the succeeding centuries.

While the Freemasons were working on the York Minster, other guilds of Freemasons, or, rather, branches of the same guild, were employed in the construction of other cathedrals in different parts of England.

Thus the Cathedral of Canterbury was repaired and greatly enlarged about the year 1174; that of Salisbury was begun in 1220 and finished in 1260; that of Ely was begun in 1235 and finished in 1252, and Westminster Abbey was begun in 1245 and finished in 1285.

If the Fabric Rolls of these edifices should hereafter be discovered, ample evidence will doubtless be furnished of the existence of a common guild of Freemasons everywhere in England, similar to that which we now know existed at York during the same period of time, namely from the middle of the 14th to the middle of the 16th century, which was precisely the age of our oldest manuscript Constitutions.

The history of Operative Freemasonry at York and in the north of England was about the same as it was in London and in the south of the kingdom.

There were times when it flourished, and times when it began to decay.

In another respect there was a similarity in the character of the guilds of both localities.

The York Lodge, like the lodges of London, and indeed of every other country, at first consisting only of practical workmen, began in time to admit into its association men who were not craftsmen - men of rank or wealth or influence, who became honorary members, and in the course of time gradually infused a Speculative element into the lodges.

There is really no historical evidence whatever that during the period in which the Freemasons were occupied in the construction of the Minster there was any other lodge than that which was connected with the works, and under the control of the Cathedral Chapter. It is, however, very presumable that from long continuance it had abandoned the nomadic character so common with the Traveling Freemasons of the Middle Ages, and had assumed a permanent form, and thus become the parent of that Lodge which we find existing in 1705 in the city of York.

Anderson asserts that the tradition was "firmly believed by the old English Masons," that on December 27, 1561,[200] Queen Elizabeth sent an armed force to break up the annual Grand Lodge that was then meeting at York.

"But Sir Thomas Sackville, Grand Master," says Anderson, "took care to make some of the chief Men sent Freemasons, who then joining to that communication made a very honorable report to the Queen, and she never more attempted to dislodge or disturb them."

This story has been repeated by Preston and by others after him; but as all of them give it on the mere authority of Anderson, and as no other evidence has ever been adduced of its truth, we shall be compelled to reject it as historical, and receive it only as Anderson has called it a "tradition." Were it true, it would settle the question that there was a Grand Lodge at York in active existence in the 16th century.

In the "Manifesto" of the Lodge of Antiquity in 1778, it is asserted that "in the year 1567 the increase of lodges in the south of England being so great . . . it was resolved that a person under the title of Grand Master for the south, should be appointed with the approbation of the Grand Lodge at York, to whom the whole Fraternity at large were bound to pay tribute and acknowledge subjection."

If this statement were authentic it would not only confirm the fact that there was a Grand Lodge of York in the 16th century, but also that it exercised a supremacy over all the lodges of the kingdom.

Unfortunately for the interests of history the "Manifesto" of the Lodge of Antiquity was written for a particular object, which renders it partisan in character and suspicious in authority. And since there is no other evidence that in 1567 there was a Grand Lodge at York, or that it then appointed a Grand Master for the south of England, we are forced to dismiss this narrative of the Lodge of Antiquity with the Sackville story to the realm of fable, or at least of unsupported tradition.

The theory of the existence of a lodge at the city of York at the beginning of the 17th century is founded on the fact that in the year

---

[200] Bro. Woodford, in his very able article on "The Connection of York with the History of Freemasonry in England," appended to Bro. Hughan's "Unpublished Records of the Craft" (p. 170), seems to attribute the particularizing of this date to the unknown author of "Multa Paucis." But the fact is that this date is first mentioned by Dr. Anderson, in the 2d edition of the "Book of Constitutions," p. 81.

1777 there was in the possession of the Lodge of York a manuscript Constitution of the date 1630, which is presumed to have been written at the time for the lodge in that city.

Such is the implied reasoning of Bro. Woodford, and although not absolutely conclusive, it may be accepted as probable, especially as Bro. Hughan tells us that there is evidence that a lodge existed there in 1643.[201]

But the authentic history of that Society of Freemasons which met in the city of York, really begins with the year 1706.[202]

In the Inventory of Regalia and Documents which were in the possession of the Grand Lodge of all England taken by a committee in 1779, and which inventory is still in possession of the Lodge at York, one of the articles is recorded as being "A narrow folio Manuscript Book, beginning 7th March 1705-6, containing sundry Accounts and Minutes relative to the Grand Lodge."

This manuscript is now unfortunately mislaid or lost, but the report of the committee is satisfactory evidence that it once existed, and hence we have a sufficient proof that there was a lodge in the year 1706 and very probably long before in the city of York.

In a work entitled the Stream of English Freemasonry, by Dr. J.P. Bell, a list is inserted of Grand Masters, as the author calls them, from the year 1705. But as Bro. Hughan observes, the presiding officers were always styled Presidents or Masters until 1725, when the Grand Lodge was organized and the office of Grand Master adopted.

Now, between 1705 or 1706, when we get the first authentic records of the existence of a lodge of Freemasons in the city of York, until the year 1725, when it assumed the rank and title of a Grand Lodge, the condition of guild Masonry or Freemasonry appears, so far as we can judge from existing records, to have been in about the same condition as it was in London just before the establishment of a Grand Lodge in that city at nearly the same period, with this difference, that in London there were four lodges and in York only one.

We have seen that from a very early period the guild of Operative Freemasons had existed in independent lodges established near

---

[201] "London Masonic Magazine," vol. iii., p. 259.

[202] It has been usual to quote the date of the commencement of the Minute Book of old York Lodge as 1705. But in the original the date is "7th March 1705-6." But March 7, 1705, of the old style is, according to the new style, March 18, 1706. So also, some writers speak of the first meeting of the four lodges in London as occurring in 1716, because Anderson's date is February, 1716-17. They should remember that February, 1716-17, means always 1717.

the cathedrals or other public buildings in the construction of which they were engaged. We have seen this system pursued at the building of the Cathedral of York, and the written Constitutions which governed them then and there are extant in the Fabric Rolls of the Minster which have been published by the Surtees Society.

At that time the lodges were purely operative in their character.

Subsequently, as in Scotland and in the south of England, persons of distinction, who were not working Masons, were admitted among the Craft, and thus the system of Theoretic or Honorary Members of the lodge was established.

The result was the same here as it had been elsewhere. The Operative element gradually yielded to the Speculative, which at the beginning of the 18th century had become in York more completely dominant than it was in London at the same period.

The manuscript book of Minutes beginning in March, 1706, has been lost, but there is extant a Roll which begins March 19, 1712, or rather 1713, for it appears that there is the same confusion of styles. The next minutes according to Bro. Hughan are of June, August, and December, 1713, which clearly shows that the minutes for March are of the same year, unless we suppose that there was a lapse of more than a year in the meetings - a thing not at all supnosable.

At the lodge in March several members were sworn and admitted by Geo. Bowes, Esq., Deputy President. The Master was at that time a Speculative Freemason. In December, 1713, a "Private Lodge" was held, at which, says Hughan, "gentlemen were again admitted members, and at which Sir Walter Hawksworth, Knight and Baronet, was the President."

A General Lodge of the Honorable Society and Company of Freemasons," so ran the Minutes, was held on Christmas, 1716, by St. John's Lodge, when John Turner, Esq., was admitted to the Society. These Minutes are signed, "Charles Fairfax, Esq. Dep. Prest. "

All of which prove that at that time the Freemasons of York knew nothing of a Grand Lodge or a Grand Master, and that there was, even then, much more of the Speculative than of the Operative element in the Society.

From 1713 to 1725 there appears to have been but one lodge in the city of York, which did not, however, assume the title of a Grand Lodge, but in its minutes is called a "Private Lodge," and on a few occasions a "General Lodge." The presiding officer was called the President, who was assisted by a Deputy President.

There were at that time in the north of England many purely Operative lodges, and these as well as the York Lodge, which was more Speculative than Operative in its character, paid little or no attention to the proceedings of the Speculative Masons in London.

They gave no adherence to the Grand Lodge established in 1717, and were for a long time averse to the newly invented system by which Operative Freemasonry was displaced by a purely Speculative organization.

Still there were no signs of dissension while they all, in their implicit belief in the Legend of the Craft, assigned to the city of York the honor of being the birthplace of English Freemasonry. The Mother Lodge, as it was supposed to be, beheld without opposition the organization of the Grand Lodge at London, nor did it resist the Constitution in 1724 by that body of a lodge at Stockton-upon-Tees, in the adjoining county of Durham, nor of another in 1729 at Scarborough, in the county of York.

The fact is, that from 1713 to 1725 the 'Old Lodge at York,as Anderson calls it, appears to have exercised but little energy. From 1713 to 1716 it held, says Findel, but one or two yearly meetings, and none at all from 1717 to 1721, and only three meetings in the following two years.[203]

But the publication in 1723 of its Book of Constitutions by the Grand Lodge at London, appears to have awakened the Lodge of York into a new life.

For unless we suppose an improbable coincidence, it is very evident that some stimulus must have been applied to its energies, since in 1725 it met eleven and in 1726 thirteen times.[204]

The year 1725 was to the Lodge at York what the year 1717 had been to the four lodges of London. The same result was achieved, though the course adopted for attaining it was different.

The Grand Lodge at London had been formed by the union of four lodges, a method that has ever since been followed, except as to the precise number, in the organization of all modern Grand Lodges.

The Grand Lodge of York was established, if we can depend on the very meager details of history that have been preserved, by the simple change of title from that of a Private Lodge to that of a Grand Lodge. This change took place on December 27,1725, when the Grand Lodge was formed by the election of Charles Bathurst as Grand Master with a Bro. Johnson as his Deputy, and Bros. Pawson and Francis Drake as

---

[203] Findel, "History of Freemasonry," Lyon's Translation, p. 160
[204] Findel, ibid.

Wardens. Brothers Scourfield and Inigo Russel were respectively the Treasurer and Clerk.[205]

The Grand Lodge now openly denied the superior authority of the body which had been established in London eight years before, and while it was content that that organization should be known as the "Grand Lodge of England," it assumed for itself the more pretentious title of the "Grand Lodge of all England."

In thus constituting itself a Grand Lodge by a mere change of title, and the assumption of more extensive prerogatives, the Old Lodge at York" had asserted its belief in its own interpretation of the Legend of the Craft.

"You know," says Bro. Drake, its first Junior Grand Warden, Awe can boast that the first Grand Lodge ever held in England was held in this city; where Edwin, the first Christian king of the Northumbers, about the sixth hundredth year after Christ, and who laid the foundation of our cathedral, sat as Grand Master. This is sufficient to make us dispute the superiority with the lodges at London.

But as nought of that kind ought to be among so amicable a fraternity, we are content they enjoy the title of Grand Master of England; but the Totgus Angliae we claim as our undoubted right."

Francis Drake, the author of this passage, which is taken from a speech delivered by him before the Grand Lodge at its session of December 27, 1726, was an antiquary who is well known by a work in folio published by him in 1735 on the History and Antiquities of the City of York. He was in respect to Freemasonry the Desauliers of the Northern Grand Lodge. To him it was indebted for its first establishment and for the defense of its right to the position it had assumed.

Though he had been initiated only a year before his advancement to the position of Grand Warden, he seems to have taken at once a great interest in the institution and to have cultivated its history.

He was the first to advance the theory that the Edwin who is said in the Legend of the Craft to have convoked the General Assembly at York, was not the brother of Athelstan, but the converted King of Northumbria, and that the date of the Convocation was not in the 10th, but in the 7th, century.

This theory is now accepted by a great number of Masonic historians as the most plausible interpretation of the Legend.

---

[205] Hughan, "History of Freemasonry in York," p. 57, and Findel, p. 61.

Drake also exhibited in his speech a very sensible idea of what was the true origin of Freemasonry. He traces it to a purely Operative source, an opinion which is the favorite one of the historians of the present day.

The Grand Lodge at York, thus constructed by a mere change of title, had, in reality, by that act acquired a more plausible claim to be called a Revival" than the Grand Lodge at London. It assumed to be a resumption of its functions by a Grand Lodge which had always been in existence since the days of Edwin of Northumbria, and which had been dormant for only a few years.

If this theory were sound, most undoubtedly the establishment of the Grand Lodge in 1725 would have been a real revival. Unfortunately, the facts are wanting which could support such a theory. There is not the slightest evidence, except that which is legendary, that there ever was a Grand Lodge or a Grand Master in the city of York until the year 1725.

The fact is that, according to the modern principles of Masonic jurisprudence, the Grand Lodge of all England, as it styled itself, was not legally constituted, unless it be admitted that it was a mere continuation or revival of a former Grand Lodge at the same place. But this fact has not been established by any historical proof. The Grand Lodge was, therefore, really only a "Mother Lodge."

This system, where a private lodge assumes the functions and exercises the prerogatives of a Grand Lodge, under the title of a "Mother Lodge," was first invented by the French innovators at a later period, and never has been acknowledged as a legal method of constitution in any English- speaking country.[206]

Laurence Dermott[207] has asserted that to form a Grand Lodge it was necessary that the representatives of five lodges should be present. He had selected this number designedly to invalidate the Constitution of the Grand Lodge of England, which had been formed by four lodges. His authority on Masonic law is not considered as good, and now the principle appears to be settled by the constant usage of America, and by

---

[206] This is the very epithet applied by Drake to the Grand Lodge in his celebrated speech. He calls it "the Mother Lodge of them all." See the extract from the speech farther on in this chapter.
Except in Scotland, where the Lodge of Kilwinning assumed the title of "Mother Lodge," and issued warrants for Daughter Lodges. But the act was never recognized as legal by the Grand Lodge of Scotland.
[207] "Ahiman Rezon," p. xiii.

its recognition in Great Britain and Ireland, that the requisite number of constituent lodges shall be limited to not less than three.

Some idea of the kind seems to have prevailed at an early period among the Masons of the south of England, although it had not been formulated into a statute, for Anderson, in 1738, spoke of the body which had been established, not as the "Grand Lodge," but as "the old Lodge of York City."[208]

So much I have deemed it necessary to say as a curious point of history, but the question of the legal constitution of the Grand Lodge of York is no longer of any judicial importance, as it has long since ceased to exist, and the lodges which were constituted by it were, on its dissolution, legitimately enrolled on the register of the Grand Lodge of England.

Besides the change from a Private Lodge to a Grand Lodge, which was made in 1725, others were adopted at the same time, which are worthy of notice.[209]

In 1725 and afterward the meetings of the Grand Lodge, which heretofore had been held in private houses, were transferred to taverns, in which they followed the example of their southern brethren. The "Star Inn" and the "White Swan" are recorded in the minutes of the first places of meeting.

In the earlier minutes we find the Craft styling themselves "the Honourable Society and Company of Freemasons." In 1725 they adopted the designation of the "Worshipful and Ancient Society of Free and Accepted Masons." The adoption of the word "Accepted" assimilated the Freemasons of York to those of London, from whose Book of Constitutions the former evidently borrowed it.

The minutes after 1725 record the initiation of "gentlemen," and the speech of Junior Warden Drake at the celebration in 1726 refers to three classes, the "working Masons," those who "are of other trades and occupations," and "gentlemen."

---

[208] "Constitutions," 2d edition, p. 196.
[209] Findel and Hughan both visited the city of York at different periods and made a personal inspection of the lodge records. It is to the "History of Freemasonry," by the former, and to the "History of Freemasonry in York," by the latter, that I am indebted for many of my facts. Preston, though furnishing abundant details, is neither accurate nor impartial, and Anderson and his successors, Entick and Northouck, supply scarcely any information. Some intimation of the character of the Grand Lodge at the time of its establishment may be derived from the speech by Bro. Drake in 1726.

But there are many proofs in the records of the lodge that the second and third classes predominated, and that the Grand Lodge of York was earnestly striving, by the admission of non-Masons as members, to eliminate the Operative element, and, like its predecessor at London, to assume an entirely Speculative character.

It does not appear that at York there was that opposition to the change which had existed at London, where the Speculative element did not gain the control of the Society until six years after the organization in 1717.

The Lodge at York had begun to prepare for the change twelve years before it assumed the rank of a Grand Lodge, for, in 1713, at a meeting held at Bradford, eighteen "gentlemen" were admitted into the Society.

From the records we learn also that the "Regulations" adopted by the Grand Lodge at London were adopted for the government of the body at York. Indeed, it is very probable that the publication of these "Regulations" in 1723 had precipitated the design of the York Freemasons to organize their Grand Lodge.

There is no doubt that in the general details of their new system they followed the "Regulations" of 1723. The titles of the presiding officers were changed in accordance with the London system from President and Deputy President to Grand Master and Deputy Grand Master, and it is supposable that other changes were made to conform to the new "Regulations."

Indeed, Anderson expressly states that the lodge at York had "the same Constitutions, Charges, Regulations, etc., for substance as their Brethren of England," that is, of London.

But, in addition to the London "Regulations," the lodge at York had another set of rules for its government, which are still extant in the archives of the present York Lodge. They are contained on a sheet of parchment which is indorsed, "Old Rules of the Grand Lodge at York, 1725, No. 8."

These rules are said by both Findel and Hughan to have been adopted in 1725 by the new Grand Lodge. This is probable, because they are signed by "Ed. Bell, Master," who is recorded as having been the Grand Master in 1725; and they are subsequently referred to in the minutes of July 6, 1726, with the title of the "Constitutions."

But I think it equally probable that they were originally the rules which were made for the regulation of the lodge long before it assumed the rank and title of a Grand Lodge.

As the Constitution of a Grand Lodge, these rules are in remarkable contrast with the "Regulations" which were compiled by Payne for the use of the Grand Lodge at London and were published in the first edition of the Book of Constitutions.

They are nineteen in number, and with the exception of a single article - the eighth - they have the form of a set of rules for the regulation of a social and drinking club rather than that of a code of laws carefully prepared for the inauguration of a great moral and philosophical institution such as Speculative Freemasonry soon became, and such as it was evidently the design of Desaguliers, Payne, and Anderson to make it.

But even as the rules of a mere club they are interesting, inasmuch as they make us acquainted, by an official authority, with the condition of Speculative Freemasonry at York, and with the social usages of the Craft there, in the second and third decades of the 18th century.

As they have been published in full only by Bro. Hughan in his History of Freemasonry in York, a most valuable work but of which both the English and American editions were unfortunately too limited in the number of copies to make it generally accessible, I have, therefore, thought that it would not be unacceptable to the reader to find them reprinted here. A few marginal annotations have been added which are partly intended to prove the truth of the opinion that the rules were not framed in 1725 after the Grand Lodge had been established, but had been previously used for the government of the private lodge, and were only continued in force by the Grand Lodge.

Rules Agreed to be Kept and Observed by the Ancient Society of Freemasons in the City of York, and to be Subscribed by Every Member Thereof at Their Admittance Into the Said Society.[210]

Imprimis. 1. That every first Wednesday in the month a lodge shall be held, at the house of a Brother according as their turn shall fall out.[211]

---

[210] It will be remarked that the title "Ancient Society of Free and Accepted Masons" which was adopted by the Grand Lodge is not here used, but the "Ancient Society of Freemasons," which was the form employed by the "Private Lodge" in all the minutes prior to 1725. This is a very strong proof that the Rules were not framed after the Grand Lodge had been organized.

[211] Monthly meetings at the houses of different members in turn though appropriate enough for a private lodge, would scarcely have been adopted as a regulation by a Grand Lodge. In this article we clearly see what was the usage of the old lodge before it promoted itself to a higher rank.

2. All subscribers to these articles, not appearing at the Monthly lodge, shall forfeit sixpence each time.

3. If any Brother appear at a lodge that is not a subscriber to these articles, he shall pay over and above his club the sum of one shilling.[212]

4. The Bowl shall be filled at the monthly lodges with Punch once, Ale, Bread, Cheese and Tobacco in common, but if anything more shall be called for by any brother, either for eating or drinking, that Brother so calling shall pay for it, himself, besides his club.[213]

5. The Master or Deputy shall be obliged to call for a Bill exactly at ten o'clock, if they meet in the evening and discharge it.[214]

6. None to be admitted to the Making of a Brother but such as have subscribed to these articles.[215]

7. Timely notice shall be given to all the Subscribers when a Brother or Brothers are to be made.

---

[212] This article was evidently designed not for a Grand Lodge, but for the private lodge pursuing the social usages of a club. Freemasons who were not members of it might appear as visitors, but every visitor in addition to his "club," or share of the expenses of the evening which were equally distributed among all, was required to pay an additional shilling for the privilege of the visit.

[213] This article must satisfy us that the "Old Lodge at York" had adopted the usages of the age, and while it cultivated Masonry from its ancient associations, it, like other societies of that period in England, indulged its members with the rational enjoyment of moderate refreshment, but strictly provided, by regulation, against all excess. The bowl was to be filled with punch only once. Other lodges elsewhere had similar regulations; they firmed a part of the lodge organization in the beginning of the last century, when almost all associations assumed the form of clubs. But this very fact warrants us in believing that the rule was made for the government of the lodge, before it declared itself to be a Grand Lodge.

[214] The calling for the bill and the settlement of the expenses of the night's meeting is a rule that was universally adopted by all clubs. But mark the use of the word "Master" instead of "Grand Master." If these rules had been framed by the Grand Lodge in 1725, we may suppose that the latter title would have been employed.

[215] The Amaking" of Masons is no part of the business of a Grand Lodge. The London "Regulations," it is true, for a short time prescribed that Fellow-Crafts and Master Masons should be made in the Grand Lodge, but the "making of Masons," that is, the initiation of candidates into the Society, was always done in a particular or subordinate lodge. The Grand Lodge of York having, when it was established, no constituents, since it was formed by a self-transmutation from a lodge to a Grand Lodge, must, of course, have continued to initiate or make brothers. But the rule most probably was made when the lodge was in its primary condition.

8. Any Brother or Brothers presuming to call a lodge with a design to make a Mason or Masons, without the Master or Deputy, or one of them deputed, for every such offense shall forfeit Five Pounds.[216]

9. Any Brother that shall interrupt the Examination of a Brother shall forfeit one shilling.

10. Clerk's Salary for keeping the Books and Accounts shall be one shilling, to be paid him by each Brother at his admittance, and at each of the two Grand days he shall receive such gratuity as the Company shall think proper.

11. A Steward to be chose for keeping the Stock at the Grand Lodge, at Christmas and the Accounts to be passed three days after each lodge.[217]

12. If any dispute shall arise, the Master shall silence them by a knock of the Mallet; any Brother that shall presume to disobey, shall immediately be obliged to leave the Company or forfeit five shillings.[218]

13. A Hour shall be set apart to talk Masonry.[219]

14. No person shall be admitted into the lodge but after having been strictly examined.[220]

---

[216] We must not suppose that "to call a lodge" denoted to hold a new lodge without warrant. If that were the meaning, the rule must have been enacted by a Grand Lodge. But the true meaning was that no brothers should call a meeting of the lodge without the consent of the Master. This is strictly a lodge rule. And here again we mark that the authority for calling was to come, not from the Grand Master of the Grand Lodge, but from the Master of the lodge.

[217] In the whole of the nineteen rules this is the only one in which we find the title "Grand Lodge." The epithet "Grand," or perhaps the entire article was inserted, it is to be supposed, when the rules of the Old Lodge were adopted, confirmed or continued by it, when it became a self-constituted Grand Lodge. It was necessary to appoint a Treasurer, here called a Steward, to take charge of the stock or fund of the Grand Lodge and to account for all expenditures. I am inclined to believe that the rule, like the other eighteen, was originally framed by the lodge, but on account of the financial importance of the subject made more specific when it was adopted by the Grand Lodge, so as to define precisely what fund it was, that had been entrusted to the Steward.

[218] Note again the use of "Master" and not "Grand Master."

[219] "But one half-pennyworth of bread to this intolerable deal of sack!" An hour "to talk Masonry," once a month! Still, thankful for small favors, we recognize in this Article the connection of the club with the ancient Craft.

[220] That visitors were required to submit to an examination proves that the ritual practiced by the lodge at York was the same as that in common use by the Craft elsewhere. Otherwise there could be no satisfactory examination of visiting strangers.

15. No more persons shall be admitted as Brothers of this Society that shall keep a Public House.[221]

16. That these articles shall at lodges be laid upon the Table, to be perused by the Members, and also when any new Brothers are made, the clerk shall publickly read them.

17. Every new Brother, at his admittance, shall pay to the Waits,[222] as their Salary, the sum of two Shillings, the money to be lodged in the Steward's hands and paid to them at each of the Grand days.[223]

18. The Bidder of the Society shall receive of each new Brother, at his admittance, the sum of one shilling as his Salary.[224]

19. No money shall be expended out of the Stock after the hour of ten, as in the fifth article.

These rules appear to me to throw very considerable light upon the rather uncertain subject of the condition of Freemasonry in the city of York before and at the time of the establishment of what is known as the "Grand Lodge of all England."

Whether the usual theory that York was the birthplace of English Freemasonry, and that it was founded there in the Ioth century by Prince Edwin, the brother of King Athelstan, as the old manuscripts

---

[221] This was a very general and necessary rule with the clubs of the 18th century. As they were almost always held at taverns, it was deemed expedient to avoid any more friendly relation with the landlord than that of hired host and guests who paid their scot as they went.

[222] Waits, says Mr. Raine, in his "Glossary of the Fabric Rolls," are "musicians who still (1859) parade the towns in the north of England at Christmas-time. At Durhan they had a regular livery and wore a silver badge. Their musical abilities at the present time are not of the most striking character, but formerly they were deemed worthy enough to assist the choristers of the Minster." In the "Fabric Rolls" under the date of 1602 there is a charge "to the Waites for their musicke to the same do. Imbassiador, 13s. 4d." It was the Spanish Ambassador who was thus complimented at the expense of the Chapter during his visit to York. It is possible that as an extraordinary occasion a supper may have followed the initiation of a new brother, when the musical service of the Waites would be required to give zest to the entertainment.

[223] Grand Days, says Brady (Clavis, Calendaria I., 164), were Candlemas Day, Ascension Day, Midsummer Day, and All Saints' Day. They were so called in the Inns of Court. The lodge might, however, have had, as its Grand Days, the festivals of St. John the Baptist and of St. John the Evangelist. This is merely problematical.

[224] The members were to receive "timely notice" when a Brother was to be made (Rule 7). He who served the notices and summoned the members was called the " Bidder."

say, or in the 7th century by Edwin, King of Northumbria, as was, for the first time, advanced by Drake in his speech made in 1726 - whether this theory is to be considered as an historical statement, or merely an unsupported tradition, is a question that need not now be discussed.

The architectural history of the church, cathedral, or, as it is now commonly called, the Minster of York, may be comprised in a few lines.

In 627 a wooden church was built by Edwin, King of Northumbria, at the suggestion of Bishop Paulinus, who had converted him to Christianity. [225]

In 669 Bishop Wilfrid, the successor of Paulinus, made many important repairs and furnished the interior anew.

In 741, according to Roger Hovedon, the Minster was destroyed by fire.

In 767, according to Alcuin, who assisted in the work, Archbishop Albert erected a most magnificent basilica. This church, Raine thinks, was in existence at the time of the Norman Conquest, but in 1069 it was destroyed by fire.

In 1070 Bishop Thomas, the Norman, rebuilt the church from its foundations.

This church remained without alteration until 1171, when Archbishop Roger began to build a new choir. Raine doubts the story that the church of Archbishop Thomas was, in 1137, destroyed by fire.

In 1240 Archbishop Roger built the south transept, and immediately after commenced the building of the north transept.

In 1291 Archbishop John Romain laid the first stone of a new nave, which was completed in 1340 by Archbishop Melton. [226]

It is at about this period that we become, through the Fabric Rolls, familiarly acquainted with the usages of the Freemasons who were employed from that time to its completion in the construction of the Minster under the direction of the Chapter of the church.

In 1361 the Presbytery was begun and completed in 1373 by Archbishop Thoresby.

---

[225] Bede says that the wooden church was temporarily erected for the public baptism of the king, but that immediately afterward he began a large stone edifice which included the wooden one, which was finished by his successor, Oswald. "Hist. Eccles.," ii., 14

[226] So far I have been indebted for dates to the authority of Raine. Preface to "Fabric Rolls," pp. vii. et seq. What follows has been derived from R. Willis, "Architectural History of York Cathedral," p. 47.

In 1380 the choir was commenced, and the works being carried on without interruption, it was completed in 1400.

In 1405 the work of the central tower was begun and finished at an uncertain period.

In 1432 the southwestern tower was begun, and at a later date the northwestern tower was erected, both being completed about 1470, when the painted vault of the central tower was set up and finished.

In 1472, the work having been completed, the Cathedral was reconsecrated.

It is thus seen that for the long period of eight hundred and forty-five years, with intervals of cessation, the great work of building a cathedral in the city of York was pursued by Masons, most of whom were brought from the continent.

Roger, the Prior of Hexham, who lived in the 12th century, tells us that Bishop Wilfrid, while building the first stone church at York, brought into England Masons and other skillful artisans from Rome, Italy, France, and other countries wherever he could find them.[227]

Of the usages and regulations of these Masons, or of their organization as a guild or fraternity, we have no knowledge except that which is derived from conjecture or analogy.

But it is historically certain from the authority of the Fabric Rolls, to which such frequent reference has been made, that from the beginning of the 14th century Freemasons were employed in the construction of the cathedral which was then in course of erection, and that these Freemasons were organized into a body similar in its organization to that of the workmen who were engaged in the building of the cathedrals of Cologne and of Strasburg.

It is a singular coincidence, if it be nothing more, and it is certainly of great historical importance, that no manuscript Constitution yet discovered is claimed to have an older date than that of the 14th century, and about the time when the Freemasons of York were occupied in the construction of the cathedral of that city.

Hence it would not be an unreasonable hypothesis to suppose that the Freemasons who built the Cathedral of York in the 14th century were the original composers of the first of the "Old Constitutions," and of the Legend of the Craft which they all contain.

---

[227] De Roma, quoque, et Italia, et Francia, et de aliis terris ubicumque invenire poterat, cementarios, et quoslibet alios industries artifices secum retinuerat, et ad opera sua facienda secum in Angliam adduxerat. Roger, Prior, Hagulst. liber i., cap. 5.

This would rationally account for the fact that in this Legend the origin of Freemasonry in England, as a guild, is attributed to Masons who congregated in the city of York, and there held a General Assembly.

If the Freemasons of the southern part of England had been the fabricators of the first copy of these Constitutions, they would have been more likely in framing the Legend to have selected London or some southern city as the birthplace of their guild, than to have chosen for that honor a city situated in the remotest limits of the kingdom, and of which, from the difficulties of intercommunication, they would have no familiar knowledge.

But, on the other hand, nothing could be more natural than that the Freemasons who were living and working at York in the 14th century should have had a tradition among themselves that at some time in the remote past their predecessors had held a great convocation in their own city, and there and then framed that body of laws which were to become the Constitution of the Craft.

It is a self-evident proposition that there must have been a time when, and a place where, the first manuscript Constitution was written, and the Legend of the Craft was first committed to writing.

As to the time, we know of no manuscript that is older than the 14th century. The earliest is the Halliwell poem, and it has been assigned by competent authority to the year 1390. But there are good reasons for believing that the work published by Mr. Halliwell is really a compilation made up of two preceding poems, which might have been composed a few years before, and which would thus be brought to the very period when the Freemasons were at work on the York Cathedral.

As to the place where, we have only the internal evidence of the Legend of the Craft which, as I have before said, would indicate from the story of the Assembly at York that the Legend was fabricated by the Freemasons of that city out of a tradition that was extant among them.

That the Halliwell poem does not particularize the city of York by name as the place where the General Assembly was held, is no proof that it was not so stated in the unwritten tradition out of which the poem was constructed. The tradition was probably so well known, so familiar to the Masons at York, that the writer of the poem did not deem it necessary to define the Assembly further than by the name of him who called it. But two centuries after, when the Freemasons of the south of England began to make copies of the Legend, they found it necessary to follow the tradition more closely and to define York as the place where the Assembly was held.

And then, too, these southern English Freemasons sought to impair the claim of their northern Brethren, and thus in the Cooke MS., written more than a century after the Halliwell poem, the " Legend of St. Alban" is introduced, and the Masons of Verulam are said, instead of those of York, to have had "charges and maners" that is, Masonic laws and usages, "first in England."[228] But the later manuscripts admit the decay of Masonry after the death of St. Alban, and its subsequent revival at York.

Now, as the Halliwell poem speaks of the Assembly as having been held at "that syte," and as the subsequent manuscripts name that city as York, and retain the same tradition as the poem, we may, as Bro. Woodford justly says, fairly conclude that the "syte" or city in the Halliwell poem refers to York.

We need not absolutely determine, even if we could, whether Freemasonry was first established in England as a guild, at the city of York, as the earliest manuscript and the prototype of all the others says; or whether after its decadence subsequent to the rule of St. Alban, it was only revived in that city. Nor need we seek to settle the question whether the General Assembly was held and the Charges instituted by Edwin, the brother of Athelstan, in the Ioth century, as all the old manuscripts say, or by Edwin, King of Northumbria, in the 7th, as was first advanced by Mr.Drake in 1726 (a theory which has since been adopted by several scholars), or finally by the Freemasons who built the York Cathedral in the 14th century, which appears to me to be the most plausible of all the hypotheses.

This need not, however, affect the probability of the fact that similar organizations existed among the Freemasons who at the same time were employed in the constructions of cathedrals in other parts of England and Scotland, of whose existence we have historical certainty, but of whose customs and regulations we have no knowledge because their Fabric Rolls have been either irrecoverably lost or have not yet been discovered.

Accepting, then, any of the three theories which have just been alluded to, we will arrive at the conclusion that Freemasonry assumed at the city of York that form which was represented at first by the building corporations or Craft guilds, known as Operative lodges in the 14th, 15th, 16th, and 17th centuries, and which in the 18th underwent a transmutation into that system of Speculative Freemasonry of which the Masonic lodges of the present day are the lineal offspring.

---

[228] Cooke MS., line 608.

It is true that such an hypothesis is based on tradition only and on a recorded legend. But this tradition is so universal and is sustained by so much of logical inference and by so many collateral authentic circumstances, which can only be explained by a reference to that tradition, that the tradition itself becomes invested with an almost historical character.

Resuming, then, the history of the rise and progress of the Grand Lodge of all England, we find its germ in the guild of those Operative Freemasons who, certainly in the 14th and 15th centuries, were employed in the construction of the Cathedral of York, even if we do not choose to trace them to a remoter period.

There is no reason to suppose that there was a cessation of the labors of the York Lodge when the Cathedral was completed in 1472.[229] We infer not only that it continued to exist, but that it extended its influence, for there is abundance of proof that there were many lodges in other parts of England, and the old manuscript charges show that these lodges were all regulated by one common law and by similar usages.

But of the especial history of the lodge at York during the 16th century we have no authentic information. We infer, however, that it was in existence early in the 17th, because a manuscript copy of the "Old Constitutions" and the "Legend" was prepared for it in 1630. This manuscript was in the archives of the lodge in 1777, but was afterward lost.

There is also in the archives of the York Lodge another and a later manuscript Constitution which is still extant, and which bears the date of 1693. The lodge was, we may presume, at that time in active operation.

We have next an authentic record that the minutes of the lodge as early as 1704 were at one time in existence. These minutes have been unfortunately mislaid or lost, and the earliest records of the lodge which have been preserved, commence with the year 1712.

I will not cite the unreliable statements of Preston and some other writers, that there was a Grand Lodge and a Grand Master at York in the 16th century, because they are entirely without proof. We are studying history, not amusing ourselves with fiction.

But we do know that there was an Operative lodge at York about the close of the 14th century and for many years previous, and we

---

[229] As the church had been in fact rebuilt, it was reconsecrated on July 3, 1472, and that day was deemed to be the feast of the dedication of the church of York in future. Willis, "Architectural History of York Cathedral," p. 47.

also know that there was an Operative lodge in the same city about the beginning of the 17th century which was continued until the beginning of the 18th, and with no evidence to the contrary, we rightly infer that the one was the descendant or successor of the other.

Dr. J. P. Bell, in a work entitled the Stream of English History, gives a list of the presiding officers of the lodge from 1705 to 1781. I have not been able to get access to a copy of this work, and I am indebted for what I know of it to Bro. Hughan, who refers to it in his History of Freemasonry in York.

Hughan says that the List may be relied on. The author is, however, in error in assigning the title of Grand Master to the officers who presided from 1705 to 1724. They were, until the latter date, called "Presidents" or "Masters," and it was not until the lodge assumed the rank of a Grand Lodge in 1725 that the title of "Grand Master" was adopted.

Up to the year 1725 the lodge at York was strictlywhat it called itself, a "Private Lodge," and in its minutes it bears the name of St. John's Lodge.

Preston says that in 1705 there were several lodges in York and its neighborhood. But I fail to find any other proof of this fact than his own assertion. Unfortunately, the disputes between the Lodge of Antiquity, of which Preston was a member, and the Grand Lodge of England, in which the Grand Lodge of York took a part, had created such a partisan feeling in Preston and his friends against the former and for the latter body, that his authority on any subject connected with York Masonry is of doubtful value. His natural desire was to magnify the Grand Lodge which had taken his own lodge under its protection, and to depreciate the one against which it had rebelled.

Until the contrary is shown by competent authority we must believe that in 1705 there was but one lodge at York, the same which twenty years afterward assumed the title and functions of a Grand Lodge.

From its earliest records we find that, though this was an Operative lodge in name, because at that time all Masonic lodges were of that character, yet the Theoretic members greatly predominated in numbers over the practical or working Masons. It was thus gradually preparing the way for that change into a purely Speculative institution which about the same time was taking place in London.

It appears from the speech of the Junior Grand Warden, Drake, delivered before the Grand Lodge in 1726, that there were at that time three classes of members in the York Lodge, namely, "working

Masons, persons of other trades and occupations, and Gentlemen." To the first of these classes he recommended a careful perusal of the Constitution, to the second class he counselled obedience to the moral precepts of the Society, and attention to their own business, without any expectation of becoming proficients in Operative Masonry. "You cannot," he says, "be so absurd as to think that a tailor, when admitted a Freemason, is able to build a church; and for that reason, your own vocation ought to be your most important study." On the "gentlemen" only, did he impress the necessity of a knowledge of the arts and sciences, and he especially recommended to them the study of geometry and architecture.

Francis Drake,[230] the author of this Speech, was a scholar of much learning and an antiquary. Like his contemporary, George Payne, of the London Grand Lodge, whom he resembled in the nature of his literary pursuits, his ambition seems to have been to establish a system of pure Speculative Freemasonry, to be created by its total severance from the Operative element.

Something of this kind he distinctly expresses in the close of his Speech before the Grand Lodge.

"It is true," he says, addressing the Gentlemen or Theoretic members, "by Signs, Words, and Tokens, you are put upon a level with the meanest brother; but then you are at liberty to exceed them as far as a superior genius and education will conduct you.

I am creditably informed that in most lodges in London, and several other parts of this kingdom, a lecture on some point of geometry or architecture is given at every meeting. And why the Mother Lodge of them all should so far forget her own institutions can not be accounted for, but from her extreme old age. However, being now sufficiently awakened and revived by the comfortable appearance of so many worthy

---

[230] He was born in 1695, and in early life established himself at York as a surgeon and practiced, Britton says, with considerable reputation, but the investigation of antiquarian researches was his favorite pursuit. He published a "Parliamentary History of England to the Restoration" and many essays in the "Archaeologia" and in the "Philosophical Transactions." His principal work, however, and the one by which he is best remembered, was published at London in 1736 under the title of "Eboracum," or the "History and Antiquities of the City of York from its Original to the Present Time." From its title we learn that Drake was a Fellow of the Royal Society and a member of the Society of Antiquaries of London. The work is in two folio volumes and illustrated by many engravings, which, considering the most of them were donations to himself and his work, made by his wealthy patrons, might have been executed in a better style of art.

sons, I must tell you that she expects that every Gentleman who is called a Freemason should not be startled at a problem in geometry, a proposition in Euclid, or, at least, be wanting on the history and just distinctions of the five orders of architecture."

On December 27, 1725, the lodge resolved itself into a Grand Lodge (I know not how to use a better term), and Charles Bathurst, Esq., was elected Grand Master, with Mr. Johnson for his Deputy, and Messrs. Pawson and Drake, both of whom had been initiated in the previous September, as Grand Wardens.[231]

On the festival of St. John the Evangelist, in the following year,[232] Bathurst was again elected Grand Master, and the Society marched in procession to Merchants' Hall, where a Speech was delivered by Bro. Francis Drake, the Junior Grand Warden.

Like its sister of London, the Grand Lodge at York was troubled with schism at a very early period of its existence. [233]William Sourfield had convened a lodge and made Masons without the consent of the Grand Master or his Deputy. For this offense he was expelled, or as the Minutes say, "banished from the Society for ever."

It was agreed that John Carpenter, W. Musgrave, Th. Alleson, and Th. Preston, who had assisted Sourfield in his illegal proceedings, should, on their acknowledging their error and making due submission, be restored to favor.

Findel gives the following account of the subsequent proceedings which was taken by him from the Minutes of the Grand Lodge

"After the Minutes of December 22, 1726, a considerable space is left in the page,[234] and then follow the Minutes of June 21, 1729, wherein it is said that two Gentlemen were received into the St. John's Lodge and their election confirmed by vote: Edw. Thompson, Esq., Grand Master; John Willmers, Deputy Grand Master; G. Rhodes, and Reynoldson, Grand Wardens. The Grand Master on his part appointed

---

[231] Bro. Findel, who had inspected the Minutes while on a visit to York, says these officers are there called Wardens, and not Grand Wardens. "History of Freemasonry," p. 161.

[232] Findel gives this date as 1725, but he is clearly in error, as the printed title of the Speech states that it was delivered "on St. John's Day, December 27, 1726."

[233] The reader is reminded of the schismatic proceedings at the London Grand Lodge in 1722 in reference to the election of the Duke of Wharton as Grand Master.

[234] In Dr. Bell's List, heretofore cited, there are no names of Grand Masters in 1722 and 1728.

a Committee of seven brothers, amongst whom was Drake, to assist him in the management of the lodge, and every now and then support his authority in removing any abuses which might have crept in.

"The lodge was, however, at its last gasp, and therefore the Committee seem to have effected but little; for on May 4, 1730, it was found necessary to exact the payment of a shilling from all officers of the lodge who did not make their appearance and with this announcement the Minutes close."[235]

At this time, according to Findel, there were no lodges subordinate to the Grand Lodge. His statement, however, that after the meeting in May, 1730, it was inactive until 1760, is shown by the records to be not precisely accurate.

The fact is that the lodge, or the Grand Lodge, after 1729, must for some years have dragged out a life of inactivity. Bell's list shows that there were no Grand Masters (probably because there were no meetings) in 1730, 1731, and 1732. John Johnson, M.D., is recorded as Grand Master in, 1733, and John Marsden, Esq., in 1734.

There are no records of Grand Masters or of Proceedings from 1734 until 1761. During that period of twenty years, while the Grand Lodge of England was diffusing the light of Speculative Freemasonry throughout the world, the Grand Lodge of all England was asleep, if not actually defunct.

From this long slumber it awoke in the year 1761, and the method of its awaking is made known to us in the Minutes of the meeting which have been preserved.

As this event is one of much importance in the history of Freemasonry at York, I do not hesitate to copy the Minute in full.

The Ancient and Independent Constitution of Free and Accepted Masons, belonging to the City of York, was, this Seventeenth day of March, in the year of our Lord 1761, Revived by Six of the Surviving Members of the Fraternity by the Grand Lodge being opened, and held at the House of Mr. Henry Howard, in Lendall, in the said City, by them and others hereinafter named.

When and where it was farther agreed on that it should be continued and held there only the Second and Last Monday in every Month.

PRESENT:
Grand Master,

---

[235] "History of Freemasonry," p. 164

Brother Francis Drake, Esq., F.R.S.
Deputy G. M.
Brother George Reynoldson.
Grand Wardens
Brother George Coates and Thomas Mason.

VISITING BRETHREN:
Tasker, Leng, Swetnam, Malby, Beckwith, Frodsham, Fitzmaurice, Granger, Crisp, Oram, Burton, and Howard.

Minutes of the Transactions at the Revival and Opening of the said Grand Lodge:
Brother John Tasker was, by the Grand Master and the rest of the Brethren, unanimously appointed Grand Secretary and Treasurer, he having just petitioned to become a Member and being approved and accepted Brother Henry Howard also petitioned to be admitted a Member, who was accordingly ballotted for and approved Mr. Charles Chaloner, Mr. Seth Agar, George Palmes, Esq., Mr. Ambrose Beckwith, and Mr. William Siddall petitioned to be made Brethren the first opportunity who, being severally ballotted for, were all approved of This Lodge was closed till Monday, the 23d day of this instant Month, unless in case of Emergency.

The Grand Lodge, thus revived, had at first and for some years but one constituent lodge under its obedience, or, to speak more correctly, the Grand Lodge of all England and the Lodge at York were really one and the same body. While it claimed the title and the prerogatives of a Grand Lodge, it also performed the functions of a private lodge in making Masons. But it afterward increased its constituency, and in the year 1769 granted Warrants for opening lodges at Ripon, at Knaresborough, and at Iniskilling.

In 1767 the Grand Lodge of England, at London, had addressed a report of the business done at its quarterly communication to a lodge held at the Punch Bowl, in the city of York, and to which lodge it had granted a Warrant, as No. 259, on the 12th of January, 1761.

But this lodge having ceased to exist, the document appears to have fallen into the hands of the Grand Master of the York Grand Lodge. It was laid before the Grand Lodge at a meeting held on the 14th December, 1767, when it was resolved that a letter should be sent by the Grand Secretary to the Grand Lodge at London.

In this letter the pretensions of the York Grand Lodge are set forth in very emphatic terms. It is stated that "the Most Ancient Grand Lodge of all England, held from time immemorial in this city (York), is the only Lodge held therein."

It is also stated that "this Lodge acknowledges no Superior, that it exists in its own Right, that it grants Constitutions and Certificates in the same manner as is done by the Grand Lodge in London, and as it has from Time immemorial had a Right and used to do, and that it distributes its own Charity according to the true principles of Masons."

Hence it does not doubt that the Grand Lodge at London will pay due respect to it and to the Brethren made by it, professing that it had ever had a very great esteem for that body and the brethren claiming privileges under its authority.

Findel says that "a correspondence with the Grand Lodge of England in London, in the year 1767, proves that the York Lodge was then on the best of terms with the former."[236]

I confess that I fail to find the proof of this feeling simply because there is no proof of the correspondence of which Findel speaks. A correspondence is the mutual interchange of letters. The Grand Lodge in London had sent an official communication to a lodge in the city of York, ignoring, in so doing, the Grand Lodge of York. This was itself an act of discourtesy. The lodge having been discontinued, this communication comes into the possession of the Grand Lodge at York, for which it had not been originally intended. It sends to the Grand Lodge at London a letter in which it asserts its equality with that Grand Lodge and the immemorial right that it had to grant Warrants, which right it trusts that the Grand Lodge in London will respect.

It appears to me that this language, if it means anything, is a mild protest against the further interference of the London Grand Lodge, with the territorial jurisdiction of the Grand Lodge in York.

It is true that in the close of the letter the York Grand Lodge expresses its esteem for the Body at London and its willingness to concur with it in anything that will affect the general good of Masonry.

The letter was dignified and courteous. It asserted rights and prerogatives, which it need not have done if they had not been invaded, and it made the offer of a compact of friendship.

To this letter there is no evidence that the Grand Lodge of England deigned to make a reply. It was treated with frigid silence, and hence there was no correspondence between the two bodies.

---

[236] "History of Freemasonry," p. 166.

Bro. Hughan, however, concurs with Bro. Findel, so far as to say that this letter is of much consequence in proving that the two Grand Lodges were on excellent terms.[237]

I am very reluctant to differ with two such authorities on Masonic history, but I can not consider that the conclusion to which Bro. Hughan has arrived is a legitimate one. The letter certainly shows a desire on the part of the Grand Lodge of York to cultivate friendly relations with that in London. But there is no evidence that the amicable feeling was reciprocated.

On the contrary, all the records go to show that the Grand Lodge at London was aggressive in repeated acts which demonstrated that it did not think it necessary to respect the territorial rights of the Masonic authority at York.

In 1738 Dr. Anderson speaks of it not as a Grand Lodge, but as "the Old Lodge at York" which he says "affected independence." It was evidently, in his opinion, merely a lodge that was unwilling to place itself under obedience to his own Grand Lodge.

That the Grand Lodge of England refused to recognize the authority of the lodge at York in its sovereign capacity as a Grand Lodge having territorial jurisdiction over the north of England or even over the two Ridings of Yorkshire is shown by the records. In 1729, four years only after the lodge at York had assumed the title of a Grand Lodge, the Grand Lodge of England constituted a lodge at Scarborough; in 1738 another at Halifax; in 1761, a third and fourth at the city of York, and at Darlington the one two months before and the other three months after the York Grand Lodge had been resuscitated; in 1762, a fifth at Orley; in 1763, a sixth at Richmond; and in 1766, a seventh at Wakefield, all situated within the county of York, and one in the very city where the Grand Lodge held its sessions.

It is not surprising that the York Grand Lodge in time resorted to reprisals, and as will presently be seen, most decidedly invaded the jurisdiction of the Grand Lodge at London.

Dr. Bell, in his History of the Grand Lodge of York,[238] says that "the two Grand Lodges continued to go on amicably until the year 1734, when in consequence of the Grand Lodge of England having granted Warrants, out of its prescribed jurisdiction, shyness between the lodges ensued."

---

[237] "History of Freemasonry in York." p. 70.
[238] "History of the Provincial Grand Lodge of North and East Yorkshire, Including Notices of the Ancient Grand Lodge of York," cited by Bro. Hughan in his "History of Freemasonry in York," p. 45.

Both Bell and Findel, who make the same statement as to a lodge warranted in 1734, are wrong as to the date, for no lodge was constituted in York by the Grand Lodge of England in that year. But as it had constituted one in 1729, I am ready to give credit to the account of the "shyness." The mistake of a date will not affect the existence of the feeling.

Preston commits the same error as Bell and Findel concerning the Constitution of two lodges in York in 1734.[239] But he adds what is of importance, considering his intimacy with the subject, that the Grand Lodge in York highly resented the encroachments of the Grand Lodge of England on its jurisdiction and "ever after seems to have viewed the proceedings of the Brethren in the South with a jealous eye; as all friendly intercourse ceased, and the York Masons from that moment considered their interests distinct from the Masons under the Grand Lodge in London."[240]

Soon after the revival of the Grand Lodge it was visited by Preston and Calcott, two distinguished Masonic writers, and Hughan supposed that about this time the Royal Arch degree was introduced into the York system by the latter. This subject will, however, be more appropriately considered in a distinct chapter devoted to the history of that degree.

From the time of its re-opening in 1761 until near the close of the 18th century the Grand Lodge appears to have flourished with considerable activity.[241]

---

[239] It is from Preston that Bell and Findel have derived their authority for the statement of lodges having been constituted in 1734. Bro. Hughan investigated the subject with his wonted perseverance and says that "there is no register of any lodge being warranted or Constituted in Yorkshire or neighborhood in A.D. 1734. We have searched every List of Lodges of any consequence from A.D. 1738 to A.D. 1784, including the various editions of the Constitutions, Freemason's Calendars, Companions and Pocket Books, etc., but can not find any "Deputation granted within the jurisdiction of the Grand Lodge of all England, during 1734 by the Grand Lodge of England." "History of Freemasonry in York," p. 47.

[240] Preston, Jones edition, p. 214.

[241] Findel says that from 1765 the name of "Bro. Drake is seldom mentioned." If we consider that at that date Drake had reached the seventieth year of his age, and that five years afterward, in 1770, he died, we will find ample cause in the infirmities of age for his withdrawal from participation in the active duties of Masonic labor.

The festival of St. John the Evangelist was celebrated in 1770 by a procession to church, and a sermon on the appropriate text "God is love." Representatives from the three lodges at Ripon, Knaresborough, and Iniskilling were present. Sir Thomas Gascoigne was elected Grand Master.[242]

In the same year a Warrant was granted for the Constitution of a lodge at Macclesfield in Cheshire, so that there were now at least four subordinates acknowledging obedience to the York Grand Lodge.

A controversy having sprung up between the Lodge of Antiquity in London and the Grand Lodge of England, the former body withdrew from its allegiance to the latter, and in 1778 received a Warrant from the Grand Lodge of York, authorizing it to assemble as a Grand Lodge for all that part of England situated to the south of the river Trent.

This episode in the history of the Freemasonry of England, which involved very important results, demands and must receive a more detailed consideration in a distinct chapter.

It is scarcely necessary to pursue the minute history of the Grand Lodge of York from that period to the date of its final collapse.

The last reference in the minutes of the lodge at York to the Grand Lodge of all England has the date of August 23, 1792. It is a rough minute on a sheet of paper, which records the election of Bro. Wolley as Grand Master, George Kitson as Grand Treasurer, and Richardson and Williams as Grand Wardens.[243]

We have no evidence from any records that the Grand Lodge ever met again. It seems to have silently collapsed; the lodge at York continued its existence as a private lodge, and finally came under the jurisdiction of the Grand Lodge of England.

---

[242] This baronet was a lineal descendant of Nicholas Gascoigne, the brother of that celebrated Chief Justice who in the reign of Henry IV. committed the heir apparent to the throne, the "Merry Prince Hal," to prison for contempt of court. He was a native and resident of Yorkshire, having seats at Barstow, Lasingcroft, and Parlington, all in the county.
See Kimber and Johnson's "Baronetage of England," London, 1771, vol.iii., P. 352.
[243] Hughan, " History of Freemasonry in York," p. 79.

In fact, as the Rev. Bro. Woodford has stated, the York Grand Lodge was never formally dissolved, but simply was absorbed, so to say, by the predominance of its more prosperous southern rival of 1717.[244]

In bringing this history of the rise and progress of Speculative Freemasonry in the city of York to a close, I am almost irresistibly impressed with the opinion that the "Old Lodge at York" was never, in the legal sense of the word, a Grand Lodge. It was not formed, like the Grand Lodge at London, by the union and co-operation of several private lodges.

It was never recognized as such by the Grand Lodge of England, but was always known as the "Old Lodge at York."

Anderson so called it in 1738, and his successor, Northouck, writing in 1784, says of it that "the ancient York Masons were confined to one lodge, which is still extant, but consists of very few members, and will probably be soon altogether annihilated."[245]

It was simply, like the lodges of Kilwinning in Scotland and of Marseilles in France, a "Mother Lodge," a term which, in Masonic language, has been used to denote a private lodge which, of its own motion, has assumed the prerogatives and functions of a Grand Lodge by granting Warrants. This title was applied to it by Drake, its Junior Grand Warden, when he delivered his "Speech" in 1726, the year after it had assumed the attitude of a Grand Lodge.

But it continued at all times to exercise the function of a "making Masons," a function which has been invariably delegated by Grand Lodges to their subordinates.

As late as the year 1761, when, after a long slumber, the Grand Lodge was revived, one of its first acts was to ballot for five candidates who were, on the first opportunity, initiated by it.

In the rules adopted for its government in 1725 the title of "Lodge" is used by it five times as the designation of the Society, and that of "Grand Lodge" only once in reference to the funds.

Their rules are signed by Ed. Bell, who calls himself not "Grand Master," but simply "Master." In the vacillating position in which the Freemasons of York had placed themselves, between a desire to imitate their London brethren by establishing a Grand Lodge and a reluctance to abandon the old organization of a private lodge, they entirely lost

---

[244] The connection of York with the "History of Freemasonry in England," by A.F.A. Woodward, A.M., in Hughan's "Unpublished Records of the Craft," p. 172.
[245] Northouck, " Book of Constitutions," p. 240.

sight of the true character of a Grand Lodge, as determined by the example of 1717.

It is not, therefore, surprising, as Bro. Hughan remarks, that these rules should offer a strange contrast to the Constitutions of the Grand Lodge of England which had been published two years before.

There can, however, be little or no doubt, as the same astute writer has observed, that in consequence of the publication of the London Constitutions the Freemasons of York is began to stir themselves and to assume the prerogatives of a Grand Lodge."

It is to be regretted that in borrowing from their Brethren the title of a Grand Lodge, the York Freemasons did not also follow their example by adopting the same regularity of organization.

In view of all these facts it is impossible to recognize the body at York in any other light than that of a Mother Lodge, a body assuming, without the essential preliminaries, the prerogatives of a Grand Lodge, while to the body established at London in 1717 must be conceded the true rank and title of the Mother Grand Lodge of the World, from which, directly or indirectly, have proceeded as its legitimate offspring all the Grand Lodges which have been organized in the 18th and 19th centuries.

Now, what must we infer from these historical facts? This and no more nor less: that there never was, as a legitimate organization, a Grand Lodge of York or a Grand Lodge of all England, but only a Mother Lodge in the city of York, which assumed the title and prerogatives of a Grand Lodge, but exercised the functions both of a Grand and a private lodge - an anomaly unknown to and unrecognized by Masonic law.

CHAPTER XL

ORGANIZATION OF THE GRAND LODGE OF SCOTLAND

It is much easier to write the history of the organization of the Grand Lodge of Scotland than that of England. The materials in the former case are far more abundant and more authentic, and the growth of the organization was more gradual, and each step more carefully recorded.

In England almost the only authority or guide that we have for the occurrences which led to the establishment of the Grand Lodge, in the year 1717, is the meager history supplied by Anderson in the second edition of the Book of Constitutions.

The four old Lodges suddenly sprung, as we have already seen, into being, with no notification of their previous existence, and no account of the mental process by which their members were led to so completely change their character and constitution from the Operative to a purely Speculative institution.

In Scotland, on the contrary, the processes which led to the change are well marked - the previous condition of the lodges is recorded, and we are enabled to trace the distinct steps which finally led to the establishment of the Grand Lodge in the year 1736.

It would appear from historical evidence that in the 17th century there were three methods by which a new lodge could be formed in Scotland.

The first of these was by the authority of the King, the second by that of the General Warden, perhaps the most usual ways and the third was by members separating from an old and already established lodge, and with its concurrence forming a new one, the old lodge becoming, in technical terms, the mother, and the new one. the descendant.

All of these methods are referred to in a minute of the Lodge of Edinburgh in the year 1688. A certain number of the members of that lodge having left it, without its sanction formed a new lodge in the Cannongate and North Leith. Whereupon the Lodge of Edinburgh declared the Cannongate and Leith Lodge to have acted "contrary to all custom, law, and reason," inasmuch as it had been formed in contempt of the Edinburgh Lodge, and " without any Royal or General Warden's authority." This is said to be "Mason Law," and for its violation the lodge was pronounced illegal, all communication with its members, or with those who were entered or passed in it, was prohibited, and it was forbidden to employ them as journeymen under a heavy penalty. In a word, the lodge was placed in the position of what, in modern parlance, we should call "a clandestine lodge."

But the old law for the organization of new lodges seems by this time to have become obsolete, and the denunciation of the Edinburgh Lodge amounted to a mere brutum fulmen. The Cannongate and Leith Lodge continued to exist and to flourish, and almost a half century afterward was recognized, notwithstanding its illegal birth, as a regular body, and admitted into the constituency of the Grand Lodge.

We may therefore presume that at or about the close of the 17th century the Scottish lodges began to assume the privileges which Preston says at that time belonged to the English Masons, when any number could assemble and, with the consent of the civil authority, organize themselves into a lodge.

At the beginning of the 18th century there were many lodges of Operative Masons in Scotland, which had been formed in one of the three ways already indicated. The two moist important of these were the Lodge of Edinburgh and that of Kilwinning. The latter especially had chartered several lodges, and hence was by its adherents called the Mother Lodge of Scotland, a title which was, however, disputed by the Lodge of Edinburgh and never was legally recognized.

A preliminary step to the establishment of a Speculative Grand Lodge must have necessarily been the admission into the ranks of the Operative Craft of non-professional members. We have seen the effect of this in the organization of the Grand Lodge of England. In Scotland the evidences of the result of the admission of these non-professionals is well shown in the minutes of the Lodge of Edinburgh. The contentions between the Operative and the non-operative elements for supremacy, and the final victory of the latter, are detailed at length. If such a spirit of contention existed in England, as an episode in the history of its Grand Lodge, no record of it has been preserved.

The earliest instance of the reception of a non-professional member is that of Lord Alexander, who was admitted as a Fellow Craft in the Lodge of Edinburgh on July 3, 1634. On the same day Sir Alexander Strachan was also admitted.

But the mere fact that these are the first recorded admissions of non- operatives among the Craft does not necessarily lead us to infer that before that date non-operatives were not received into lodge membership.

On the contrary, there is a minute of the date of the year 1600 which records the fact that the Laird of Auchinleck was present at a meeting of the Lodge of Edinburgh, and as one of the members took part in its deliberations. William Schaw, who was recognized as the General Warden and Chief Mason of Scotland in 1590, was, most probably, not an Operative Mason. Indeed, all the inferential evidence lies the other way.

Yet his official position required that he should be present at the meetings of the lodges, which would lead to the necessity of his being received into the Craft. The same thing is pertinent to his predecessors, so that it is very evident that the custom of admitting non-operatives among the Craft must have been practiced at a very early period, perhaps from the very introduction of Masonry into Scotland, or the 13th century.

It will be seen hereafter how this non-operative element, as it grew in numbers and in strength, led, finally, to the establishment of a non- operative or Speculative Grand Lodge.

But attention must now be directed to another episode in the history of Scottish Masonry, namely, the contests between the Masters and the Journeymen, which also had its influence in the final triumph of Speculative over Operative Masonry.

Taking the Lodge of Edinburgh as a fair example of the condition and character of the other lodges of the kingdom, we may say that during all of the 17th century there was observed a distinction between the Master Masons or employers and the Fellow Crafts or Journeymen who were employed.

The former claimed a predominant position, which the latter from necessity but with great reluctance conceded. It was only on rare occasions that the Masters admitted the Fellows to a participation in the counsels of the lodge.

This assumption of a superiority of position and power by the Masters was founded, it must be admitted, upon the letter and spirit of the Schaw Statutes of 1598 and 1599.

In these Statutes the utmost care appears to have been taken to deprive the Fellows of all power in the Craft and to bestow it entirely on the Wardens, Deacons, and Masters.

Thus the Warden was to be elected annually by the Masters of the lodge, all matters of importance were to be considered by the Wardens and Deacons of different lodges to be convened in an assembly called by the Warden and Deacon of Kilwinning; all trials of members, whether Masters or Fellows, were to be determined by the Warden and six Masters; all difficulties were to be settled in the same way. In a word, these Statutes seem to have passed over the Fellows in the distribution of power and concentrated it wholly upon the Masters.

But this evidently very unjust and unequal distribution of privileges appears toward the middle of the 17th century, if not before, to have excited a rebellious spirit in the Fellows.

This is very evident from the fact that from the year 1681 enactments began to be passed by the Lodge of Edinburgh against the encroachments of the Fellows or Journeymen, who must have at or before that time been advancing their claim to the possession of privileges which were denied to them. "Though there can be no doubt," says Lyon, "that all who belonged to the lodge were, when necessity required, participants in its benefits, the journeymen appear to have had the feeling that it was not right that they should be entirely dependent, even for fair treatment, on the good-will of the Masters."

It was in fact but a faint picture of that contest for supremacy between capital and labor, which we have since so often seen painted in much stronger colors. The struggle in the Masonry of Scotland began to culminate in the year 1708, when a petition was laid before the Lodge of Edinburgh from the Fellows, in which they complained that they were not permitted to inspect the Warden's accounts.

The lodge granted the petition, and agreed that thereafter "six of the soberest and discretest Fellow-Craftsmen" should be appointed by the Deacon to oversee the Warden's accounts. The lodge also granted further concessions and permitted the Fellow Crafts to have a part in the distribution of the charity fund to widows.

But these concessions do not appear to have satisfied the Fellows, who, as Lyon supposes, must have been guilty of decided demonstrations, which led the lodge in 1712 to revoke the privilege of inspecting the accounts that had been conferred by the statute of 1708.

This seems to have brought matters to a climax. At the same meeting the Fellow Crafts who were present, except two, left the room and immediately proceeded to organize a new lodge known afterward as the Journeymen's Lodge. Every attempt on the part of the Masters' Lodge to check this spirit of independence and to dissolve the schismatic lodge, though renewed from time to time for some years, proved abortive. The Journeymen's Lodge continued to exercise all the rights of a lodge of Operative Masons, and to enter Apprentices and admit Fellows just as was done by the Masters' Lodge from which it had so irregularly emanated.

Finally, in 1714, the most important and significant privilege of giving the "Mason Word" was adjudged to the Lodge of Journeymen by a decree of Arbitration.

The lodge, now perfected in its form and privileges, flourished, notwithstanding the occasional renewal of contests, until the organization of the Grand Lodge, when it became one of its constituents.

There can, I think, be no doubt that this independent action of the Journeymen Masons of Edinburgh led to an increase of lodges, when the prestige and power of the incorporated Masters had been once shaken.

Twenty-four years after the establishment of the Journeymen's Lodge we find no less than thirty-two lodges uniting to organize the Grand Lodge of Scotland.

Another event of great importance in reference to the history of the Grand Lodge is now to be noticed. I allude to the process through which the Masons of Scotland attained to the adoption of a Grand Master as the title of the head of their Order.

There can be no doubt that the Grand Lodge of Scotland was organized upon the model of that of England, which had sprung into existence nineteen years previously. As the English Grand Lodge had bestowed upon its presiding officer the title of Grand Master, it was very natural that the Scotch body, which had derived from it its ritual and most of its forms, should also derive from it the same title for its chief.

But while we have no authentic records to show that previous to 1717 the English Masons had any General Superintendent, under any title whatever, it is known that the Scottish Masons had from an early period an officer who, without the name, exercised much of the powers and prerogatives of a Grand Master.

On December 28, 1598, William Schaw enacted, or to use the expression in the original document, "sett down" certain "statutes and ordinances to be observed by all Master Masons" in the realm of Scotland. In the heading of these Statutes he calls himself "Master of Work to his Majesty and General Warden of the said Craft." In a minute of the Lodge of Edinburgh, of the date of 1600, he is designated as "Principal Warden and Chief Master of Masons."

Now in the Statutes and Ordinances just referred to, as well as in a subsequent code of laws, ordained in the following year, there is ample evidence that this General Warden exercised prerogatives very similar to those of a Grand Master and indeed in excess of those exercised by modern Grand Masters, though Lyon is perfectly correct in saying that the name and title were unknown in Scotland until the organization of the Grand Lodge in 1736.[246]

The very fact that the Statutes were ordained by him and that the Craft willingly submitted to be governed by codes of laws emanating from his will - that he required the election of Wardens by the lodges to be submitted to and to be confirmed by him, "that he assigned their relative rank to the lodges of Edinburgh, of Kilwinning, and of Stirling," and that he delegated or "gave his power and commission" to the lodges to make other laws which should be in conformity with his Statutes - proves, I think, very conclusively that if he did not assume the title of Grand Master of Masons of Scotland, he, at all events, exercised many of the prerogatives of such an office.

It is true that it is said in the preamble to the Statutes of 1598 that they are "sett down" (a term equivalent to "prescribed") by the General Warden "with the consent of the Masters;" but the acceptance of such consent was most likely a mere concession of courtesy, for the Statutes of 1599 are expressly declared in many instances to be "ordained by the General Warden," and in other instances it is said that the law or regulation is enacted because "it is thought needful and expedient by the General Warden." All of which shows that the Statutes were the result of the will of the General Warden and not of the Craft. That the Masters accepted them and consented to them afterward was very natural as a matter of necessity. There might have been a different record had they been uncompliant and refused assent to regulations imposed upon them by their superior.

Therefore, though the theory of the existence of Grand Masters in Scotland under that distinctive title at a period anterior to the organization of the Grand Lodge must be rejected as wholly untenable, it

---

[246] Except in 1731, when the Lodge of Edinburgh elected its presiding officer under the title of Grand Master. This was, however, entirely local, and was almost immediately abandoned.

can hardly be denied that William Schaw, under the name of General Warden, did, at the close of the 16th century, exercise many of the prerogatives of the office of Grand Master.

Schaw died in 1602, and with him most probably died also the peculiar prerogatives of a General Warden, but the Scottish Craft appear not to have been in consequence without a head.

This leads us to the consideration of the St. Clair Charters, documents of undoubted authenticity but which have been used by Brewster in Laurie's History, under a false interpretation of the existence of the office of Grand Master of Masons in Scotland, from the time of James II., an hypothesis which has, however, been proved to be fallacious and untenable.

There are two ancient manuscripts in the repository of the Grand Lodge of Scotland, which are known by the title of the St. Clair Charters. The date of the first of these is supposed to be about the year 1601, and is signed by William Schaw as Master of Work, and by the office-bearers of five different lodges. The date of the other is placed by Lyon, with good reason, at 1628. It is signed by the office-bearers of five lodges also.

In the Advocates' Library of Edinburgh there is a small manuscript volume known as the "Hays MSS." which contains copies of these charters, not materially or substantially varying from the originals in the repository of the Grand Lodge.

The genuineness of these original manuscripts is undeniable. Whatever we can derive from them in relation to the position as signed by the Scottish Craft to the St. Clairs of Roslin in the beginning of the 17th century will be of historical value.

By them alone we may decide the long-contested question whether the St. Clairs of Roslin were or were not Hereditary Grand Masters of the Masons of Scotland. The Editor of Laurie's History of Freemasonry asserts that these charters supply the proof that the grant to William Sinclair as Hereditary Grand Master was made by James II. Mr. Lyon contends that the charters furnish a conclusive refutation of any such assertion. The first of these opinions has for a long time been the most popular. The last has, however, under more recent researches been now generally adopted by Masonic scholars. An examination of the precise words of the two charters will easily settle the question.

The first charter, the date of which is 1601, states (transmuting the Scottish dialect into English phrase) that "from age to age it has been observed among us that the Lords of Roslin have ever been patrons and protectors of us and our privileges, and also that our predecessors have obeyed and acknowledged them as patrons and protectors, which within these few years has through negligence and slothfulness passed out of use." It proceeds to state that in consequence the Lords of Roslin have been deprived of their just rights and the Craft subjected to much injury by being "destitute of a patron, protector, and overseer." Among the evils complained of is that various controversies had arisen among the Craftsmen for the settlement of which by the ordinary judges they were unable to wait in consequence of their poverty and the long delays of legal processes.

Wherefore the signers of the charter for themselves and in the name of all the Brethren and Craftsmen agree and consent that William Sinclair of Roslin shall for himself and his heirs purchase and obtain from the King liberty, freedom, and jurisdiction upon them and their successors in all time to come as patrons and judges of them and all the professors of their Craft within the realm (of Scotland) of whom they have power and commission.

The powers thus granted by the Craft to the Lord of Roslin were very ample. He and his heirs were to be acknowledged as patrons and judges, under the King, without appeal from their judgment, with the power to appoint one or more deputies. In conclusion the jurisdiction of the Lords of Roslin was to he as ample and large as the King might please to grant to him and his heirs.

The second charter was issued in 1628 by the Masons and Hammermen of Scotland. It repeats almost in the same words the story contained in the first that the Lords of Roslin had ever been patrons and protectors of the Scottish Craft, and adds the statement that there had been letters patent to that effect issued by the progenitors of the King, which had been burnt with other writings in a fire which occurred in a year not stated within the Castle of Roslin.

The William Sinclair to whom the previous charter had been granted having gone over to Ireland, the same evils complained of in the beginning of the century were renewed, and the Craft now in this second charter grants to Sir William Sinclair of Roslin the same powers and prerogatives that had been granted to his father, as their "only protector, patron, and overseer."

The contents of these two charters supply the following facts, which must be accepted as historical since there is no doubt of the genuineness of the documents.

In the first place there was a tradition in the beginning of the 17th century, and most probably at the close of the 16th, if not earlier, that the Sinclairs of Roslin had in times long passed exercised a superintending care and authority over the Craft of Scotland.

This superintendence they exercised as protectors, patrons, and overseers, and it consisted principally in settling disputes and deciding controversies between the brethren without appeal, which disputes and controversies would otherwise have to be submitted to the decision of a court of law.

The tradition implied that this office of protectorate of the Craft was hereditary in the house of Roslin, but had not been exercised continuously and uninterruptedly, but on the contrary had, in the beginning of the 17th century, been long disused.

It is true that there is no reference in the first charter to any crown grant, at least in explicit terms, but it speaks of the Lord of Roslin as lying out of his "just right" by the interruption in the exercise of the prerogative of patron, and if he had or was supposed to have such "just right," then the implication is strong that it was founded on a royal grant. The second charter is explicit on this subject and asserts that the record of the grant had been destroyed by a conflagration. This statement is very probably a myth, but it shows that a tradition to that effect must have existed among the Craft.

We may imply also from the language of the first charter that the Craft were in some doubt whether by this non-user the hereditary right had not been forfeited, since it is required by them that Sinclair should "purchase and obtain" from the King permission to exercise the jurisdiction of a patron and judge. In fact the sole object of the charter was to authorize William Sinclair to get the royal authority to resume the prerogatives that had formerly existed in his family. Whether the Craft were correct in this judgment, and whether by lying in abeyance the hereditary right had lapsed and required a renewal by the royal authority are not material questions. It is sufficient that such was the opinion of the Scottish Masons at the time.

Lastly, the two charters are of historical importance in proving that at the time of their being issued, the title of Grand Master was wholly unknown to the Craft.

The Editor of Laurie's History is, therefore, entirely unwarranted in his theory, which, however, he presents as an undoubted historical fact that the Sinclairs of Roslin were "Hereditary Grand Masters of Scotland."

Equally unwarranted is he in making Kilwinning, in Ayrshire, the seat of his mythical Grand Lodge, not, as has been urged by Bro.

Lyon, because the Sinclairs[247] had no territorial connection with Ayrshire, but simply because there is not the least historical evidence that Kilwinning was the center of Scottish Masonry, though the lodge in that village had assumed the character of a Mother Lodge and issued charters to subordinates.

The true historical phase which these charters seem to present is this: In the 17th century, or during a part of it, the Operative Masons of Scotland adopted the family of Sinclair of Roslin as their patrons and protectors, and as the umpires to whom they agreed to refer their disputes, accepting their decisions without appeal, as a much more convenient and economical method of settling disputes than a reference to a court of law would be. Out of this very simple fact has grown the mythical theory, encouraged by fertile imaginations, that they were Grand Masters by royal grant and hereditary right.

The immediate superintendence of the Scottish Masons seems, however, to have continued to be invested in a General Warden. In 1688, when there was a secession of members from the Lodge of Edinburgh, who established an independent lodge in the Canongate, one of the charges against them was that they had "erected a lodge among themselves to the great contempt of our society, without any Royal or General Warden's authority."

But the St. Clairs were the patrons and the General Wardens were the Masters of Work, while no reference was made to nor any word said of the title or the prerogatives of a Grand Master.

The point is, therefore, historically certain that there never was a Grand Master in Scotland until the establishment of the Grand Lodge, in 1736.

As early as the year 1600 we find the record of the admission of a non- professional into the Lodge of Edinburgh. The custom of admitting such persons as honorary members continued throughout the whole of the 17th century. Before the middle of the century, noblemen, baronets, physicians, and advocates are recorded in the minutes as having been admitted as Fellow-Crafts. The evidence that at that time the Speculative element had begun to invade the Operative is not confined to the minutes of the Lodge of Edinburgh. There are records proving that the same custom prevailed in other lodges.

Much importance has rightly been attached to the fact that there is an authentic record of the admission of two gentlemen into an

---

[247] The modern spelling of the name is St. Clair, but I have for the present retained the form of Sinclair to be in conformity with the orthography of the charter.

English lodge of Operative Masons in the year 1646. There are numerous instances of such admissions before that time in Scottish lodges. Indeed it has been well proved by records that it was a constant habit, from about 1600, in the Scottish lodges, to admit non-masons into the Operative lodges.

There ought not to be a doubt that the same practice prevailed in England at the same time. That there is no proof of the fact is to be attributed to the absence of early English lodge minutes. The Scottish Masons have been more careful than the English in preserving their records.

The minutes of the Scottish lodges, and the one authentic record contained in Ashmole's Diary, furnish sufficient evidence that in the 17th century the Operative Masons were admitting into their society men of wealth and rank, scholars, and members of the learned professions. This was undoubtedly the first step in that train of events which finally led to the complete detachment of the theoretic from the practical element, and the organization of the present system of Speculative Freemasonry.

The change from an Operative to a Speculative system was very sudden in England. At least, if the change was gradual and foreseen, we can not now trace the progress of events because of the absolute want of records.

In Scotland the change was well marked and its history is upon record. It was much slower than that in England. It was not until nineteen years after the Grand Lodge of England was organized that a similar organization took place in Scotland. And whereas the English lodges all assumed the Speculative character at once, after the Grand Lodge was established, and abandoned Operative Masonry altogether, some of the Scottish lodges, for many years after their connection with the Grand Lodge of Speculative Masonry, retained an Operative character, mingled with the Speculative.

The closing years of the 17th century were marked in Scotland by contests between the Masters and the Journeymen Masons, the former having long secured the dominant power. These contests led in the Lodge of Edinburgh to a secession of the Fellow Crafts, who having been denied certain privileges, formed an independent lodge, which after some years of conflict with the Mother Lodge received by a decree of arbitration the power of admitting Apprentices and Fellow-Crafts and what appears to have been deemed of vast importance, the privilege of communicating the "Mason Word."

This seems to have been at that time the sum of esoteric instruction received by candidates on their admission.

Another cause of contest in Scottish Masonry at that period was the growing custom of receiving non-professional members into the lodges of Operative Masons. This custom had originated at least a century before, and there are records in the 17th century from its very commencement of the presence in the lodges as members of persons who were not Operative Masons. But in the early part of the 18th century the practice grew to such an extent that at a meeting of the Lodge of Edinburgh in the year 1727, out of sixteen members present only three were operative Masons. And in the same year a lawyer was elected as Warden or presiding officer of the lodge.

In the year 1700 there were several lodges in various parts of Scotland.

Although perhaps all of them contained among their members some persons of rank or wealth who were not Masons by profession, still the lodges were all Operative in their character.

Seventeen years afterward the English Operative Masons had merged their society into a Speculative Grand Lodge. The influence of this act was not slow to extend itself to Scotland, where the non-professionals began slowly but surely to dominate over the professional workmen.

In 1721 Dr. John Theophilus Desaguliers, who was the principal founder of the Grand Lodge of England, paid a visit to Edinburgh. He was received as a brother by the lodge, and at two meetings held for the purpose, several gentlemen of high rank were admitted into the fraternity.

As the records of these meetings are of historic importance, as showing the introduction of the new English system of Speculative Masonry into Scotland, I shall not hesitate to give them in the very words of the minute- book, as copied from the original by Bro. Lyon.

"Likeas (likewise) upon the 25th day of the sd moneth (August 1721) the Deacons, Warden, Masters, and several other members of the Societie, together with the sd Doctor Desaguliers having mett att Maries Chapell, there was a supplication presented to them by John Campbell Esqr. Lord Provost of Edinbr., George Preston and Hugh Hathorn, Bailies; James Nimo, Thesuarer, William Livingston Deacon convener of the Trades thereof; and Geroge Irving Clerk to the Dean of Guild Court, - and humbly craving to be admitted members of the sd Societie; which being considered by them, they granted the desire thereof, and the saids honourable persons were admitted and receaved Entered Apprentices and Fellow Crafts accordingly.

"And siclike upon the 28th day of the said moneth there was another petition given in by Sr. Duncan Campbell of Locknell, Barronet; Robert Wightman Esqr., present Dean of Gild of Edr.; George Drummond Esq., late Theasurer thereof; Archibald McAuley, late Bailly there; and Patrick Lindsay, merchant there, craveing the like benefit, which was also granted, and they receaved as members of the societie as the other persons above mentioned. The same day, James Key and Thomas Aikman servants to James Wattson, deacon of the Masons, were admitted and receaved Entered Apprentices and payed to James Mack, Warden the ordinary dues as such."

There can be no doubt that the object of Desaguliers in visiting Scotland at that time was to introduce into the Scottish lodges the esoteric ritual so far as it had been perfected by himself and his colleagues for the Masons of England. Bro. Lyon very properly suggests that the proceedings of the lodge on that occasion "render it probable that taking advantage of his social position, he had influenced the attendance of the Provost and Magistrates of Edinburg and the other city magnates who accompanied them as applicants for Masonic fellowship in order to give a practical illustration of the system with which his name was so closely associated with a view to its commending itself for adoption by the lodges of Scotland."[248]

Hence in these two meetings we see that the ceremonies of entering and passing were performed a or, in other words, that the two new degrees of Entered Apprentice and Fellow-Craft, as practiced in the Grand Lodge of England, were introduced to the Scottish Masons. The degree of Master was not conferred, and for this omission Bro. Lyon assigns a reason which involves an historic error most strange to have been committed by so expert and skilled a Masonic scholar as the historian of the Lodge of Edinburgh and the translator of Finders work.

Bro. Lyon's words are as follows: "It was not until 1722-23 that the English regulation restricting the conferring of the Third Degree to Grand Lodge was repealed. This may account for the Doctor confining himself to the two lesser degrees."[249]

But the facts are that the regulation restricted the conferring of the Second as well as the Third degree to the Grand Lodge; that this regulation, instead of being repealed in 1722-23, was not promulgated until 1723, being first published in the Thirty-nine Articles contained in

---

[248] Lyon, "History of the Lodge of Edinburgh," p. 152.
[249] Ibid., p. 153.

the Book of Constitutions of that date; and that it was not repealed until 1725.

Now if it be said that the restriction existed before it was promulgated, having been approved June 24, 1721, and was known to Desaguliers, it would have prevented him from conferring the Second as well as the Third degree.

If, however, the regulation was in force in England in 1721, which I have endeavored heretofore[250] to prove to be very doubtful, Desaguliers, in violating it so far as respected the Second degree, showed that he did not conceive that it was of any authority in Scotland, a country which was not under the jurisdiction of the Grand Lodge of England.

If so, the question arises, why did he not, at the same meeting, confer the Third degree?

The answer is that the Third degree had not yet been fabricated. In the task of formulating a ritual for the new system of Speculative Masonry, Desaguliers, Anderson, and the others, if there were any who were engaged with them in the task, had, in 1721, proceeded no further than the fabrication of the ritual of the First and Second degrees. These degrees only, therefore, he communicated to the Masons of Edinburgh[251] on his visit to the lodge there. Subsequently, when the Third degree had received its form, it was imparted to the Masons of Scotland. Of the precise time and manner of this communication we have no record, but we know that it took place before the Grand Lodge of Scotland was organized. Lyon says that the year 1735 is the date of "the earliest Scottish record extant of the admission of a Master Mason under the modern Masonic Constitution."[252]

The visit of Desaguliers and the events connected with it develop at least two important points in the history of Scottish Masonry.

In the first place, we notice the great increase of non-professional members over the working craftsmen, so that in six or seven years after that visit the Speculative element had gained the supremacy over the Operative which led, in the second place, to the adoption of various forms indicative of the growing influence of Speculative Masonry, such as the change of the title of the presiding officer from

---

[250] When treating of the origin of the three degrees.
[251] The connection of this visit of Desaguliers to Edinburgh with the history of the fabrication of the three degrees of Symbolic Masonry has already been discussed in a previous chapter devoted to that subject.
[252] "History of the Lodge of Edinburgh," p. 213.

"Warden" to that of "Master," and the substitution, in the nomenclature of the Craft, of the word "Freemason" for the formerly common one of "Mason."

From all this, and from certain proceedings in the years 1727, 1728, and 1729 connected with the contests between the Theoretic and the Operative members of the lodges, "it may be inferred," says Bro. Lyon, "that, departing from the simplicity of its primitive ritual and seizing upon the more elaborate one of its Southern contemporaries, and adapting it to its circumstances, the ancient lodge of the Operative Masons of Edinburgh had, in a transition that was neither rapid nor violent, yielded up its dominion to Symbolical Masonry and become a unit in the great Mystic Brotherhood that had started into existence in 1717."[253]

The next step that was naturally to be taken was the establishment of a Grand Lodge in close imitation in its form and Constitution of that of the similar body which had been previously instituted in the sister kingdom.

The record of the occurrences which led to this event is much more ample than the meager details preserved by Anderson of the establishment of the Grand Lodge of England, so that we meet with no difficulty in writing the history.

It had long been supposed, on the authority of the History attributed to Laurie, that the Scottish Masons had been prompted to first think of the institution of a Grand Lodge in consequence of a proposition made by William St. Clair of Roslin to resign his office of "Hereditary Grand Master." This is said to have been done in 1736. Lyon, however, denies the truth of this statement, and says that more than a year before the date at which St. Clair is alleged to have formally intimated his intention to resign the Masonic Protectorate, the creation of a Grand Mastership for Scotland had been mooted among the brethren.[254]

The authentic history is perhaps to be found only in the pages of Lyon's History of the Lodge of Edinburgh, and from it I therefore do not hesitate to draw the material for the ensuing narrative.

On September 29, 1735, at a meeting of Canongate Kilwinning Lodge, a committee was appointed for the purpose of "framing proposals to be laid before the several lodges in order to the choosing of a Grand Master for Scotland." At another meeting, on October 15th, the same

---

[253] "History of the Lodge of Edinburgh," p. 160.
[254] Ibid., p. 167

committee was instructed to "take under consideration proposals for a Grand Master."

On August 4, 1736, John Douglas, a surgeon and member of the Lodge of Kirkcaldy, was affiliated with the Lodge of Canongate Kilwinning and appointed Secretary, that he might make out "a scheme for bringing about a Grand Master for Scotland."

On September 20th the lodge was visited by brethren from the Lodge Kilwinning Scots Arms, who made certain proposals on the subject.

The matter was now hastening to maturity, for on October 6th the Canongate Kilwinning Lodge met for the purpose, as its minutes declare, of "concerting proper measures for electing a Grand Master for Scotland." Proposals were heard and agreed to. The four lodges of Edinburgh were to hold a preliminary meeting, when proper measures were to be taken for accomplishing the desired object.

Accordingly delegates from the four Edinburgh lodges, namely, Mary's Chapel, Canongate Kilwinning, Kilwinning Scots Arms, and Leith Kilwinning, met at Edinburgh on October 15, 1736. It was then resolved that the four lodges in and about Edinburgh should meet in some convenient place to adopt proper regulations for the government of the Grand Lodge, which were to be sent with a circular letter to all the lodges of Scotland. A day was also to be determined for the election of a Grand Master, when all lodges which accepted the invitation were to be represented by their Masters and Wardens or their proxies.

The circular, which brought a sufficient number of lodges together at the appointed time to institute a Grand Lodge and elect a Grand Master, is in the following words:

"Brethren: The four lodges in and about Edinburgh, having taken into their serious consideration the great loss that Masonry has sustained through the want of a Grand Master, authorized us to signify to you, our good and worthy brethren, our hearty desire and firm intention to choose a Grand Master for Scotland; and in order that the same may be done with the greatest harmony, we hereby invite you (as we have done all the other regular lodges known by us) to concur in such a great and good work, whereby it is hoped Masonry may be restored to its ancient luster in this kingdom. And for effectuating this laudable design, we humbly desire that betwixt this and Martinmas day next, you will be pleased to give us a brotherly answer in relation to the election of a Grand Master, which we propose to be on St. Andrew's day, for the first time, and ever thereafter to be on St. John the Baptist's day, or as the Grand Lodge shall appoint by the majority of voices, which are to be collected from the Masters and Wardens of all the regular lodges then present or by proxy to any Master Mason or FellowCraft in any lodge in Scotland; and the election is to be in St. Mary's Chapel. All that is hereby proposed is for the advancement and prosperity of Masonry in its greatest and most charitable perfection. We hope and expect a suitable return; wherein if any lodges are defective, they have themselves only to blame. We heartily wish you all manner of success and prosperity, and ever are, with great respect, your affectionate and loving brethren."

This circular letter was accompanied by a printed copy of the regulations which had been proposed and agreed to at the meeting. By these regulations the Grand Master was to name the new Grand Wardens, Treasurer, and Secretary, but the nomination was to be unanimously approved by the Grand Lodge, and if it was not these officers were to be elected by ballot. The requirement of unanimity would be very certain to place the choice of most occasions in the Grand Lodge. The Grand Master was to appoint his own Deputy, provided he was not a member of the same lodge. There were to be quarterly communications, at which the particular lodges were to be represented by their Masters and Wardens with the Grand Master at their head. There was to be an annual visitation by the Grand Master with his Deputy and Wardens of all the lodges in town. There was to be an annual feast upon St. John's day, and several other regulations, all of which were evidently copied from the Articles adopted in 1721 by the Grand Lodge of England and published in 1723 in the first edition of its Book of Constitutions.

There were several meetings of the four Edinburgh lodges, and finally, on November 25, 1736, it was agreed that the election of Grand Master should take place in Mary's Chapel on Tuesday, November 30, 1736.

But while these preliminary meetings were being held a rivalry sprung up (as might have been anticipated from the nature of human passions) between two of the lodges, in the choice of the proposed Grand Master.

The Lodge of Edinburgh nominated for that office the Earl of Home, who was one of its members. But the Canongate Kilwinning Lodge, which was really the prime instigator of the movement for the institution of a Grand Lodge, was unwilling to surrender to another lodge the honor of providing a ruler of the Craft.

William St. Clair, who, notwithstanding the high claims advanced for his family does not appear to have taken any interest in Masonry, had been received as an Apprentice and Fellow-Craft only six months before (May 18, 1736) by the Canongate Kilwinning Lodge, and had been raised to the Third degree only eight days before the election, was placed before the fraternity by the lodge of which he was a recent member, as a proper candidate for the Grand Mastership It will be seen in the subsequent details of the election that the Canongate Kilwinning Lodge availed itself of a strategy which might have been resorted to by a modern politician.

What Lyon calls "the first General Assembly of Scotch Symbolical Masons" was, according to agreement, convened at Edinburgh on Tuesday, November 30, 1736. There were at that time in Scotland about one hundred particular lodges. All of them had been summoned to attend the convention, but of these only thirty-three were present, each represented by its Master and two Wardens.

While in this scanty representation, only one-third of the lodges having responded to the call, we see that the interest in the legal organization of the Speculative system and the complete abandonment of the Operative had not been universally felt by the Scottish Craft, we find in the method of conducting the meeting that the spirit and forms of the English Constitution had been freely adopted by those who were present.

The list of the lodges which united in the establishment of a Grand Lodge is given both by Laurie's Editor and by Lyon, and it is here presented as an important part of the historical narrative. The lodges present were as follows:

Mary's Chapel, Dumfermling, Kilwinning, Dundee, Canongate Kilwinning, Dalkeith, Kilwinning Scots Arms, Aitcheson's Haven, Kilwinning Leith, Selkirk, Kilwinning Glasgow, Inverness, Coupar of Fife, Lesmahagoe, Linlithgow, St. Brides at Douglas, Lanark, Peebles, Strathaven, Glasgow St. Mungo's, Hamilton, Greenock, Dunse, Falkirk, Kirkcaldy, Aberdeen, Journey Masons of Edinburgh, Mariaburgh, Kirkintilloch, Canongate and Leith, Biggar, Leith and Canongate, Sanquhar, Montrose.

After the roll had been called, and the draft of the Constitution with the form of proceedings had been submitted and approved, St. Clair of Roslin tendered a document to the convention which was read as follows:

"I, William St. Clair of Roslin, Esquire, taking into my consideration that the Masons in Scotland, did, by several deeds, constitute and appoint William and Sir William St. Clairs of Roslin, my ancestors and their heirs to be their Patrons, Protectors, Judges or Masters; and that my holding or claiming any such jurisdiction, right or privilege might be prejudicial to the Craft and vocation of Masonry, whereof I am a member, and I being desirous to advance and promote the good and utility of the said Craft of Masonry, to the utmost of my power, do therefore hereby, for me and my heirs, renounce, quit claim, overgive and discharge all right, claim or pretence that I or my heirs, had, have or anyways may have, pretend to or claim, to be Protector, Patron, Judge or Master of the Masons in Scotland, in virtue of any deed or deeds made and granted by the said Masons, or of any grant or charter made by any of the Kings of Scotland, to and in favour of the said William and Sir William St. Clairs of Roslin, my predecessors; or any other manner or way whatsoever, for now and ever.

And I bind and oblige me and my heirs to warrant this present renunciation and discharge at all hands. And I consent to the registration hereof in the books of Council and Session or any other judges' books competent, therein to remain for preservation, and thereto I constitute . . .

my procurators, etc. In witness whereof I have subscribed these presents (written by David Maul, Writer to the Signet) at Edinburgh, the twenty- fourth day of November, one thousand seven hundred and thirty-six years, before these witnesses, George Frazer, deputy auditor of the excise in Scotland, Master of the Canongate Lodge, and William Montgomery, Merchant in Leith, Master of the Leith Lodge."

This document was signed by W. St. Clair and attested by the two witnesses above mentioned. The reading of it at the opportune moment, just before the election of Grand Master was entered upon, is the strategical point to which reference has already been made. It succeeded in securing, as had been expected by the promoters of the scheme, the immediate election of William St. Clair as the first Grand Master of the Grand Lodge of Scotland.

As a legal instrument the renunciation of his ancestral rights by St. Clair is worthless. Whatever prerogatives he may have supposed that he possessed as a Masonic "Protector, Patron, Judge and Master," referred exclusively to the Guild of Operative Masonry, and could not by any stretch of law have been extended to a voluntary association of Speculative Masons, the institution of which was expressly intended to act as a deletion of the Operative organization whose design and character were entirely cancelled and obliterated by the change from a practical art to a theoretical science. The laws of Operative Masonry can be applied to Speculative Masonry only by a symbolic process. If the Lords of Roslin had even been the "Hereditary Grand Masters" of the stonecutters and builders who were congregated in a guild spirit in the

Operative lodges of Scotland, it did not follow that they were by such hereditary right the Grand Masters of the scholars and men or rank, the clergymen, physicians, lawyers, and merchants who, having no connection or knowledge of the Craft of Masonry, had united to establish a society of an entirely different character.

But in a critical point of view in reference to the traditional claims of the St. Clairs to the Hereditary Grand Mastership, this instrument of renunciation is of great value.

It is but recently that the historians of Freemasonry have begun to doubt the statement that James II. of Scotland had conferred by patent the office of Grand Master on the Earl of Orkney, the ancestor of the St. Clairs and on his heirs. Brewster had boldly asserted it in the beginning of the present century, and although it has been more recently doubted whether such patent was issued, the statement continues to be repeated by careless writers and to be believed by credulous readers.

Now the language used by St. Clair its his renunciation before the Grand Lodge of Scotland must set this question at rest. He refers not to any patent granted to his original ancestors the Earls of Orkney, but to the two charters issued in 1601 and 1628 in which not the king but the Masons themselves had bestowed the office of patrons and protectors, first on William St. Clair and afterward on his son.

James Maidment, Advocate, the learned Editor of Father Hay's Genealogie of the Saint Claires of Roslyn, comes to this conclusion in the following words:

AThus the granter of the deed, who it must be presumed was better acquainted with the nature of his rights than any one else could be, derives his title from the very persons to whom the two modern charters were granted by the Masons; and in the resignation of his claim as patron, etc., exclusively refers to these two deeds or any 'grant or charter made by the Crown,' not in favor of William Earl of Orkney, but of William and Sir William St. Clair, the identical individuals in whose persons the Masons had created the office of patron."

But in the excitement of the moment the representatives of the lodges were not prepared to enter into any such nice distinctions.

The apparent magnanimity of Mr. St. Clair in thus voluntarily resigning his hereditary claims had so fascinating an influence that though many of them had been instructed by their lodges to vote for another candidate, St. Clair was immediately elected Grand Master with great unanimity.

The remaining offices were filled by the election of Capt. John Young as Deputy Grand Master; Sir William Baillie as Senior Grand

Warden; Sir Alexander Hope as Junior Grand Warden; Dr. John Moncrief as Grand Treasurer; John Macdougal, Esq., as Grand Secretary; and Mr. Robert Alison, Writer, as Grand Clerk.

Upon the institution of the Grand Lodge nearly all the lodges of the kingdom applied for Warrants of Constitution and renounced their former rights as Operative lodges, acknowledging thereby the supreme jurisdiction of the Grand Lodge as the Head of Speculative Masonry in Scotland.

In a review of the proceedings which finally led to the establishment of a Speculative Grand Lodge in Scotland, several circumstances are especially worthy of remark.

It has been seen that from a very early period, as far back as the close of the 16th century, theoretical Masons, or persons who were a part of the working Craft, had been admitted as members of the Operative lodges.

The custom of receiving non-professionals among the brethren was gradually extended, so that in the early years of the 18th century the non- professional members in some of the lodges greatly exceeded the professional.

In this way the transition from Operative to Speculative Masonry was made of easy accomplishment, so that when the Grand Lodge was established, several of the leading lodges which were engaged in the act of organization were already Speculative lodges in everything but the name.

Another event, which exerted a great influence in hastening the change in Scotland, was the visit of Desaguliers in the year 1721 to Edinburgh. He brought with him the ritual of Speculative Masonry, so far as it had then been formulated in England, and introduced it and the newly adopted English lodges into Scotland. Lyon refers to the formation of the Lodge Kilwinning Scots Arms in February, 1729, as one of the results of the Masonic communication between the northern and the southern capitals, which had been opened by this visit of Desaguliers. It was from the beginning a purely Speculative lodge, all of its original members having been theoretical Masons, chiefly lawyers and merchants. It was one of the four Edinburgh lodges which were engaged in the preliminary steps for the organization of the Grand Lodge.

As an evidence of how extensively the theoretical principle had spread, so that the scheme of abandoning the Operative character of the institution must have been easily effected, it may be stated that of the twelve hundred brethren returned to the Grand Lodge as members of the several lodges represented at the first election of officers in that body, one half were persons not engaged in mechanical pursuits.[255]

The influence of English Masonry is also seen in the fact that in the middle of the 17th century the English Legend of the Craft was known to and used by the Aitcheson's Haven Lodge of Musselburg and the Lodge of Edinburgh as well as other Scottish lodges and was in all probability used in the initiation of candidates. As the two manuscripts which still remain in Scotland are known from their form and language to have been copies of some of the old English Records of the "Legend" and "Charges," no better evidence than the use of them by Scottish lodges could be needed to prove that the English Masonry had been constantly from the 17th century exerting a dominating influence upon the Craft in Scotland which finally culminated in the organization of the Grand Lodge.

Finally, the Grand Lodge of Scotland presents an important and marked peculiarity in the cause and manner of its institution.

The first Grand Lodge of Speculative Masons ever established was the Grand Lodge of England organized in the year 1717 at London. From this Grand Lodge every other Grand Lodge in the world, with one exception, has directly or indirectly proceeded. That is to say, the Grand Lodge of England established in foreign countries either lodges which afterward uniting, became Grand Lodges, or it constituted Provincial Grand Lodges which, in the course of time and through political changes, assumed independence and became national supreme bodies in Masonry.

But however instituted as Grand Lodges, they derived, remotely, the authority for their legal existence from the Grand Lodge of England, so that that venerable body has very properly been called the "Mother Grand Lodge of the World."

The single exception to this otherwise universal rule is found in the Grand Lodge of Scotland. Of all Grand Lodges it alone has derived no authority for its constitution from the English body. The Scottish lodges existed contemporaneously with the English; at a very early period they admitted non-professional members and they began at the beginning of the 18th century to take the preliminary steps for their conversion from an Operative to a Speculative character. In this they were undoubtedly influenced by the English Masons, who about the same time had begun to contemplate the expediency of a similar conversion.

---

[255] Lyon, "History of the Lodge of Edinburgh," p. 176.

But although while the Scottish lodges, in organizing their Grand Lodge, were undoubtedly led to take the necessary steps by the previous action of the English lodges, and while they borrowed much of the forms and imitated the example of their English brethren, they derived from them no authority or warrant of Constitution.

The Masonry of Scotland produced from its own Operative lodges its Speculative Grand Lodge, precisely as was the case with the Masonry of England. And in this respect it has differed from the Masonry of every other country where the Operative element never merged into the Speculative, but where the latter was a direct and independent importation from the Speculative Grand Lodge of England, wholly distinct from the Operative Masonry which existed at the same time.

CHAPTER XLI

THE ATHOLL GRAND LODGE, OR THE GRAND LODGE OF ENGLAND
ACCORDING TO THE OLD INSTITUTIONS

THE first important event in the history of English Freemasonry which seriously affected the harmony of the Fraternity, was the schism which occurred in the year 1753. The interposition of a new and rival authority in the north of England by the self-constitution of a Grand Lodge at the city of York in the year 1725, seems to have created no embarrassment, save in its immediate locality, to the Grand Lodge at London.

The sphere of its operations was limited to its own narrow vicinity, nor, until nearly half a century after its organization, did it seek, by traveling beyond those meager limits, to antagonize, in the south of the kingdom, the jurisdiction of the body at London.

But the schism which commenced at London and in the very bosom of the Grand Lodge in the year 1753, and to the history of which this chapter shall be dedicated, was far more important in its effects, not only on the progress of Speculative Masonry in England, but also in other countries.

The Grand Lodge, which in the above-mentioned year was organized as a successful rival and antagonist of the regular Grand Lodge, has received in the course of its career various names. Styling itself officially the "Grand Lodge of England according to the Old Institutions," it was also called, colloquially, the "Grand Lodge of Ancients," both designations being intended to convey the vain-glorious boast that it was the exponent of a more ancient system of Freemasonry than that which was practiced by the regular Grand Lodge, which had been in existence only since 1717. Upon that later system, as it was asserted to be, the Schismatics bestowed the derogatory designation of the "Grand Lodge of Moderns." And so the schismatic body having been formed by a secession from the regular and constitutional Grand Lodge, its members were often called the "Seceders." Subsequent writers have been accustomed to briefly distinguish the two rival bodies as the "Moderns" and the "Ancients;" without however any admission on the part of the former of the legal fitness of the terms, but simply for the sake of avoiding tedious circumlocutions.

Another and a very common title bestowed upon the schismatic body was that of the "Atholl Grand Lodge," because the Dukes of Atholl, father and son, presided over it for many successive years, and it has also been sometimes called the "Dermott Grand Lodge," in allusion to Laurence Dermott, who was once its Deputy Grand Master, and for a long time its Grand Secretary, and who was one of its founders, its most able defender, and the compiler of its Ahizman Rezon, or Book of Constitutions.

In the present sketch this body will, for convenience, be distinguished as the "Atholl Grand Lodge," and its members as the "Ancients," without, however, the remotest idea of conceding to them or to their Grand Lodge the correctness of their claim for a greater antiquity than that which rightly belongs to the Constitutional Grand Lodge, established in 1717.

The progress of the schism which culminated in the organization of the Atholl Grand Lodge was not very rapid. As far back as 1739, complaints were made in the Grand Lodge against certain brethren, who, as Entick euphemistically phrases it, were "suspected of being concerned in an irregular making of Masons."[256]

But the inquiry into this matter was postponed.

At a subsequent quarterly Communication held in the same year the inquiry was resumed, and the offending brethren having made submission and promised good behavior, they were pardoned, but it was ordered by the Grand Lodge that the laws should be strictly enforced against any brethren who should for the future countenance or assist at any irregular makings.[257]

The language of Entick is not explicit, and it authorizes us to suppose either that the pardon granted by the Grand Lodge was consequent on the submission of the offenders which had been made

---

[256] Entick, "Book of Constitutions," p. 228.
[257] Ibid., p. 229

before the pardon was given, or that it was only promissory and depended on their making that submission.

Some may have made the submission and received the pardon, but the reconciliation was by no means complete, for Northouck[258] tells us that the censure of the Grand Lodge irritated the brethren who had incurred it, and who, instead of returning to their duty and renouncing their error, persisted in their contumacy and openly refused to pay allegiance to the Grand Master or obedience to the mandates of the Grand Lodge.

"In contempt of the ancient and established laws of the Order," says Northouck, "they set up a power independent, and taking advantage of the inexperience of their associates, insisted that they had an equal authority with the Grand Lodge to make, pass, and raise Masons."

In the note, whence this passage is taken, and in which Northouck has committed several errors, he has evidently anticipated the course of events and confounded the "irregular makings" by private lodges which began about the year 1739, with the establishment of the Grand Lodge of Ancients, which did not take place until about 1753.

This body of disaffected Masons appears, however, to have been the original source whence, in the course of subsequent years, sprang the organized Grand Lodge of the Ancients.

The process of organization was, however, slow. For some time the contumacious brethren continued to hold their lodges independently of any supreme authority. Nor is it possible, from any records now existing, to determine the exact year in which the Grand Lodge of the Ancients assumed a positive existence.

Preston tells us that the brethren who had repudiated the authority of the Constitutional Grand Lodge held meetings in various places for the purpose of initiating persons into Masonry contrary to the laws of the Grand Lodge. [259]

Preston also says that they took advantage of the breach which had been made between the Grand Lodges of London and York, and assumed the title of "York Masons." In this statement he is, however, incorrect. There was never any recognition by the London Grand Lodge of the body calling itself the Grand Lodge of York, nor was that Grand Lodge in active existence at the time, having suspended its labors from 1734 to 1761.

The name of "York Masons," adopted by these seceders, was derived from the old tradition contained in the Legend of she Craft, that

---

[258] Northouck, "Book of Constitutions," p. 240, note.
[259] Preston, "Illustrations," p. 210, Oliver's edition.

the first Grand Lodge in England was established by Prince Edwin in 926 at the city of York.

Northouck assigns this reason for the title when he says that "under a fictitious sanction of the Ancient York constitutions, which was dropped at the revival of the Grand Lodge in 1717, they presumed to claim the right of constituting Lodges."[260]

The Grand Lodge at London now committed an act of folly, the effects of which remain to the present day. Being desirous to exclude the seceding Masons from visiting the regular lodges, it made a few changes in the ritual by transposing certain significant words in the lower degrees, and inventing a new one in the Third.

The opportunity of raising the cry of innovation (a phrase that has always been abhorrent to the Masonic mind) was not lost. But availing themselves of it, the seceders began to call themselves "Ancient Masons," and stigmatize the members of the regular lodges as "Modern Masons," thus proclaiming that they alone had preserved the old usages of the Craft, while the regulars had invented and adopted new ones.

At this day, when the turbulence of passion has long ceased to exist, and when the whole Fraternity of English Masons is united under one system, it is impossible duly to estimate the evil consequences which arose from this measure of innovation adopted by the Grand Lodge.

If it had made no change in its ritual, but confined itself to the exercise of discipline according to constitutional methods, provided by its own laws, it is probable that the irregular lodges would have received little countenance from the great body of the Craft, and as they would have had no defense for their contumacy, except their objection to the stringency of the Grand Lodge regulations, that objection could have been easily met by showing that the regulations were stringent only because stringency was necessary to the very existence of the institution.

Unsustained by any justification of their rebellion, they would, under the general condemnation of the wiser portion of the Fraternity, have been compelled in the course of time to abandon their independent and irregular lodges and once more to come under obedience to their lawful superior, the Grand Lodge of England.

But the charge that the landmarks had been invaded and that innovations on the ancient usages had been introduced, had a wonderful effect in giving strength to the cause of those who thus seemed in their rebellion to be only defenders of the old ways.

---

[260] Northouck, "Constitutions," p. 240, note.

"Antiquity," says one who was himself an Ancient York Mason, "is dear to a Mason's heart; innovation is treason, and saps the venerable fabric of the Order."[261]

And so the seceders, instead of returning to their allegiance to the legitimate Grand Lodge, persisted in their irregularities, and making new converts, sometimes of individuals and sometimes of entire lodges, which were attracted by their claim of antiquity, at length resolved to acquire permanent life and authority by the establishment of a Grand Lodge to which they gave the imposing name of "The Grand Lodge of England according to the Old Institutions."

But the seceders themselves were not less obnoxious to the charge of innovating on the landmarks. One change in the existing ritual introduced by them was far more important than any mere transposition of passwords. This innovation having been extended by them into all the foreign countries where the Grand Lodge of the Ancients subsequently established lodges or Provincial Grand Lodges, and afterward compulsorily accepted by the Grand Lodge of the Moderns, at the union of the Grand Lodges at London in 1813, has entirely changed the whole system of Freemasonry from that which existed in the constitutional Grand Lodge of England during the 18th century.

This innovation consisted in a mutilation of the Third degree or "Master's Part," and the fabrication of a Fourth degree, now known to the Fraternity as the Royal Arch degree.

"The chief feature in the new ritual," says Brother Hughan, "consisted in a division of the Third degree into two sections, the second of which was restricted to a few Master Masons who were approved as candidates and to whom the peculiar secrets were alone communicated."[262]

From the year 1723 and onward throughout the 18th century and the early portion of the 19th the Grand Lodge of Moderns practiced only three degrees. The adoption of a Fourth degree by the Grand Lodge of Ancients gave to that body a popularity which it probably would not otherwise have obtained. "Many gentlemen," says Hughan, in the work just cited, "preferred joining the 'Grand Lodge of Four Degrees,' to associating with the society which worked only three." And hence when, in 1813, the two rival bodies entered into a union which produced the present Grand Lodge of England, the Moderns were forced to abandon their ritual of three degrees, and to accept that of the Ancients. So in the second article of the Compact, it was declared "that pure Ancient

---

[261] Dalcho, "Ahiman Rezon of South Carolina." second edition, p. 191.
[262] "Memorials of the Masonic Union," p. 5.

Masonry consists of three degrees and no more; viz., those of the Entered Apprentice, the Fellow-Craft, and the Master Mason, including the Supreme Order of the Holy Royal Arch."

This was evidently a compromise, and compromises always indicate some previous attempt at compulsion. The constitutional Grand Lodge sought to preserve its consistency by recognizing only three degrees, while it immediately afterward, and in the same sentence, sacrificed that consistency by admitting that there was a Fourth, called the Royal Arch.

The Ancients had clearly gained a victory, but without this victory the union could never have been accomplished. But this subject of the Royal Arch will be more fully discussed when we come to the consideration of the origin and history of that degree.

I have already said that it is impossible to determine the precise year in which the Grand Lodge of Ancients was established. Before its actual organization the brethren of the different lodges appear to have combined under the title of the "Grand Committee." This body, it would seem, subsequently became the Grand Lodge.

The earliest preserved record of the transactions of this Committee has the date of July 17, 1751.[263] On that day there was an Assembly of Ancient Masons at the "Turk's Head Tavern," in Greek Street, Soho, when the Masters of the seven lodges which recognized the Grand Committee as their head, [264]namely, lodges Nos. 2, 3, 4, 5, 6, and 7, "were authorized to grant Dispensations and Warrants and to act as Grand Master."

The first result of this unusual and certainly very irregular authority conferred upon all the Masters of private lodges to act as Grand Master was the Constitution in the same year of a lodge at the "Temple and Sun," Shire Lane, Temple Bar, which took the number 8, and this appears to have been the first Warrant issued by the Ancients.

The Warrant, which is in favor of James Bradshaw, Master, and Thomas Blower and R.D. Guest, as Wardens, is signed by the Masters of lodges Nos. 3, 4, 5, and 6. This would imply that the authority and prerogatives of a Grand Master were conferred not upon each Master,

---

[263] Cited by Bro. Robert Freke Gould in his work on "The Atholl Lodges" (p. 2), to which work I am also indebted for valuable information in the way of quotations from the "Atholl Records." This is the earliest date cited in the "Atholl Records."

[264] Bro. Gould thinks that this "Grand Committee," which subsequently was developed into a Grand Lodge, was no doubt originally the senior private lodge of the Ancients. Ibid., Preface, p. ix.

individually, but upon the whole of them, collectively, or at least upon a majority of them.

These Masters constituted a body which in its exercise of the prerogatives of a Grand Master has since found its analogue in the "Council of the Order" into which the Grand Orient of France has for some years merged its Grand Mastership, though the mode of organization of the latter body materially differs from that of the former.

This "Grand Committee," whose presiding officer was called the "President," exercised the functions of a Grand Lodge without the name until the close of the year 1752. In 1751 it granted Warrants for two other lodges, numbered respectively 9 and 10; in 1752 it constituted five more, respectively numbered as 11, 12, 13, 14, and 15.

It will be seen that in its legislation the Grand Committee refers only to No. 2 as its oldest lodge. No. 1 must, however, have existed, though not named as such in the records. But in the list of Atholl Lodges given by Bro. Gould, No. 1 is stated to have been called the "Grand Master's Lodge," and its Warrant is dated August 13, 1759. In 1751 and 1752 it could not, however, have borne this title, because during those years there was no Grand Master recognized by the Ancients.

It was probably the senior lodge, the first which seceded from the legitimate Grand Lodge, and with which Nos. 2, 3, 4, 5, 6, and 7 subsequently united.

These were lodges which on account of their irregularities and schismatic proceedings had been stricken from the roll of the Grand Lodge of England, and having assumed the name of Ancient Masons, had enrolled themselves under the lead of the oldest of their companions in secession.

This older lodge appears to have been the body known at first as the Grand Committee and which, some time after the organization of a Grand Lodge, received the title of "The Grand Master's Lodge" and the precedence of lodges as No. 1.

It is only in this way that we can reasonably explain the apparent anomaly that of the seven lodges which must have been engaged in 1751 in the work of the Ancients, no mention is made of No. 1, but that upon No. 2, with the five other lodges of later numbers, was conferred the functions of a Grand Master and the power of warranting lodges, while no mention is made of No. 1, the oldest of the seven. The fact was that No. 1 constituted the really governing body, known until a Grand Lodge was established as the Grand Committee. Bro. Gould, who has very carefully investigated the history of the Atholl lodges, entertains the same opinion.

He says: "The 'Grand Committee' of the 'Ancients,' which subsequently developed into their 'Grand Lodge,' was, no doubt, originally their senior private lodge, whose growth, in this respect, is akin to that of the Grand Chapter of the Moderns,' which, commencing in 1765 as a private Chapter, within a few years assumed the general direction of the R. A. Masonry, and issued Warrants of constitution."[265]

Of this Grand Committee John Morgan was, in 1751, the Secretary. He appears to have been very remiss in the performance of his duties. His successor, Laurence Dermott, who was elected Secretary or Grand Secretary of the Committee February 5, 1752, reported that he had received "no copy or manuscript of the Transactions" from Morgan, and did not believe that that officer had ever kept a book of records. This neglect has thrown much obscurity on the early periods of the history of the Ancients.

The "Grand lodge of England, according to the old Institutions, appears to have been organized as a Grand Lodge on December 5, 1753, for on that day Robert Turner, the Master of Lodge No. 15, was elected the first Grand Master. Laurence Dermott, who was at that time the Secretary of the Grand Committee, became the Grand Secretary of the new Grand Lodge, and continued in that office until the year 1770.

In writing a sketch of the Grand Lodge of "Ancients," it would not be fitting to the prominent position he occupied in its history to give to Dermott only an incidental notice. First as its Grand Secretary, and afterward as Grand Master, he gave to the scheme of organizing a body rivaling that of the Constitutional Masons, a factitious luster which secured it an extraordinary share of popularity. It must be admitted that this was, in great part, accomplished by scandalous statements, devoid of truth; while such a course must detract from his moral character, we can not deny to him the reputation of being the best informed and the most energetic worker of all the disciples and adherents of the so-called "Ancient Masonry." In the early years of the Grand Lodge of a "Ancients" we look in vain for the name of any officer or member distinguished for social rank or literary reputation. We look in vain, among those who were prominent in its history, for such scholars as Anderson or Payne or Desaguliers. The name of Dermott shows the only star in its firmament, not indeed peculiarly effulgent in itself, but whose

---

[265] "The Atholl Lodges," Preface, p. ix.

brilliance is owing to contrast with the obscurity of those which surround it.

In some well written "Studies of Masonic History," published in Mackey's National Freemason, Bro. J.F. Brennan has thus described the successful efforts of Dermott to establish the popularity of his Grand Lodge.

"The history of that period, so far as concerns Laurence Dermott's strenuous and persistent determination to establish upon a firm foundation his Grand Lodge, has, except in slight degree, never been published, if it has ever been written. Enough to say, that notwithstanding the most earnest antagonism manifested towards him by the 1717 organization, or its then succession, he triumphantly did succeed, and not only divided the profits of Grand Lodgeism with the earlier organization in London, but as well led the Grand Lodges of Ireland and Scotland to believe that the 1717 organization was a spurious body and therefore unworthy of recognition by those Grand Lodges while his Grand Lodge was really and properly the true Grand Lodge of English Freemasons. And not only did he thus succeed, but he also induced Freemasons in the then British American Colonies, which subsequently became the United States, particularly in Pennsylvania, Massachusetts, New York, North Carolina, Virginia and South Carolina to believe that in his Grand Lodge of Ancient York Masons, alone was true Freemasonry extant; and so well did he succeed that while in several of those colonies he established under his Charter lodges assuming to be Grand Lodges, in Pennsylvania, notably, he induced all the lodges there already and for several years established to surrender their Charters and accept from him Charters preferably, and as authority for their practice of what he designated the real Ancient York and only true Masonry recognized or properly recognizable, and his Ahiman Rezon, a plagiaristic adaptation of the 1723[266] publication of Anderson, the only correct >Book of Masonic Constitutions.' "[267]

Of a man so successful in intrigue we know but little, save what we derive from his connection with the body which he served so faithfully. Unlike Anderson and Desaguliers and Payne and Folkes and other lights of the legitimate Grand Lodge, he wrote nothing and did nothing, outside of Masonry, which could secure his memory from oblivion.

---

[266] Brennan is here in error; the plagiarism, of which there is no doubt, is of the 1738 and not the 1723 edition of Anderson's " Constitutions."

[267] Mackey's " National Freemason," Washington, 1872, vol. i., p. 302.

Laurence Dermott was born in Ireland in the year 1720. In 1740 he was initiated into Freemasonry in a Modern lodge at Dublin, and on June 24, 1746, was installed as Master of Lodge No. 26 in that city.

It is undeniable that Dermott was a man of some education. Brother Gould says[268] that "besides English and his native Irish, Dermott seems to have been conversant with the Jewish tongue. All the books kept by him as Grand Secretary are plastered over with Hebrew characters, and the proceedings of the Stewards' lodge record, under date of March 21, 1764, 'Heard the petition of G.J. Strange, an Arabian Mason, with whom the Grand Secretary conversed in the Hebrew language. The Ahiman Rezon, while the title indicates a smattering at least of Hebrew, gives several proofs that Dermott was a man of some reading. He was not a profound scholar, but he was far from being illiterate.

In what year he removed to England is not known, but he afterward joined a lodge under the jurisdiction of the Constitutional Grand Lodge. In 1751 he removed his membership to Lodge No. 1, on the registry of the "Ancients," and was a member of it when on February 5, 1752, he was elected Grand Secretary of the seceders' Grand Lodge. From that time he devoted all his energies and what abilities he possessed to the advancement of the cause of the "Ancients," with what success has already been seen.

He was appointed Deputy Grand Master on March 2, 1771, by the third Duke of Atholl, who had just been elected Grand Master. On December 27, 1777, he resigned that position, and at his request W. Dickey was appointed as his successor by the fourth Duke of Atholl. He was again appointed Deputy on December 27, 1783, and was, at his own request, succeeded, on December 27, 1787, by James Perry, who was appointed by the Earl of Antrim, Grand Master at that time. Dermott's last appearance in the Grand Lodge was on June 3, 1789, after which period he is lost sight of.

During this long period of thirty-seven years Laurence Dermott was untiring in his devotion to the interests of the "Grand Lodge of England according to the Old Institutions," and to the propagation of what was called "Ancient York Masonry."

Six years after its organization the legitimate Grand Lodge, established in 1717, had prepared and published a Book of

---

[268] Cited in the AKeystone." November 6. 1880.

Constitutions. Dermott felt it necessary that his own Grand Lodge should also have a code of laws for its government.

Accordingly, in 1756 he published the Constitutions of the Grand Lodge of which he was the Grand Secretary, under the following title:

Ahiman Rezon: or a Help to a Brother, showing the Excellency of Secrecy and the first cause or motive of the Institution of Freemasonry; the Principles of the Craft and the Benefits from a Strict Observance thereof etc., also the Old and New Regulations, etc. To which is added the greatest collection of Masons' Songs, etc. By Laurence Dermott, Secretary.

Other editions, with the title much abbreviated, were published subsequently, the last, by Thomas Harper, in 1813, the year before the union of the two Grand Lodges.

The third edition, published in 1778, has a much briefer title. It is the Ahiman Rezon: or a Help to all that are, or would be Free and Accepted Masons, with many Additions. By Lau. Dermott, D.G.M.

In this work, partly in an address "To the Reader" (pages i-xxi), and in what he calls "A Phylacterial[269] for such Gentlemen as may be inclined to become Free-Masons " (pages xxii to xxviii), he gives a confused history of the origin of the Grand Lodge of Moderns and of his own Grand Lodge, claiming, of course, for the latter a priority of date, and decrying the former as a spurious innovation on genuine Freemasonry.

His attempted history is, on account of its meager details and its assumptions, unsupported by any authority, utterly without value. As a specimen of its worthlessness as an historical document, the following narrative of the Grand Lodge at London in 1717 affords a fair sample:

"About the year 1717," he writes, "some joyous companions who had passed the degree of a craft (though very rusty) resolved to form a lodge for themselves in order (by conversation) to recollect what had been formerly dictated to them, or if that should be found impracticable, to substitute something new, which might for the future pass for masonry amongst themselves. At this meeting the question was asked

---

[269] This is a Greek word, but improperly spelt by Dermott, and signifies a precaution or warning. Dermott appears to have been, like most smatterers, fond of using words borrowed from the dead languages, and incomprehensible or puzzling to plain readers. Witness his "Ahiman Rezon," the name which he gives to his Book of Constitutions the prayer which he calls "Ahabath Olam," and this APhilacteria." "A little learning," says Pope, "is a dangerous thing, and that seems to have been Dermott's infirmity.

whether any person in the assembly knew the Master's part, and being answered in the negative, it was resolved, that the deficiency should be made up, with a new composition, and what fragments of the old order found amongst them should be immediately reformed, and made more pliable to the humors of the people."[270]

In this absurd way he proceeds to account for the invention of a ritual by the "Moderns," which they adopted as a substitute for the genuine possessed by the "Ancients."

Recent researches into the history of the ritual and the formation of the three degrees which, with the addition of the Royal Arch, constitute what is called "Ancient Craft Masonry," make it unnecessary to prove by an argument that all of Dermott's statements on this subject are utterly false and the mere figment of his own invention.

It is indeed extraordinary that this unscrupulous writer should have had the audacity to assert that he and his followers were in possession of a system of Speculative Freemasonry much older than that which was practiced by the Grand Lodge, organized in 1717, and that they derived their authority to open and hold their lodges from this more ancient system.

The fact is that Dermott himself, like every one of those who before his appearance on the stage had separated from the Constitutional Grand Lodge and established what they called "Lodges of Ancient Masons," was originally made in a lodge of Moderns. Whatever he knew of Speculative Freemasonry was derived from a lodge in Ireland which had derived its authority and learned its lessons from the 1717 Grand Lodge at London.

The first schism, which took place in 1738, was not pretended to be based on the fact that the seceders were desirous of practicing an older and purer Masonry than that professed by the Grand Lodge at London. It was because they were unwilling to submit to the constitutional regulations which had been established by the Grand Lodge and because their irregular proceedings, in violation of those regulations, had met with necessary censure and deserved punishment.

It is true that after the secession and consequent erasure from the roll of these contumacious lodges, the Constitutional Grand Lodge, to prevent the visits of irregular Masons, had most unwisely made a few alterations in the modes of recognition.

These alterations were not adopted by the seceders, but retaining the old methods which had been in use, certainly as far back as

---

[270] Dermott's "Ahiman Rezon," third edition, p. 35.

1723, some of them still earlier, they claimed to be "Ancient Masons," because they adhered to the old forms, while they stigmatized the Masons who still maintained their allegiance to the Constitutional Grand Lodge as "Moderns," because they practiced the new methods.

And this is in fact all there really is about this dispute concerning "Ancients" and "Moderns," which for so many years distracted the English Craft, and the remembrance of which is to this day preserved and perpetuated in America, where Dermott Masonry at one time prevailed to a very great extent, by the title assumed by several Grand Lodges of "Ancient York Masons."

The hypothesis that there was any Speculative Freemasonry distinct from Operative Freemasonry that can be traced to an earlier origin than that of the Grand Lodge established in 1717, was a fiction invented by its propagators under the influence of interested motives and ignorantly accepted by their successors as an historical fact.

We know from documents now extant that Laurence Dermott, who was entered, passed, and raised in a lodge of what he afterward called a lodge of "Moderns," who afterward presided over a lodge of the same character in Ireland, and on his removal to England renewed his connection with a Modern lodge, and so remained until he was elected the Grand Secretary of the Grand Lodge of "Ancients."

It is almost impossible to believe, that with the knowledge which he must have had of current events, he could have honestly been of the opinion that there was any Speculative Freemasonry, or any Grand Lodge of Speculative Freemasonry, older than that established in 1717.

He must have known, too, while he was stigmatizing this body as illegal and sarcastically styling the system which it practiced "the memorable invention of modern masonry," that from it, and from it alone, every lodge of Speculative Masons, his own lodges included, either directly or indirectly had derived the authority for their existence.

Nothing more clearly shows the insincerity of Dermott's denunciation of the Grand Lodge of "Moderns" than his conduct in reference to the Regulations. It is known that in 1721 the Grand Lodge approved the "General Regulations of the Free and Accepted Masons," which had been compiled the year before by Grand Master Payne. In 1723 these were published by authority of the Grand Lodge, together with the "Old Charges," which had been "collected from the old Records" and "the manner of Constituting a New Lodge" as practiced by Grand Master the Duke of Wharton.

In 1738, by authority of the same Grand Lodge, a second edition of the Book of Constitutions was published under the editorship of Dr. Anderson.

In this edition Anderson made some material changes in the language of the "Old Charges," and in "the manner of Constituting a New Lodge," so as to adapt them to the changes in the Ritual by which the Master Mason superseded the FellowCraft as the crowning degree of Speculative Freemasonry. He also published the "General Regulations" in two columns; in the first were the "Old Regulations," printed without change, and in the other column, opposite to them, were "the New Regulations, or the Alterations, Improvements or Explications of the Old, made by several Grand Lodges since the first edition."

Now this second edition, having after inspection of the manuscript been "approved and recommended" by the Grand Lodge, "as the only Book of Constitutions for the use of the lodges,"[271] became the law for the government of those whom Dermott had called the "Modern Masons," and the organization of which he had declared to be "defective in number and consequently defective in form and capacity."[272]

If such were his honest opinion, then he must have believed that the Grand Lodge of 1717, so constituted, was an illegal body, and consequently incapable of enacting any laws or regulations or instituting any ceremonies which could be of binding force upon the Fraternity which derived its existence from an older institution.

But we find that so far from repudiating the laws enacted by this illegal and defective organization, he adopted them in full for the government of his own Grand Lodge, which he had claimed to be the only perfect and legal one.

Therefore, when he compiled his Ahiman Rezon and bestowed it upon the "Ancients" as their Book of Constitutions, Dermott, instead of seeking laws for its government in that older system, whose parentage he claimed, deliberately appropriated from the 1738 Book of Constitutions, without a change, except here and there a brief marginal comment, the whole of the "Old Charges," the "Old and New Regulations," and "the manner of Constituting a New Lodge."

---

[271] Anderson's "Constitutions," edition of 1738, p. 199. In the next edition the editor, Entick, restored the original phraseology of 1723, but the "Charges" and "Regulations" in the edition of 1738 continued to be the law of the Grand Lodge for eighteen years, and were so when Dermott adopted them for the government of his Grand Lodge.

[272] Dermott's "Ahiman Rezon," p. xiv.

The irresistible conclusion from this is that while pretending to believe that the organization of 1717 was invalid and an innovation on an older system from which he and his adherents denied their existence, Dermott actually knew and felt that the organization was valid and legitimate, that the Grand Lodge then formed was regular and constitutional, and that the laws and regulations adopted by it were the only constitutional authority for the government of the Craft.

There can be no doubt that Dermott was insincere in his professions and consciously untruthful in his statements, and that while the Masonic schism was made by him the instrument for advancing his own interests, he was well aware that all his pretensions as to the superior antiquity of his own Grand Lodge, and his denunciations of the Grand Lodge of 1717 as a modern and illegal organization, were false.

But the rapid progress made by the Grand Lodge of "Ancients" in the popular regard, which, in the beginning was mainly attributable to the untruthful statements and the specious arguments of Dermott, for many years threw a veil over the defects of his character.

"Throughout his eventful career," says Hughan, "he always managed to secure a good working majority in his favor, and the extraordinary success of the schism was an argument in confirmation of his views, which the most of his followers acknowledged."[273]

Success, says Seneca, makes some crimes honorable, and Dermott, the falsifier of history, had for a long time an honorable name in England and America among the adherents of the Grand Lodge of which he was, if not the founder, certainly the chief supporter.

It is here proper to say a few words in relation to Dermott's connection with the fabrication of the Royal Arch degree. This degree, which Dermott enthusiastically calls "the root, heart, and marrow of masonry,"[274] was, undoubtedly, one of the most efficient elements in giving popularity to the lodges of the "Ancients," because it presented as an additional and much extolled degree, an incentive to candidates which was wanting in the lodges of the " Moderns."

It is, however, incorrect to credit Dermott (as has been done by many writers) with its invention or even its introduction into the system of the "Ancients." It was known to and practiced by the schismatic lodges, who were censured for their "irregular makings" as early as 1738, by the Constitutional Grand Lodge. Dermott, as we have seen, was made in a "Modern" lodge in Ireland, became affiliated with a Modern lodge in London when he removed to England, and could have known

---

[273] Hughan, "Memorials of the Masonic Union," p. 8.
[274] Dermott, "Ahiman Rezon," second edition, 1764, p. 46.

nothing of the Royal Arch degree until he joined No. 9, an "Ancient," in 1751.

That he afterward cultivated and perhaps enlarged or improved the degree, and gave to it a prominence which it did not at first possess, is not improbable. But it is an error to attribute to him its invention.

But this subject will be more appropriately and more fully treated in the Chapter to be devoted to the History of the Origin of the Royal Arch degree.

The third and fourth Dukes of Atholl played so prominent a part in the history of the Grand Lodge of "Ancients" as to give to that body, as has already been said, the distinctive title of the "Atholl Grand Lodge." It is indeed to the social influence of these noblemen, combined with the shrewdness and indomitable energy of Laurence Dermott, that the Grand Lodge was indebted for the remarkable success which it achieved.

The Grand Lodge at the date of its organization out of the "Grand Committee" had elected, on December 5, 1753, Robert Turner, who was the Worshipful Master of Lodge No. 15, as Grand Master. In 1754 Edward Vaughan was elected to that office. In 1756 the Earl of Blessington received the Grand Mastership, and was succeeded in 1760 by the Earl of Kelly, who, after five years of service, was followed in 1766 by the Hon. Thomas Mathew, who served until 1771.

In 1771 John, the third Duke of Atholl, was elected Grand Master. The Duke was a member of the Scottish Craft, and in the following year was elected Grand Master of the Grand Lodge of Scotland, so that, as he continued in his English office until his death, in 1774, he was at the same time Grand Master both of the Grand Lodge of Scotland and of the "Ancient" Grand Lodge of England. The effect of this unusual concurrence of two offices, whereby the leader ship of the Craft in two countries was vested in the same person, was seen in a close union which about that time was cemented between the Grand Lodge of Scotland and that of the "Ancients" in England.

In 1782 the Earl of Antrim was elected Grand Master, and served until 1790. From 1773 to 1779 the Earl had been Grand Master of the Grand Lodge of Ireland.

This shrewd policy of electing leading Masons in the two sister kingdoms to the highest position in the "Ancient " Grand Lodge of England, very soon displayed the effect which Dermott had wisely expected to be produced.

On September 2, 1771, the Grand Lodge of "Ancients," meeting at the "Half Moon Tavern" in Cheapside, [275]Laurence Dermott being in the chair as Deputy Grand Master, adopted the following resolution, which the Grand Secretary was ordered to transmit to the Grand Lodge of Ireland:

"It is the opinion of this Grand Lodge that a brotherly connection and correspondence with the Right Worshipful Grand Lodge of Ireland has been and will always be found productive of honor and advantage to the Craft in both kingdoms."

At the same time it was ordered that the Grand Secretary should annually transmit to the Grand Lodge of Ireland the names of officers elected and any other information that might be of interest to the Craft.

It was further ordered that no Mason made under the sanction of the Grand Lodge of Ireland should be admitted as a member nor partake of the General Charity of the Grand Lodge of England unless he produced a certificate from the Irish Grand Secretary.[276]

At the same meeting, on the proposition of Dermott, a correspondence was ordered to be opened with the Grand Lodge of Scotland.

The response from both the Grand Lodges of Ireland and of Scotland was very satisfactory to the "Ancients."

On November 5, 1772, the Grand Lodge of Ireland, Viscount Dunluce being Grand Master, adopted a resolution which declared that it entirely agreed with the Grand Lodge of England that a brotherly connection and correspondence between the two Grand Lodges had been and always would be found of honor and advantage to the Craft in both kingdoms. [277]

---

[275] The Half Moon in Cheapside was, during the 17th and 18th centuries, a tavern of some notoriety. Ashmole records in his Diary, under date of March 11, 1682, that he was at "a noble dinner given at the Half Moon Tavern in 'Cheapside.= A The Grand Lodge of Ancients met there, but subsequently removed to the Crown and Anchor.

[276] Dermott had previously opened a correspondence with Thomas Corker, the Deputy Grand Secretary of Ireland, to prepare the way for this action. See "Ahiman Rezon," edition of 1778, p. lvi.

[277] The use of the word "continued" and the phraseology in the resolution of both bodies that a brotherly connection and correspondence "have been and always will be" would indicate that such a connection and correspondence had previously existed between the two Grand Lodges.

It was also ordered that the particular occurrences of the Grand Lodge of Ireland should from time to time be continued to be transmitted to the Grand Secretary of England, and that "hereafter no English Mason shall be considered worthy of their charity without producing a certificate from the Grand Lodge of England."

The letter suggested by Dermott was sent to the Grand Lodge of Scotland. It was of the same purport and almost in the same language as that transmitted to Ireland, except that the Grand Lodge of England expressed the opinion that a brotherly connection and correspondence with the Grand Lodge of Scotland "will be found productive of honor and advantage to the fraternity in general."

There is no reference, as I have stated in the preceding note, to any former correspondence, but only the proposal for a future one.

On November 30, 1772, the Earl of Dumfries being Grand Master, and the Duke of Atholl being present as Grand Master elect, the letter and resolution of the "Grand Lodge of England according to the Old Institutions" being read (so says the record), "the Grand Lodge were of opinion that the brotherly love and intercourse which the Right Worshipful Grand Lodge of England were desirous to establish would be serviceable to both Grand Lodges and productive of honor and advantage to the fraternity."[278]

The Grand Lodge of Scotland accordingly commenced the correspondence by transmitting the names of the officers that day elected, and ordered the same to be done yearly, together with any other information that might be of honor and advantage to the Craft.

It also ordered "that no Mason, made under the sanction of the Grand Lodge of England according to the Old Institutions,' shall be admitted a member of the Grand Lodge of Scotland, nor partake of the general charity without having first produced a certificate of his good behavior from the Secretary of the Grand Lodge of England."[279]

The reader will notice a very important difference in the phraseology of the orders of the two Grand Lodges of Ireland and Scotland, which if intentionally made would indicate the feelings of each to the Constitutional Grand Lodge of England.

The Grand Lodge of Ireland, addressing the Grand Lodge of "Ancients," calls it a the Grand Lodge of England," and refuses

---

This phraseology is not used by the Grand Lodge of England in the resolution sent to the Grand Lodge of Scotland, nor is it employed by that body in its responsive resolution. In both, the reference is only to a future correspondence.
[278] Laurie, "History of Freemasonry," p. 208. Dermott, "Ahiman Rezon," p.lx.
[279] Laurie, "History of Freemasonry," p. 208. Dermott, "Ahiman Rezon," p. lx.

recognition to any "English Mason" who does not produce a certificate from it.

The necessary effect of this order would be to repudiate the Grand Lodge of "Moderns" and to place all its members under the ban as illegal Masons. It is very evident that no member of a lodge of "Moderns" would seek or obtain a certificate from the Grand Lodge of "Ancients," and without this, if he visited Ireland, he would be debarred by the terms of the Order from all his Masonic rights and privileges. Such an order would, according to the views of the present day, be considered as a recognition of the Grand Lodge of "Ancients" as the only regular Masonic authority in England.

The Grand Lodge of Scotland was more prudent in its choice of language.

It specifically designated the body in England with which it was about to establish a brotherly correspondence as "the Grand Lodge of England according to the Old Institutions," and required only Masons made under its sanction to present its certificates. Thus we may justly infer that Masons made under the sanction of the Grand Lodge of "Moderns" were not excluded from Masonic visitation if they had the certificate of their own Grand Lodge.

The Grand Lodges of Ireland and Scotland, however, subsequently reconsidered their action and eventually assumed the position of neutrality or indifference in the contest, but, says Hughan, "during the period that they especially countenanced the refractory brethren, the latter made considerable out of the fact, and proclaimed their alliance with these two Grand Lodges far and near."[280]

Looking at the subject from the legal stand-point of the present day, one can not but be greatly surprised at the action taken by the Irish and Scottish Masons.

Here are two Grand Lodges, the former of which was indebted to the legitimate Grand Lodge of England for its organization and the latter for its ritual, deliberately ignoring that body and acknowledging as legitimate a schismatic association which their ancient ally had declared to be irregular.

Evidently Masonic jurisprudence had not then assumed those formal principles by which it is now distinguished and by which it governs the institution.

Scarcely less surprising is it that the Constitutional Grand Lodge of England appears to have taken no notice of these proceedings,

---

[280] Hughan, "Masonic Memorials," p. 14.

nor entered any protest against their want of comity. Neither Preston nor Northouck, in their chronicle of the times, make any reference to this manifest invasion of legitimate authority. It is passed over by both in silence as something which they either deemed inexplicable or not worthy of mention.[281]

The Grand Lodge itself, when four or five years after it repeated its denunciation of the "Ancients," treated the two Grand Lodges which had sustained its rival with a courtesy which under similar circumstances at this day it would hardly repeat.

On April 7, 1777, the Constitutional Grand Lodge held an "extraordinary" communication to take into consideration "the proper means of discouraging the irregular assemblies of persons calling themselves ancient masons," when the following resolution was passed:

"It is the opinion of this Grand Lodge, that the persons calling themselves ancient masons, and now assembling in England or elsewhere, under the patronage of the Duke of Atholl are not to be considered as masons, nor are their meetings to be countenanced or acknowledged by any lodge or mason acting under our authority. But this censure shall not extend to any mason who shall produce a certificate or give other satisfactory proof of his having been made a mason in a regular lodge under the Constitution of Scotland, Ireland, or any foreign Grand Lodge in alliance with the Grand Lodge of England."

So the Grand Lodges of Ireland and Scotland were recognized by the Constitutional Grand Lodge as in friendly alliance with it, notwithstanding that the one had repudiated all English Masons who were not "Ancients," and the other had acknowledged the Grand Lodge of "Ancients" as a regular and legally constituted organization.

The comparison which is thus afforded of the energy of the "Ancients" and the apathy of the "Moderns" would alone sufficiently account for the rapid success and growing popularity of the former body, were there no other causes existing to produce the same result.

It was very natural that the "Ancient" Grand Lodge, elated by this success and popularity, should in an official document issued in 1802 have declared that its members "can not and must not receive into the body of a just and perfect lodge, nor treat as a Brother any person who has not received the obligations of Masonry according to the " Ancient" Constitutions as practiced by the United Grand Lodges of England, Scotland, and Ireland, and the regular branches that have sprung from their sanction."[282]

---

[281] Northouck. "Constitutions." p. 323.
[282] See the edition of the "Ahiman Rezon," 1804, p. 130.

The schismatics had now claimed to be regular, and the regular Masons were relegated by them to the realms of schism. It is the nature of men, says the Italian historian Guicciardini, when they leave one extreme in which they have been forcibly held to rush speedily to the opposite. Just before the middle of the 18th century the "Ancient" Masons, who were embraced in only a few lodges, were accepting the censures of the Constitutional Grand Lodge for their irregularities, and were humbly but not sincerely making promises of reformation. At its close they were denouncing their old masters as irregular and proclaiming themselves to be the only true Masons in England.

Mention has been frequently made of the successful progress of the "Ancients" in the propagation of their system. The authentic records of the time afford the most satisfactory evidence of this fact.

Commencing its organized opposition to the regular Grand Lodge in 1751, under a superintending head styled the " Grand Committee," which was in fact the premier lodge, and six others, it constituted in 1751 and 1752 seven others. In 1753 these lodges organized the "Grand Lodge of England according to the Old Institutions." In the course of the next four years it constituted thirty additional lodges in London and ten more in various parts of the kingdom, namely, two at Bristol, three at Liverpool, and one each at Manchester, Warrington, Coventry, Worcester, and Deptford, so that at the end of the year 1757 there were or had been fifty-four lodges in England acknowledging allegiance to the "Ancient " Grand Lodge.

But its operations were not confined to the narrow limits of the kingdom.

Lodges and a Provincial Grand Lodge were established in Nova Scotia as early as 1757, and in a few years there were lodges and Provincial Grand Lodges in Canada, in the American colonies, in the West, at Minorca in the Mediterranean, in the distant island of St. Helena, and in the East Indies.

In 1774 the third Duke of Atholl died, being at the time, as he had been since 1771, the Grand Master of the "Ancients."

His son and the successor to his title, John the fourth Duke, was not a Mason at the time of his father's death. On February 25, 1775, as we learn from the Minutes of the Grand Committee,[283] he received the first three degrees in the Grand Master's Lodge of Ancient Masons, and was immediately chosen as Master of that lodge. On March 1st, in

---

[283] Cited by Bro. Gould in his "Atholl Lodges," p. i.

the same year, only four days after his initiation, he was unanimously elected to succeed his father as Grand Master.

The object of Dermott and his companions in thus elevating a mere tyro to the magistral chair was simply to retain for their Grand Lodge the great influence and patronage of the Scottish House of Atholl. In 1782 the Duke was succeeded by the Earl, afterward the Marquis, of Antrim, an Irish nobleman, who held the office of Grand Master until 1791.

The Duke of Atholl was then re-elected, and continued to preside over the Grand Lodge until the year 1813, when he resigned and was succeeded by the Duke of Kent, who assumed the office as a preliminary step toward the union of the two Grand Lodges, which was consummated in that year.

The following is a correct list of the Grand Masters of the "Grand Lodge of England according to the Old Institutions," or more familiarly speaking, the "Grand Lodge of Ancients," or the "Atholl Grand Lodge," from its birth to its death. It was first compiled by Bro. W.J. Hughan, and published in his Masonic Memorials. I have verified it (though verification was hardly necessary of so accurate an historian) by collation with other authorities.

1753, Robert Turner 1754-55, Edward Vaughan 1756-59, Earl of Blessington 1760-65, Earl of Kellie 1766-70, Hon. Thomas Mathew 1771-74, John, third Duke of Atholl 1775-81, John, fourth Duke of Atholl 1782-90, Earl of Antrim 1791-1813, John, fourth Duke of Atholl 1813, Duke of Kent

The following is a list of the Grand Secretaries who served during the same period:

1752, John Morgan, 1752-70, Laurence Dermott, 1771-76, William Dickey, 1777-78, James Jones, 1779-82, Charles Bearblock, 1783-84, Robert Leslie, 1785-89, John McCormick, 1790-1813, Robert Leslie.

It is inconceivable how Preston could have committed so grave an historical error as to say, "the fact is, that the 'Ancients' after their secession continued to hold their meetings without acknowledging a superior till 1772, when they chose for their grand master the Duke of Atholl."[284] He was apparently utterly ignorant of the fact, here shown, that their first Grand Master was elected in 1753, and that from that time until the dissolution of their Grand Lodge in 1813 the office was

---

[284] "Illustrations of Masonry," p. 358.

filled by an uninterrupted succession of Grand Masters. Voila justement comme on ecrit l'histoire.[285]

In conclusion it is necessary to say something of the character and pretensions of the Grand Lodge which created a Masonic schism that lasted in an organized form for sixty years, and which extended its influence into every part of the civilized world where the English language was spoken.

The Freemasons, who about 1738 seceded from the Constitutional Grand Lodge of England, and soon after began to call themselves "Ancient Masons," and who stigmatized the regular members of the Craft as "Moderns," were not incited to the secession in consequence of any innovations that had been made upon the ritual by the Grand Lodge from which they separated.

Those innovations were the consequence and not the cause of their secession. They were made by the Grand Lodge, so as to produce a change in the working that would exclude the visits of the seceders to the regular lodges. They were indeed not very important and did not at all affect the traditional history or the symbolic system of Speculative Freemasonry. The adoption of them was certainly, however, a very great error, and the seceders were not slow to avail themselves of the charge of innovation, so distasteful to the Masonic mind, to produce a feeling of sympathy in their behalf.

But the truth is that the first innovation, and this, too, a very important one, was made by the "Ancients" themselves, and the practice of it was the cause of the censures passed by the regular Grand Lodge, which was the first step that led to the final separation.

It is important to settle the nature of this innovation, because it is really the " chief corner-stone" on which the schism of the "Ancients" was founded, and because one of the almost contemporary historians of the Regular Grand Lodge has committed a grave error in respect to it.

Northouck, who in 1784 gave us the best edited edition of the Book of Constitutions, in speaking of the conduct of the Masons engaged in the "irregular makings " which in 1739 elicited the censures of the Grand Lodge, has the following passage:

"In contempt of the ancient and established laws of the Order, they set up a power independent, and taking advantage of the inexperience of their associates, insisted that they had an equal authority with the Grand Lodge to make, pass, and raise masons. At this time no private lodge had the power of passing or raising masons; nor could any

---

[285] Voltaire, "Chariot," I. p. 7.

brother be advanced to either of these degrees but in the Grand Lodge, with the unanimous consent and approbation of all the brethren in communication assembled."[286]

It is unaccountable that Northouck should ignorantly or designedly have made an assertion so entirely untruthful as that which is contained in the last clause of the above-cited paragraph.

It is true that in 1723, at about the time of the fabrication of the Second and Third degrees a clause was inserted in the 13th of the Thirty-nine Regulations which declared that "Apprentices must be admitted Masters and Fellow Crafts only here (in the Grand Lodge) unless by dispensation." This was done, in all probability, to secure the proper conferring of the newly fabricated degrees in the hands of their inventors and of experienced Masons, instead of entrusting them to Masters of lodges who might be incompetent to preserve the purity of the ritual.

But this objection was soon obviated as the degrees became more common, and the inconvenience of the Regulation being recognized, it was repealed in 1725.

On November 22, 1725, they adopted a new regulation that "The Master of a lodge with its Wardens and a competent number of the lodge assembled in due form can make Masters and Fellows at discretion."[287]

Seeing that this new regulation was published both by Anderson in 1738 and by Entick in 1756 in their respective editions of the Book of Constitutions, with which Northouck must have been familiar, especially with the latter, and seeing also that there is no provision restraining the passing and raising of Candidates by private lodges contained in the code of Regulations published by Northouck in his edition, but on the contrary, one which expressly recognizes that right,[288] it is, as I have said, unaccountable that he should have ignorantly committed the error of which he has been guilty, nor is it to be believed that he would have done so designedly.

The truth is that the act which called down upon certain Masons the censures of the Grand Lodge, and which finally produced

---

[286] Northouck's edition of " Book of Constitutions." note on p. 240.
[287] See Anderson, edition of 1738, p. 160, and Entick, edition of 1756, p. 280, where this new Regulation will be found.
[288] "Nor shall any Lodge be permitted to make and raise a brother at the same meeting, without a dispensation from the Grand Master or his Deputy, on very particular occasions. " Regulations published by Northouck in his editions of the " Constitutions," p. 392.

the separation, was not the conferring of the Second and Third degrees in their lodges, for this was a prerogative that had long before been conceded to them, but it was the conferring of the Master's degree in a form unknown to the existing ritual of the Grand Lodge, and the supplementing it with an entirely new and Fourth degree.

The "irregular making of Masons," which according to Entick[289] was complained of in 1739, was the mutilation of the Third degree and the transferring of its concluding part to another degree called the "Royal Arch."

The Chevalier Ramsey, a Freemason of much learning, was the inventor of a series of degrees supplementary to the system of Craft Masonry, which have furnished the substratum for most if not all of the Modern Rites. Among these was one now known to ritualists as the "Royal Arch of Solomon."

Ramsey went to England in the year 1728, where he received from the University of Oxford the degree of Doctor of the Laws. He sought, it is said, to induce the Grand Lodge to adopt his system of high degrees. But the leading members of that body were extremely conservative and refused to make any change in the ritual.

But there were some of the Fraternity with whom he was more successful.

It is not by any means intended to affirm that the Royal Arch degree of Ramsey was accepted in the form or even with the legend which he had invented.

This would not be true. But the theory advanced by Ramsey doubtless awakened in their minds new views and suggested ideas which were novel, but which were believed to be essential to the perfection of Masonic symbolism.

From the earliest times of Speculative Masonry the "Word," or, as it was called by the Masons of Scotland, the "Mason Word," had always held a prominent place in the Masonic ritual, and was, we have every reason to believe, one of the few symbols retained by the Speculative out of the Operative system. The triangle, it will be remembered, always in Christian Iconography an emblem of the Godhead, was a favorite architectural ornament used by the Stonemasons of the Middle Ages.

Adopted by the Speculative Freemasons, it was placed by them, when they fabricated their ritual, as a prominent symbol in the Master's

---

[289] Entick, "Constitutions," p. 228.

degree, to which it had been transferred from the original degree or ritual common to all the Craft.[290]

But the Master's degree as it was constructed by Dr. Desaguliers and his collaborators was as to the history of this "Word" imperfect. The legend detailing the method by which it had been lost to the Craft was preserved, but no provision had been made to account for its recovery.

The legend was not carried out to its denouement. The story was left unfinished, and although the "Word" was there and was communicated to the Master, no one could tell, for he was not informed, how it got there.

Now Ramsey, who was a thinker and a man of much learning, had seen this defect in the Masonic scheme and had supplied the deficiency by the invention of his "Royal Arch of Solomon." He thus perfected what he had found unfinished, and gave completeness and connection to all the details of the allegory.

Some of the English Masons had doubtless seen the fault in the system of Desaguliers which had been adopted and sanctioned by the Grand Lodge. When Ramsey arrived in England and proposed his new arrangement by which that fault was to be amended, though the Grand Lodge, as the representative of the Fraternity, refused to accept his system, and preferred to "stand on the old ways," imperfect as they were, there were brethren not so strictly conservative in their views who were impressed with the advantage of accepting the suggestions of Ramsey.

These brethren were the seceders who, about the year 1738, were concerned in "irregular makings," that is, who undertook to confer the Master's degree in a form different from that which was sanctioned by the Grand Lodge.

At this distance of time it is impossible to know, with anything like precision, what were the precise changes made by the "Ancients" in the old and accepted ritual of the "Moderns." It is, however, very satisfactorily evident, from the course of contemporaneous history and from the succession of events, that that change, whatever it was, finally led to the development of the Royal Arch degree, such as it is now practiced, as a necessary completion of the Master's part, and therefore as a recognized section of Ancient Craft Masonry.

In so far, then, the secession of the "Ancients," however unjustifiable it was in its inception as a violation of Masonic law, was in

---

[290] In primitive lodges of Scotland, and the practice prevailed in England and elsewhere, the Mason Word was communicated to Apprentices. Lyon says "this was the germ whence has sprung Symbolical Masonry". "History of the Lodge of Edinburgh," p. 23

its subsequent results of great advantage to the system of Speculative Freemasonry. It gave to Masonic symbolism a completeness and perfection that was altogether wanting under the old arrangement of only three degrees, and supplied a break in the history of the "Word" which it is strange that the ritualists of the earlier period of the 18th century had not perceived nor appreciated.

The introduction of this degree was for a long time vehemently opposed by the regular Grand Lodge as an innovation on the landmarks. They even treated it with contempt.

To a petitioner from Ireland applying for relief the Grand Secretary of the Grand Lodge of "Moderns" replied: "Our Society is neither Arch, Royal Arch, nor Ancient, so that you have no right to partake of our charity."[291]

But the innovation was advocated with such ability and became so popular that the regular Grand Lodge was compelled to succumb to what was evidently the wish of the Fraternity, and at length to adopt what they had so persistently condemned.[292]

On June 12, 1765, a Royal Arch Chapter was formed in connection with the " Moderns," which was in the subsequent year converted into a Grand Chapter. Hughan says it "was virtually, though not actually, countenanced by the Grand Lodge. It was purely a defensive organization to meet the wants of the regular brethren, and prevent their joining the Ancients for exaltation."[293]

In 1813, at the union of the Grand Lodges, the "Holy Royal Arch" was legally recognized as a constituent part of Ancient Craft Masonry.

A doubt is, however, cast over the accuracy of Bro. Hughan's assertion that in 1766 the Grand Chapter was even virtually countenanced by the Grand Lodge of "Moderns" by two contemporaneous records.

The first is the declaration already given of the Grand Secretary of the "Modern" Grand Lodge, made about that time, that they were "neither Arch, Royal Arch, nor Ancients ;" and the other a letter written on June 7, 1766, by the same Grand Secretary to the Provincial Lodge of Frankfort- on-the-Main, in which he declares that the Royal Arch is " a Society which we do not acknowledge and which we regard as an invention designed for the purpose of introducing innovations amongst

---

[291] I give this anecdote on the authority of Dermott ("Ahiman Rezon," p. xvi.), but there is no reason to doubt its truth.
[292] "Masonic Memorials," p. 8, note.
[293] Ibid

the Brotherhood and diverting them from the fundamental rules which our ancestors laid down for us."[294]

In this conflict of authority there appears to be but one reasonable explanation. It is probable that some of the "Modern" Masons, tempted by the success and popularity of the Arch degree among the "Ancients," had independently formed a chapter of their own, and soon converted it into a self-created Grand Chapter, just as the lodge at York, forty years before, had resolved itself into a Grand Lodge.

Although this was done without the sanction of the Grand Lodge, and though it was precisely the same innovation which in 1738 had met with the severe censure of that body, it is to be presumed that no notice was taken of the act, because experience had taught the Grand Lodge that the best policy would be not to endanger by opposition a second rebellion from its authority.

So Royal Arch Masonry was permitted to exist by sufferance. But the victory of the "Ancients" was fully accomplished in 1813, when the Grand Lodge of "Moderns" was compelled to recognize that which they had at first styled an innovation and to acknowledge the Royal Arch to be a component part of Ancient Craft Masonry.

Thus the two Grand Lodges continued to move in parallel but not amicable lines, both indulging at times in mutual recriminations and each denouncing the other as irregular. The "Ancients," as well as the "Moderns," extended their jurisdiction beyond the limits of England into foreign countries. They exercised this power, however, in a different manner.

The Grand Lodge of "Moderns" usually appointed Deputations or Provincial Grand Masters in various countries, by whom lodges were organized, and afterward Provincial Grand Lodges.

The "Ancients" never practiced this method. It was their usage to grant Warrants, directly, for the establishment of lodges, and these, as soon as there were a sufficient number, proceeded to organize Grand Lodges, under the incorrect title of "Ancient York Masons."

Such was the universal practice on the American Continent, where the Grand Lodges established under the obedience of the Grand Lodge of a "Moderns" and those organized by the York or Ancient Lodges preserved the distinctive principles of their parents and inherited their angry passions.

But such a condition of things was too alien to the benign and fraternal sentiments of Freemasonry to be perpetuated. Movements

---

[294] Findel cites this in his "History of Freemasonry," p. 184.

toward a reconciliation were inaugurated toward the close of the 18th century, and finally, in 1813, the Atholl Grand Lodge was forever dissolved by a fusion of the two contending bodies in England into the now existing body under the title of the "United Grand Lodge of England." This excellent example was speedily followed by similar amalgamations in all the States where the rivalry had prevailed.

But the fusion in England, which closes the history of the Atholl Grand Lodge, is too important an event to be treated otherwise than in a separate chapter.

CHAPTER XLII

THE GRAND LODGE OF ENGLAND, SOUTH OF THE TRENT;
OR THE SCHISM OF THE LODGE OF ANTIQUITY

OF the four old Lodges of London which united in the formation of a Grand Lodge in the year 1717, the one which at that time met at the "Goose and Gridiron Ale-house" in St. Paul's Churchyard, assumed the precedency as No. 1, and under all its changes of name and locality retained that precedency until the union of the two Grand Lodges in 1813, when, in casting lots, it lost its primitive rank and became No. 2, a number which it has ever since retained. Anderson calls it "the Senior Lodge whose Constitution is immemorial."[295]

About the year 1729 it removed from the "Goose and Gridiron," to the "King's Arms Tavern," also in St. Paul's Churchyard. Here it remained, except for a brief interval in 1735 until 1768, having taken in 1760 the name of the "West India and American Lodge." In 1768 it removed to the "Mitre," in Fleet Street, and in 1770 adopted the title of the "Lodge of Antiquity," which it has ever since continued to use.[296]

These four Lodges had been established previous to the formation of the Grand Lodge, under the old system which permitted a sufficient number of Masons to meet together and form a lodge, the only authority required being the consent of the chief magistrate of the place.[297]

This privilege, which they called immemorial usage, they claimed and received from the new Grand Lodge, which required all other lodges which should be constituted to previously obtain a Warrant

---

[295] In the List of lodges in the 1738 "Book of Constitutions," p. 184.
[296] Gould's "Four Old Lodges," note 9, p. 6.
[297] Preston, "Illustrations," Oliver's edition, p. 182.

from the Grand Master, but permitted the four original Lodges to act as they always had done without such authority.

The history of these four Lodges may be thus briefly told:

Lodge No. 2, which originally met at the "Crown" in Parker's Lane, became extinct in 1730.

Lodge No. 3, which met at the "Apple Tree Tavern," memory able as the place where the preliminary meeting for the organization of a Grand Lodge was held, in 1723, on account of some difference among its members, renounced its immemorial privileges and accepted a Warrant of Constitution from the Grand Lodge as No. 10.

Lodge No. 4, afterward No. 2, first held at the "Rummer and Grapes," afterward removed to the "Horn Tavern." In 1747 it was, for non- attendance of its representative at the Quarterly Communications, erased from the roll of lodges,[298] but reinstated in 1751. In 1774 it united with the Somerset Lodge, which had been warranted in 1762 as No. 269.

Preston, in a passage of his 1781 edition, asserted that by this act "the members of the lodge tacitly agreed to a renunciation of their rights as one of the four original Lodges, put themselves entirely under the authority of the Grand Lodge and claimed no distinct privilege by virtue of an immemorial Constitution."

This is not an accurate statement, and Preston did well to erase it from the subsequent editions of his book. The act of incorporation with the Somerset Lodge was really an absorption of that lodge into the Horn Lodge, whose number remained unchanged, and at the union of 1813 it was admitted on the Register without a Warrant of Constitution and as acting from "Time Immemorial."

There is not the least doubt cast upon the record of Lodge No. 1, which met at the "Goose and Gridiron," and which has for more than a century been known as the "Lodge of Antiquity." It never at any time abandoned its claim to all the privileges of a lodge dating from time immemorial and vigorously though perhaps erroneously asserted them when an attempt was made to violate them, and the "Lodge of Antiquity" has remained to the present day without a Warrant.

In Pine's List of lodges for 1729 it is stated that the lodge was established in 1691, but Hughan believes it to have been much older. It is said that the celebrated architect, Sir Christopher Wren, was made a Freemason in this lodge. Aubrey, the antiquary, in his Natural History of Wiltshire, says that on May 19, 1691, there was "a great convention at

---

[298] Entick, "Book of Constitutions," p. 248.

St. Paul's Church of the fraternity of Adopted Masons where Sir Christopher Wren is to be adopted a brother, and Sir Henry Goodrie of the Tower and divers others." It is probable that this passage suggested to the maker of Pine's List the notion of giving to the lodge the date of 1691 as the time of its establishment.

Supposing that the lodge, which in 1717 met at the "Goose and Gridiron," was the one that in 1691 admitted Wren to the Fraternity, the roll of distinguished members will be confined to the architect of St. Paul's and to William Preston, the celebrated Masonic historian. The statement that Dr. Desaguliers was initiated in it has been proved to be incorrect.

The fourth lodge, the one that met at the "Rummer and Grapes," and afterward at the "Horn Tavern," can boast a much larger list of Masonic worthies. Among them at the earliest stage of its existence are the names of Desaguliers, Payne, and Anderson, all of whom were probably made in it, either just before or immediately after the organization of the Grand Lodge. Desaguliers is said to have been made in 1712, and I am disposed to believe that both Payne and Anderson, as well as he, were Freemasons in 1717 and were personally engaged in the formation of the Grand Lodge. Between 1723 and 1738 a great many noblemen, both English and foreign, were admitted to its membership, while the roll of Nos. 1 and 2 contain no brethren of Masonic or social rank, and that of No. 3 claims only the name of Anthony Sayer, the first Grand Master.[299]

Bro. Gould thinks that in the earliest years of the Grand Lodge, Nos. 1, 2, and 3 represented the Operative and No. 4 the Speculative elements of the Society.[300] This is probably true. We know that the first three lodges were not distinguished in their membership by the name of a single personage of rank or learning, and that in 1723 the Master of No. 1 was a stonecutter. On the other hand, Desaguliers, Payne, and Anderson, the prime instigators of the change from purely Operative to purely Speculative Freemasonry, were all members of No. 4.

In after times, Lodges Nos. 2 and 3 became extinct, and No. 4 continued to exist in placid obscurity, while No. 1, having become the "Lodge of Antiquity," played a prominent part in the history of the Grand Lodge of England, and under the leadership of William Preston was the cause of a schism, which at one time threatened to be very disastrous to the cause of Freemasonry, though happily it proved to be temporary in its duration.

---

[299] Gould, "Four Old Lodges," p. 9.
[300] Gould, ibid.

It is because of the part taken by the "Lodge of Antiquity" in this schismatic proceeding, in which it sought to defend itself on the ground that it, as one of the four old Lodges, was entitled to certain privileges and exemptions from the authority of the Grand Lodge, which did not appertain to the younger lodges, that I have deemed it necessary to take a glance at the condition of these four primary lodges, as preliminary to the history of the contest in which one of them was engaged.

In this contest No. 1, or the "Lodge of Antiquity," alone was prominent.

Nos. 2 and 3 had become extinct, and No. 4 took no other part in the dispute than that of remaining loyal to the Grand Lodge.

The history of the dissensions between the "Lodge of Antiquity" and the Grand Lodge of England, which terminated in the establishment of a fourth Grand Lodge within the jurisdiction of England, may be briefly related as follows:

In the year 1777, during the Grand Mastership of the Duke of Manchester, the Master, Wardens, and a part of the members of the "Lodge of Antiquity," under a resolution of the lodge, celebrated the festival of St. John the Evangelist by attending divine service at St. Dunstan's Church, in Fleet Street, walking there and returning to the "Mitre Tavern" in the clothing of the Order, and this without having obtained a Dispensation for the procession from the Grand Master or his Deputy.

This was a flagrant violation of the law of the Grand Lodge which prescribed that no Mason should attend any public procession clothed with the badges and ensigns of the Order, unless a dispensation for that purpose was obtained from the Grand Master or his Deputy; and the penalty for a violation of this law was a forfeiture of all the rights and privileges of the Society and a deprivation of the benefits of the general fund of charity.

This law, which had been enacted in 1754, must have been well known to the Master and the members of the lodge, and its open violation by them in the face of that knowledge would lead us to assent to the statement of Findel that they wished to come to an open rupture with the authority to whom they owed allegiance.[301]

This act was very properly condemned by the Grand Lodge. "Various opinions," says Preston, "were formed on the subject, and several brethren were highly disgusted."

---

[301] "History of Freemasonry," Lyon's Translation. p. 181.

It is surprising that there should be more than one opinion of the unlawfulness of an act which palpably violates a written statute; but it is very natural that the perpetrators of an offense, if they are not penitent, should be "disgusted" with the punishment which has followed.

Another circumstance soon followed which, according to Preston, tended still further to widen the breach.

For some alleged misconduct the lodge had expelled three of its members. The Grand Lodge, deeming, as we may fairly suppose, that some injustice had been done, ordered them to be reinstated.

Preston says that the Grand Lodge interfered without proper investigation. But it can not be presumed upon the authority of a partisan that the Grand Lodge would have exercised this high prerogative of reinstatement without a fair investigation of all the circumstances connected with the original expulsion. The good old principle must here prevail that in respect to all acts of an official nature, the presumption is that they have been fairly executed, and that all has been rightly and duly performed until the contrary is shown.[302]

Unfortunately, it is almost wholly upon Preston, in his edition of 1781, that we must depend for our authority in the recital of this history. But this statement must be taken with all the allowance due to an active partisan.

Preston was a prominent actor and indeed a leader in this contest, and in telling his story might have repeated the words of Pater Eneas to the Queen of Carthage:

"..... quoque ipse miserrima vide, Et quorum pars magna fui."

The lodge vainly resisted this act of the Grand Lodge and to re-admit the expelled members "Matters," says Preston, " were agitated to the extreme on both sides; resolutions were precipitately entered into, and edicts inadvertently issued; memorials and remonstrances were presented."

Finally an open rupture ensued. The lodge withdrew the attendance of its Master and Wardens as representatives from the Quarterly communications, but continued to exercise its functions as a lodge, independently of the jurisdiction of the Grand Lodge. It issued a Manifesto in which it detailed its grievances and asserted its rights and appealed for sympathy and support to the Grand Lodges of Scotland, Ireland, and York.

---

[302] "Omnia presumuntur legitime facta donec probetur in contrium."

The Grand Lodge of England, on its part, was not less resolute. It expelled the rebellious members of the lodge, extended its protection to the three members whose expulsion had been ostensibly the original cause of all the difficulties, and recognizing them as the only legitimate representatives of the "Lodge of Antiquity," ordered, but of course in vain, a surrender to them of the property of the lodge.

The position which was now assumed by the "Lodge of Antiquity" was precisely that which it had occupied before its union in 1717 with the three other lodges in the establishment of a Grand Lodge, namely, that of a lodge, instituted without a Warrant, and by the mere consent of its founders, as all the Operative lodges had been instituted prior to the formation of a Grand Lodge.

As the Manifesto of the "Lodge of Antiquity" which was issued on December 16, 1778, is a full exposition of the grounds on which the lodge based its right to assume independency and eventually to accept from the Grand Lodge at York the rank and title of "The Grand Lodge of England south of the Trent," it is very necessary, to a correct understanding of these important transactions, that the reader should be placed in possession of a copy of the document. It is accordingly here printed, as follows:[303]

TO ALL REGULAR, FREE AND ACCEPTED MASONS.

WHEREAS, the Society of Free Masons is universally acknowledged to be of ancient standing and great repute in this kingdom, as by our Records and Printed Constitutions, it appears that the first Grand Lodge in England was held at York, in the year 926, by virtue of a Royal Charter granted by King Athelstan, and under the patronage and government of this Grand Lodge, the Society considerably increased; and the ancient charges and regulations of the Order so far obtained the sanction of Kings and Princes, and other eminent persons, that they always paid due allegiance to the said Grand Assembly.

AND WHEREAS, it appears, by our Records, that in the year 1567, the increase of lodges in the South of England, being so great as to require some Nominal Patron to superintend their government, it was resolved that a person under the title of Grand Master for the South should be appointed for that purpose, with the approbation of the Grand Lodge at York, to whom the whole Fraternity at large were bound to pay tribute and acknowledge subjection. And after the appointment

---

[303] The copy here printed is from Bro. Hughan's "History of Freemasonry in York" (American edition, p. 117), and is one of the most interesting documents in that valuable work.

of such Patron, Masonry flourished under the guardianship of him and his successors in the South, until the Civil Wars and other intestine commotions interrupted the assemblies of the Brethren.

AND WHEREAS, it also appears that in the year 1693, the Meetings of the Fraternity in their regular lodges in the South became less frequent and chiefly occasional, except in or near places where great works were carried on. At which time the "Lodge of Antiquity" or (as it was then called) the Old Lodge of St. Paul, with a few others of small note, continued to meet under the patronage of Sir Christopher Wren, and assisting him in rearing that Superb Structure from which this respectable lodge derived its Title. But on completing this Edifice, in 1710, and Sir Christopher Wren's retiring into the country, the few remaining lodges in London and its suburbs, continued without any nominal Patron, in a declining state for about the space of seven years.

AND WHEREAS, in the year 1717, the Fraternity in London agreed to cement under a new Grand Master, and with that view the Old Lodge of St. Paul, jointly with three other lodges, assembled in form, constituted themselves a nominal Grand Lodge pro tempore and elected a Grand Master to preside over their future general meetings, whom they afterwards invested with a power to constitute subordinate lodges, and to convene the Fraternity at stated periods in Grand Lodge, in order to make Laws, with their consent and approbation, for the good government of the Society at large.

BUT SUBJECT to certain conditions and restrictions then expressly stipulated, and which are more fully set forth in the 39th article of the General Regulations in the first Book of Constitutions, this article with thirty-eight others, was afterwards at a meeting of the Brethren in and about the cities of London and Westminster, in the year 1721, solemnly approved of, ratified and confirmed by them, and signed in their presence by the Master and Wardens of the Four old Lodges on the one part, and Philip, Duke of Whar.

ton, then Grand Master, Dr. Desaguliers, D.G.M., Joshua Timson and William Hawkins, Grand Wardens, and the Masters and Wardens of sixteen lodges which had been constituted by the Fraternity, betwixt 1717 and 1721, on the other part. And these articles the Grand Master engaged for himself and his successors, in all time coming, to observe and keep sacred and inviolable. By these prudent precautions the ancient Land-marks (as they are properly styled) of the four old Lodges were intended to be secured against any encroachments on their Masonic Rights and Privileges.

AND WHEREAS, of late years, notwithstanding the said solemn engagement in the year 1721, sundry innovations and encroachments have been made, and are still making on the original plan and government of Masonry, by the present nominal Grand Lodge in London, highly injurious to the institution itself, and tending to subvert and destroy the ancient rights and privileges of the Society, more particularly of those members of it under whose sanction, and by whose authority, the said Grand Lodge was first established and now exists.

AND WHEREAS, at the present time there only remains one of the said four original ancient Lodges - The Old Lodge of St. Paul, or as it is now emphatically styled, The "Lodge of Antiquity." Two of the said four ancient lodges having been extinct many years, and the Master of the other of them having on the part of his lodge, in open Grand Lodge, relinquished all such inherent rights and privileges which, as a private lodge, acting by an immemorial Constitution it enjoyed. But the "Lodge of Antiquity," conscious of its own dignity, which the Members thereof are resolutely determined to support, and justly incensed at the violent measures and proceedings which have been lately adopted and pursued by the said nominal Grand Lodge, wherein they have assumed an unlawful prerogative over the "Lodge of Antiquity," in manifest breach of the aforesaid 39th article, by which means the peaceful government of that respectable lodge has been repeatedly interrupted, and even the original independent power thereof, in respect to its own Internal Government, disputed.

THEREFORE, and on account of the Arbitrary Edicts and Laws which the said nominal Grand Lodge has, from time to time, presumed to issue and attempted to enforce, repugnant to the ancient Laws and principles of Free Masonry, and highly injurious to the "Lodge of Antiquity,"

WE, the Master, Wardens and Members of the "Lodge of Antiquity," considering ourselves bound in duty, as well as honour, to preserve inviolable the ancient rights and privileges of the Order, and as far as in our power, to hand them down to posterity in their native purity and excellence, do hereby, for ourselves and our successors, solemnly disavow and discountenance such unlawful measures and proceedings of the said nominal Grand Lodge; and do hereby declare and announce to all our Masonic Brethren throughout the Globe. That the said Grand Lodge, has by such arbitrary conduct, evidently violated the conditions expressed in the aforesaid 39th article of the General Regulations, in the observance of which article the permanency of their authority solely depended.

And in consequence thereof, WE, do by these presents retract from and recall all such rights and powers as We or our predecessors, did conditionally give to the said nominal Grand Lodge in London; and do hereby disannul and make void all future Edicts and Laws, which the said Grand Lodge may presume to issue and enforce, by virtue of such sanction, as representatives of the ancient and honorable Society of Free and Accepted Masons.

AND WHEREAS we have, on full enquiry and due examination, happily discovered, that the aforesaid truly ancient Grand Lodge at York does still exist, and have authentic Records to produce of their antiquity, long before the establishment of the nominal Grand Lodge in London in the year 1717; We do, therefore, hereby solemnly avow, acknowledge and admit the Authority of the said Most Worshipful Grand Lodge at York, as the truly ancient and only regular governing Grand Lodge of Masons in England, to whom the Fraternity all owe and are rightfully bound to pay allegiance.

AND WHEREAS, the present members of the said Grand Lodge at York have acknowledged the ancient power and authority of the "Lodge of Antiquity" in London as a private lodge and have proposed to form an alliance with the said lodge, on the most generous and disinterested principles, - We do hereby acknowledge this generous mark of their friendship towards us, and gratefully accept their liberal, candid and ingenuous offers of alliance: - And do hereby, from a firm persuasion of the justice of our cause, announce a general union with all Regular Masons throughout the world, who shall join us in supporting the original principles of Free Masonry, in promoting and extending the authority of the said truely ancient Grand Lodge at York, and under such respectable auspices in propagating Masonry on its pure, genuine and original plan.

AND LASTLY, we do earnestly solicit the hearty concurrence of all regular lodges of the Fraternity in all places where Free Masonry is legally established to enable us to carry into execution the aforesaid plan, which is so apparently beneficial to our most excellent institution, and at the present critical juncture, so essentially necessary to curb the arbitrary power which has been already exerted, or which, hereafter, may be illegally assumed, by the nominal Grand Lodge in London, and so timely prevent such unmasonic proceedings from becoming a disgrace to the Society at large.

By Order of the Right Worshipful Lodge of Antiquity, in open Lodge assembled, this with day of December A.D., 1778, A.L. 5782.

J. SEALY, Secretary.

Before proceeding to the arguments adduced in this manifesto by the "Lodge of Antiquity," to defend its action in withdrawing from the Grand Lodge, it will be proper to say, that as an historical document it is utterly worthless.

The statement that the first Grand Lodge was held at York under a Charter granted by King Athelstan in the 10th century, is founded on the mere tradition contained in the Legend of the Craft; - it was denied by the Masons of York, who attributed the origin of their society to a much earlier period; it has been doubted or disbelieved by some of the most eminent Masonic scholars of the present day; and finally there is not the slightest historical proof that there was ever a Grand Lodge or Grand Master in England prior to the second decade of the 18th century.

Again: The assertion that in 1567 the Grand Lodge at York appointed a Grand Master for the south of England, and that he and the Fraternity under him "were bound to pay tribute and acknowledge subjection" to the Grand Lodge of York, is wholly unsupported by historical evidence.

Anderson, who was ever ready to frame history out of legends, does indeed record the existence of a Grand Lodge, holding annual communications at York,[304] and tells us the apocryphal story of Queen Elizabeth and Grand Master Sackville. He also states that it was a tradition of the old Masons that in 1567, on the demission of Sir Thomas Sackville, two Grand Masters were chosen, one for the north and one for the south, but he makes no allusion to the position of the latter as subordinate to the former. He makes no further mention of the Grand Lodge at York in the subsequent pages of the Book of Constitutions, but always speaks of the Grand Master and the Grand Lodge at London as the sole Masonic authority in England. Thus, unhistorical and merely traditionary as is the authority of Anderson on this subject, it completely fails to give any support to the assertion of the writer of the Manifesto, that in the 16th century the Grand Lodge at York was the supreme Masonic power of all England, and that it delegated a subordinate rank and position to a "nominal Grand Master" for the south of the kingdom.

From this Manifesto it will be seen that the "Lodge of Antiquity" withdrew its allegiance to the Grand Lodge of England, in

---

[304] When Bro. Woodford in his Essay on the "Connection of York with the History of Freemasonry in England," asserted that the statement in the Manifesto was Athe only existing evidence that in 1567 there was a Grand Lodge at York," this passage in Anderson must have escaped his attention.

consequence of the wrong it supposed that body had inflicted upon it, by the reinstatement of certain members whom it had expelled. It then asserted its independence and attempted to resume the position which it had occupied before the organization of the Grand Lodge, as a lodge working without a Warrant.

In defense of its action, the lodge refers in the Manifesto to the 39th General Regulation, which it says had been violated by the Grand Lodge in its treatment of the "Lodge of Antiquity."

But the most liberal construction of that Regulation will fail to support any such theory.

The 39th Regulation simply recognizes the inherent power of the Grand Lodge to make new regulations or to alter the old ones, provided that the landmarks be preserved, and that the new regulation be adopted at a stated communication by a majority of the brethren present.

Now there is no distinct charge of the violation of a landmark by the Grand Lodge, and if there was there is no provision in the Regulations for its redress by the secession of a lodge.

The whole tenor of the Thirty-nine Regulations adopted in 1721, is to make the Grand Lodge a supreme Masonic power. It is, moreover, provided in the 8th Regulation that no number of Brethren shall withdraw from the lodge in which they were made and form a new lodge without the consent of the Grand Master.

The facts are briefly these. The Grand Lodge having reinstated three members who we are bound to presume had been wrongly expelled, the lodge refused to recognize the act of reinstatement, and withdrew from its allegiance to the Grand Lodge, and assuming independence, proceeded to work out a Warrant, under its old Operative Constitution and without the consent or approval of the Grand Lodge.

The Grand Lodge refused to admit the legality of this act. It continued to recognize the three members and any others who adhered to them as the true "Lodge of Antiquity," and viewed the recusant members as Masons who had violated the 8th Regulation, by withdrawing from their lodge and joining a new lodge without the Grand Master's Warrant.

Bro. Robert Freke Gould, in his History of the Four Old Lodges,[305] has advanced the doctrine that the "Lodge of Antiquity" had a legal right to secede from the Grand Lodge, and he supports his opinion

---

[305] "Four Old Lodges," p. 28.

by the very extraordinary argument that if the Grand Lodge had a right to expel a lodge from the Union, that is, to erase it from the roll of lodges, this would imply a correlative right in a subordinate lodge to withdraw or secede from the Union of lodges or the Grand Lodge. The adoption of such a doctrine would make every Grand Lodge a merely temporary organization, subject at any moment to be impaired by the arbitrary withdrawal of as many lodges as thought proper to exercise this privilege of secession. This would inevitably be a termination to all power of discipline and of coercive government. He has unfortunately sought to illustrate his views by a reference to the American Constitution which he supposes to have conceded to any one or more of the States the right of secession. He does not seem to be aware that this doctrine, generally called a "political heresy," though at one time maintained by most Southern Statesmen, was always disavowed by the people of the North, and finally forever obliterated by the severe arbitrament of a four years' intestine war.

The fact is that the four old Lodges entered voluntarily into the compact which resulted in the establishment of a Grand Lodge in London in the year 1717. The Regulations adopted by the Grand Lodge four years afterward, for its government and that of its subordinates, was approved and accepted by all the lodges then existing, among which were the four Lodges, and the names of the Master and Wardens of the "Lodge of Antiquity" head the list of the signers of the Act of Approbation. The "Lodge of Antiquity" was, therefore, forever bound by the compact, and by regulations enacted under its authority.

By the compact made prior to the enactment of the Thirty-nine Regulations, and which was entered into by the four old Lodges, it was agreed that in future every lodge should owe its existence to the consent of the Grand Master expressed by his Warrant of Constitution, and such has been the invariable practice, not only in England but in every country into which Freemasonry had penetrated.

As an act of courtesy, the four Lodges were exempted from the duty of applying for Warrants, and were permitted to continue their labors under the old system of Operative Freemasonry by authority of a self-constitution through which they had been established under the old system of Operative Freemasonry which had existed prior to the organization of the Grand Lodge.

But this was the only distinct privilege which they possessed. In all other matters, every lodge was alike subjected to the control of the Grand Lodge, and to the constant supervision of the Grand Master. This system of government, so different from that of the Operative

Freemasonry which had previously prevailed, had been accepted by the four original Lodges.

They themselves had inaugurated it; they had accepted all the consequences of the great change, and it was no longer in the power of any one of them, at any future period, to annul the contract into which they had entered.

All the regulations adopted after their compact refer in general terms to the collective body of lodges without making any exception; in favor of the four original Lodges. Especially was this the fact with respect to the Thirty-nine Regulations adopted in 1721. The laws therein enacted were just as applicable to Lodge No. 1 as to Lodge No. 20, for the former lodge had, as well as the latter, and all the intermediate ones, formerly accepted them and declared that they and the Charges, as published by Anderson, should be received in every lodge "as the only Constitutions of Free and Accepted Masons."[306]

Hence it follows, that in withdrawing from the Grand Lodge and establishing a lodge, independent of its authority, the contumacious members of the "Lodge of Antiquity" acted illegally, and violated the Constitutions which the Freemasons of England had accepted for half a century as the fundamental law of the Order.

On second sober thought, Preston himself, who had undoubtedly been the ringleader in this schism, when he was restored to the privileges of Masonry, in 1789, expressed his regret for what he had done in the past, and his wish to conform in future to the laws of the Grand Lodge.[307] As the Grand Lodge had made no concessions, Preston thus admitted the constitutionality of the law, against which as being unconstitutional, he and his colleagues had been contending for eleven years.

The recusant members of the "Lodge of Antiquity" having declared their independence of the Grand Lodge, and continued after their expulsion from the Society to hold their lodge and to perform the work of Masonry, the Grand Lodge permitted those members who had maintained their obedience to assemble as the real "Lodge of Antiquity,"

---

[306] See the act of Approbation in Anderson's 1723 edition of the "Constitutions," p. 74.
[307] The official record of the Grand Lodge for November 25, 1789, says that Preston and seven other members of the "Lodge of Antiquity," who had been expelled in 1779, had "signified their concern that through misrepresentation, as they conceived, they should have incurred the displeasure of that Assembly, and their wish to be restored to the privileges of the Society, to the laws of which they were ready to conform."

still without a Warrant, and to appear by their Master and Wardens at the Grand Communications as the representatives of the lodge.

There were thus two lodges of Antiquity in the field - the lodge recognized by the Grand Lodge, consisting of the members who had refused to take part in the schismatic proceedings; and the lodge consisting of the members who had withdrawn from their allegiance, and had established themselves as an independent body, working under the old Operative system.

Of the former lodge, it is unnecessary and irrelevant to the present history to take any further notice. It probably pursued "the even tenor of its way" quietly and unobtrusively. In the lists of lodges made during the period of the schism, its name and number are retained without alteration as the "Lodge of Antiquity No. 1, Freemasons' Tavern, Great Queen Street, formerly the 'Goose and Gridiron,' St. Paul's Church Yard."[308]

The latter lodge, the one whose existence I have sought to prove was illegal, very soon proceeded to adopt measures still more offensive in their character.

It has been commonly stated that it applied to the Grand Lodge at York for a sanction of its acts, and for authority to continue its existence as a lodge.

This is not correct. The true statement of the relative positions of the Grand Lodge at York and the independent Grand Lodge of Antiquity is fully set forth in a correspondence between certain members of the two bodies which is still extant.[309]

From this correspondence it appears that Bro. Jacob Bussey, the Grand Secretary of the Grand Lodge of York, while in London had an interview with some of the members of the "Lodge of Antiquity." Under a misapprehension of the views of these Brethren, on his return home he stated that it was their desire to obtain a Warrant of Constitution as a lodge from the York Grand Lodge. Having learned the fact of this misapprehension from a communication, made on August 29th, by Bussey, after his return to York, to Bro. Bradley, the Junior Warden of the "Lodge of Antiquity," the officers of that lodge addressed a letter on September 16, 1778, to the Grand Master and Brethren of the Grand Lodge at York. In this letter is the following explicit statement of their views:

---

[308] List of Lodges, in 1781, taken from the Calendar for 1788. See Gould, p. 68.
[309] See this correspondence in Bro. Hughan's "History of Freemasonry in York," pp. 74-76

"Though we should be happy to promote Masonry under the Banners of the Grand Lodge at York, an application by petition for a Warrant for a Constitution to act as a private lodge here was never our intention, as we considered ourselves sufficiently empowered by the Immemorial Constitution of our lodge, to execute every duty we can wish as a private lodge of Masons."

They were, however, ready, they go on to say, if satisfied by proofs of the existence of the Grand Lodge at York before the year 1717, to accept from it a Constitutional authority to act in London as a Grand Lodge for that part of England which is south of the river Trent.

The Grand Secretary, however, in his August letter, appears to have furnished the required proofs, and consequently Bradley, the Junior Warden of the "Lodge of Antiquity," wrote to him on September 22, 1778. [310]In this letter he again disclaimed any desire on the part of the "Lodge of Antiquity" to receive a Warrant as a private lodge, but expressed its willingness to accept "a Warrant or Deputation to a few members of the 'Lodge of Antiquity' to act as a Grand Lodge for that part of England, south of the Trent, with a power to constitute lodges in that division when properly applied for, and a regular correspondence to be kept up and some token of allegiance to be annually given on the part of the brethren thus authorized to act."

The same letter contained a list of the names of the brethren of the "Lodge of Antiquity" as the persons suggested to be placed in the Warrant or Deputation, should it be granted. These were as follows, and though at this distant time and place I am unable to verify the fact, it may be fairly presumed that the suggestion was accepted, and that when the Deputation was accepted, the following Brethren constituted the first officers of the new Grand Lodge:

JOHN WILSON, Esq., Master of the Lodge of Antiquity, as Grand Master.

WILLIAM PRESTON, Past Master of the same Lodge, as Deputy Grand Master.

BENJAMIN BRADLEY, Junior Warden of the same, as Senior Grand Warden.

GILBERT BUCHANAN, Secretary of the same, as Junior Grand Warden.

JOHN SEABY, Senior Steward of the same, as Grand Secretary.

Further correspondence, protracted for more than a year, followed, but finally the "Warrant of Confirmation" was sent, and on

---

[310] Benjamin Bradley's Letter of September 22d. See Hughan's "History," p. 76.

April 19th the "Grand Lodge of England South of the Trent" was inaugurated, the Grand Master installed, and the other officers appointed.

There are two things which are here worthy of notice as historical facts.

In the first place, the body thus erected was in no proper sense a sovereign and independent Grand Lodge, as Grand Lodges are known to be at this day and as was at the time the Grand Lodge at London. It was rather, though not so called by name, a sort of Provincial Grand Lodge, erected by a Grand Lodge, to which it acknowledged that it owed allegiance and to which it paid an annual contribution in money and a fee of two guineas for every Warrant of Constitution that it granted.

In the second place, it was not to the "Lodge of Antiquity" that the Deputation was granted, as it never changed its condition or its title as a private lodge. The Deputation was given, it is true, to certain of its officers, and its Master was most probably the first Grand Master, as there was no other source whence the officers could be drawn.

As soon as the new Grand Lodge was inaugurated, the "Lodge of Antiquity" became subordinate to it, and a return made in March, 1789, the lodges then under the Grand Lodge South of the Trent, are said to be, exclusive of the "Lodge of Antiquity," No. 1, or the Lodge of Perfect Observance, and No. 2, or the Lodge of Perseverance and Triumph.

These lodges were respectively Warranted on August 9th, and November 15, 1779.

The "Lodge of Antiquity," like the Grand Steward's Lodge in the Grand Lodge of England, seems to have assumed precedency without a number.

It was a right which it claimed from its "immemorial Constitution."

Preston says, in his 1781[311] edition, that "a Grand Lodge, under the banner of the Grand Lodge in York, is established in London, and several lodges are already constituted under that banner, while the 'Lodge of Antiquity' acts independent by virtue of its own authority."

If the word "several" is here properly applied, other Warrants must have been issued between July 1, 1780, when the two lodges[312] mentioned above were said to be "the only lodges" which had been

---

[311] "Illustrations of Masonry," edition of 1781, p. 295.
[312] In the subsequent editions, published after the reconciliation, these statements are omitted.

constituted, and the time when Preston made his statement. But of this we have no other evidence.

The "Grand Lodge of England South of the Trent" does not appear to have made any especial mark in Masonic history. It originated in a mistaken view, assumed by its founders, of their rights and privileges.

These views were strenuously opposed by all the other lodges which composed the Mother Grand Lodge and were finally abandoned by themselves.

At the Grand Feast of the Grand Lodge of England held in 1790, a reconciliation was effected principally through the mediation of Bro. William Birch, a Past Master of the "Lodge of Antiquity." Unanimity was happily restored; the Manifesto of the "Lodge of Antiquity," in which it had asserted its claims and defended its conduct, was revoked; the Master and Wardens of the lodge resumed, as heretofore, their seats in the Grand Lodge whence they had seceded in 1778; the Brethren of the lodge who had retained their loyalty were reunited with the original members; and the " Grand Lodge of England, South of the Trent," after an ephemeral career of little more than ten years, ceased to exist.[313]

But this episode in the history of English Freemasonry, bitter as were the feelings which the separation engendered, has not been without compensating advantages in its results.

It has permanently settled the important principle of Masonic jurisprudence, that the old Operative law or usage which recognized the right of a competent number of Freemasons to establish a lodge without the authority of a Warrant, has been forever abrogated by the transformation of the Operative Art into a Speculative Science, and that henceforth, in all time to come, the supreme authority to grant Warrants and to constitute lodges is vested solely in Grand Lodges.

This principle, so essential to the harmony and the perpetuity of Speculative Freemasonry, was almost worth a ten years' struggle to secure its permanent maintenance.

It has thus been seen that in the year 1780 there were in England four bodies claiming to be Grand Lodges.

1. The Grand Lodge of England, established in London in the year 1717.

2. The Grand Lodge of all England, established at York in the year 1725.

---

[313] See Preston, Oliver's edition, p. 249.

3. The Grand Lodge of England, according to the Old Institutions, established at London in the year 1753, and

4. The Grand Lodge of England South of the Trent, established also at London in the year 1780.

It has been heretofore shown that the second of these self-styled Grand Lodges was really a Mother Lodge, and that its pretended organization as a Grand Lodge was in violation of the law and precedent established eight years before by the Grand Lodge at London.

It has also been shown that the third and fourth of these pretended Grand Lodges were illegal secessions from the primitive Grand Lodge, and that their assumption of authority was in violation of the compact of 1721, and was unsupported by any principle of Masonic law which then prevailed and was recognized by the Craft.

It follows then, as has hitherto been said, that the first of these bodies, the one established at London in 1717, is the only really legal and regular Grand Lodge that ever existed in England, and that it is, as it has always claimed to be, the Premier and Mother Grand Lodge of the World.

Of the three irregular bodies, the Grand Lodge at York and the Grand Lodge South of the Trent were both, in the course of time, quietly absorbed into the Grand Lodge of England, and thus obscurely ceased to exist.

The Grand Lodge according to the Old Institutions, more commonly known as the Atholl Grand Lodge, or the Grand Lodge of Ancients, had a higher vitality, lived for a longer period, became prominent as a successful rival of the regular and older body, and with it was eventually merged in 1813 to the United Grand Lodge of England.

But a future chapter must be devoted to the history of this important and interesting event.

www.ingramcontent.com/pod-product-compliance
Lightning Source LLC
Chambersburg PA
CBHW071148160426
43196CB00011B/2040